"Life in India

always partakes of the nature

of a campaign . . ."

—Flora Annie Steel,
The Complete Indian Housekeeper and Cook, 1898

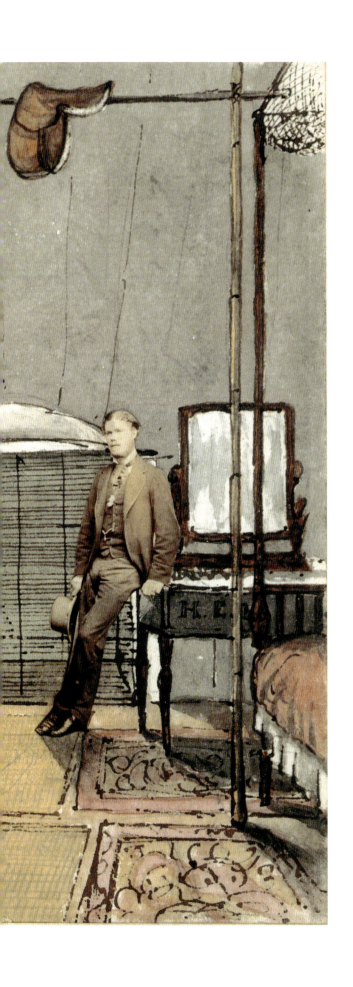

British Campaign Furniture

Elegance under Canvas, 1740–1914

Nicholas A. Brawer

Harry N. Abrams, Inc., Publishers

Editor: Elaine M. Stainton

Designer: Maria L. Miller

Pages 2–3: H. E. Malet. *Interior of My Tent, High Ground, Bangalore,* 1865. Watercolor and black and white photograph on paper. Signed and dated H. E. Malet, 1865 (on the *verso*). The British Library, Oriental and India Office Collections.

Malet places himself in this watercolor by use of a cut-out photograph. He illustrates a number of pieces of campaign furniture very similar to the "camp furniture" or "barrack furniture" advertised in 1867 by Hill & Millard and J. W. Allen. These include a portable "Douro Chair," a small book rack on top of the trestle table, the four post camp bedstead with bedside rugs, and a set of campaign shelves complete with books resting on top of a campaign chest, which has been removed from its black-painted packing crates, illustrated to the right. Of interest, Malet went to the trouble to take along a large and fragile cheval looking-glass, which sits above a carved wooden sideboard bearing the artist's monogram "H.E.M."

Endpapers: A mess tent carried by elephants, from *Bengal Troops on the Line of March. A Sketch by an Officer in that Army.* London: Day & Haghe, c. 1837.
The Anne S. K. Brown Military Collection, Brown University, Rhode Island.

Library of Congress Cataloguing-in-Publication Data

Brawer, Nicholas N.
British campaign furniture : elegance under canvas, 1740–1914 / Nicholas N. Brawer.
       p.   cm.
Includes bibliographical references and index.
ISBN 0-8109-5711-6
1. Outdoor furniture—Great Britain—History. 2. Camping—Great Britain—Equipment and supplies—History 3. Furniture industry and trade—Great Britain—Directories.
I. Title.

TS810.G7 B73 2001
749'.8'0941—dc21   00-059360

Copyright © 2001 Nicholas N. Brawer

Published in 2001 by Harry N. Abrams, Incorporated, New York
All rights reserved. No part of the contents of this book may be reproduced without the written permission of the publisher.

Printed and bound in Japan

Harry N. Abrams, Inc.
100 Fifth Avenue
New York, N.Y. 10011
www.abramsbooks.com

Contents

Foreword by Jerome Phillips — 11
Acknowledgments — 13

I. British Campaign Furniture

    Campaign Furniture as a Reflection of British Society — 19

    The End of an Era — 67

    Characteristics of British Campaign Furniture — 75

    The Accelerating Demand for Campaign Furniture in Eighteenth- and Nineteenth-Century Britain — 109

    Domestic Demand for Campaign Furniture in Eighteenth- and Nineteenth-Century Britain — 111

    Conclusion — 117

    Notes — 118

II. Elegance Abroad: A Portfolio — 121

III. Directory of British Campaign Furniture Makers, Outfitters, and Patentees — 157

    Notes to the Directory — 216

Bibliography — 218
Index — 221
Photograph Credits — 231

Interior of a Double Pole Tent

For Meredith

A. Harcourt. *Interior of a Double-Pole Tent*, 1867. Watercolor on paper. Signed and dated "A. Harcourt / Feb. 1867" (lower right). The British Library, Oriental and India Office Collections.

In this watercolor, Harcourt depicts two officers, one seated at a campaign pedestal desk, the other seated in a chair similar to the Douro Pattern chair (*see* plate 49). Other campaign furniture in the tent includes a book rack, additional chairs, draped tables and a large dhurrie rug.

John Brownrigg Bellasis (1806–1890). *Midday Halt: Marching*, c. 1825. Signed with initials and inscribed "Midday Halt." Pen and ink and watercolor on paper. H: 6¼ in.; W: 8½ in. Courtesy Martyn Gregory Gallery, London.

Express Camel from *Bengal Troops on the Line of March.*
A Sketch by an Officer in that Army.
London: Day & Haghe, c. 1837. The Anne S. K. Brown
Military Collection, Brown University, Rhode Island.

Foreword

As a dealer with a long-time interest in campaign or "knock-down" furniture, I have regretted the absence of a scholarly treatment of this fascinating subject. While there have been occasional articles and references in general works, until now no one has brought together the great wealth of information to be found on pieces made specifically for voyage, camp, and travel in the British Empire. Traveling furniture was not only durable and practical, but it was elegant, designed in the most fashionable contemporary taste; it engaged the skills of the finest makers and designers of the eighteenth and nineteenth centuries. Today, growing public interest has called for a thorough investigation into every aspect of these ingenious pieces and the circumstances in which they were made and used.

Nicholas Brawer has combined enormous enthusiasm for his subject with the patience to pursue hundreds of leads to reveal previously unknown contemporary illustrations and to unearth new facts about the pieces, their makers, and the social environment in which they were created. Whether our interest lies in innovative design, the history of furniture-making, or the historical background of British colonial expansion, this comprehensive exploration of campaign furniture will add much to our knowledge not only of individual pieces, but of the cultural context from which they emerged.

Jerome Phillips
The Manor House, Hitchin, Hertfordshire, June 2000

Lieutenant F. P. Layard. *Officer's Baggage*
from *Line of March of a Bengal Regiment of Infantry in Scinde*,
London, c. 1843. The Anne S. K. Brown Military
Collection, Brown University, Rhode Island.

Acknowledgments

During the course of researching and writing this book, I have benefited from the advice and encouragement of many people. There are several to whom I am particularly indebted. My good friend and former colleague at Sotheby's, Alice Milica Ilich, offered constant moral support from the project's start. Another good friend, Thomas Bilson, of the Courtauld Institute of Art in London, was unstinting in his help and good humor in helping me work with hundreds of photographs. Lieutenant-Colonel C. R. D. Gray, O. B. E., of Skinner's Horse and Major Donald C. McIntosh, of the Scinde Horse, both cherished friends, did me the great honor of spending many magical hours with me, recalling their years of service in India. Their generosity has helped me to put a face on British military and social life in the distant empire.

I owe an immense debt of gratitude to Jerome Phillips, who not only shared his enormous knowledge of British campaign furniture with me, but also allowed me access to his extensive photographic archives, put me in touch with numerous dealers and collectors, and offered invaluable assistance of every kind. Without his help, the book could not have been completed. Another colleague and friend, Amin Jaffer of the Victoria & Albert Museum in London, was kind enough both to allow me access to his extensive research on Indo-European furniture, and to read and comment on the manuscript. Dr. Jaffer also introduced me to Laura A. Lindey, without whose research assistance I could not have completed the Directory of British Campaign Furniture Designers, Makers, Outfitters, and Patentees.

Several scholars, collectors, and dealers have been most generous in allowing me access to their collections. Peter Bronson very kindly permitted me to have photographs taken of his fine collection of campaign furniture, and allowed me to reproduce a number of rare trade labels and advertisements. David Harvey gave me access to his extensive photographic archives, many pictures from which are included in this book. Professor and Mrs. John Ralph Willis also allowed me to photograph their important collection and graciously shared their archives with me. Simon Phillips permitted me access to the photographic archives of Ronald Phillips, Ltd., London. I would also like to thank Colin Greenway Antiques, Oxfordshire, England, for allowing me to photograph their Ross & Co. chiffonier.

Martin P. Levy, of H. Blairman & Sons, London, invited me to use his extensive library and introduced me to a number of scholars in the field of English furniture. Lennox Money shared his archives on campaign furniture and graciously introduced me to Frances Collard, Assistant Curator, Furniture and Woodwork Department, Victoria & Albert Museum, who kindly allowed me to use the museum's furniture archives. Laura Lindsay of Christie's London kindly suggested the names of several people interested in the field of campaign furniture, as did William Clegg, Harvey Ferry, and Christopher Gibbs. Susan Riley kindly showed me her family's photo albums from India.

In London my research was expedited by the staff of the Oriental and India Office Collections at the British Library, and the Department of Prints and Drawings at the British Museum. The staff of the Reading Room at the National Army Museum provided access to their archives on campaign furniture, as well as answers to a variety of queries. I am particularly grateful for the help of Sara H. Jones in the Department of Weapons, Equipment and Vehicles. Guy Savill at Phillips Fine Art Auctioneers, London, provided me with information on Ross & Co. Alison Kenney at the City of Westminster Archives Centre was a great help with my work in the Gillow Archives. Charles Webb at Spink & Son, London, kindly provided me with information on the Household Cavalry. Margaret McGreggor, of the Bristol Record Office, researched the firm of Miles & Kington. I would also like to thank Christopher Bryant for bringing to my attention the papers of Lieutenant-General Robert Ballard Long. Annamaria and Nino Calia's hospitality made it possible for me to do ongoing research in London, for which I am grateful.

On this side of the Atlantic, thanks are due to Jane Muir and to her father, William, for allowing me to use his extensive library. Donald Skinner kindly sent me images of campaign furniture, and shared his militaria collection. Jane Reed, Associate Library Director, the University Club, New York, assisted me in my research by locating numerous books for me. Helen Guittard jumped in to help me at a moment's notice, and Karl Senn offered several helpful suggestions. Alice R. McAdams introduced me to Richard G. Schneidman, who kindly allowed me to view his archives on campaign and metamorphic furniture. Ruth Mills and Randy Rosen generously shared their knowledge and expertise. William Stahl, Wendell Garrett, Simon Redburn, and Peter Lang, all of Sotheby's New York, provided assistance when it was needed. David Katz and Sipra Chakrabarty at Photobition in New York worked wonders with several of the photographic images.

Special thanks are also due to the photographers Ian Walters, Peter Trulock, Dan Morgan, Arthur Vitols, and Tom Morello. I would also like to thank Christina la Torre of the Photographic Department at the National Army Museum for her help in providing several important images. At the Public Records Office in Kew, Jo Mathews and Paul Johnson helped me obtain numerous images of Victorian patent designs. Diana Kay, Photo Library Manager, Phillips Fine Art Auctioneers, London, allowed me to use her firm's library and kindly located transparencies for me. I would also like to thank Jane Taylor, publicity manager, Heal & Son, Ltd., for her help in answering a flurry of last-minute questions. She put me in touch with Guy Baxter of the Archive of Art and Design at the Victoria & Albert Museum. Their timely assistance in procuring two important photographs is greatly appreciated. Jane Padelford, of Christie's Images, expedited my many photographic requests. Without the thoughtful and generous assistance of Martin Durrant of the V & A Picture Library, it would have been impossible to provide a number of important illustrations in this book.

I would also like to thank the following people and institutions for permission to reproduce their photographs: Peter Harrington, Curator, The Anne S. K. Brown Military Collection, Brown University; Melissa L. Gold, Assistant Registrar, Yale Center for British Art; Shaula Coyl, Rights and Reproductions Assistant, and Cheryle T. Robertson, Rights and Reproductions Coordinator, the Los Angeles County Museum of Art; Christopher Howe Antiques, London; Patrick Conner, the Martyn Gregory Gallery, London; B&T Antiques, London; Michael Sim Fine English Furniture, Kent, England; John A.

Pearson Antiques, London; Neil Wibroe, London; Patrick Adam, Galérie Le Scaphandré, Paris; James Weedon and Robert Wotherspoon, Bonham's, London; Mallett, London; Ross Hamilton Antiques Ltd., London; Sean Clarke, Christopher Clarke Antiques, Gloucestershire, England; Andrew McMillan, Boulton & Cooper, Yorkshire; Humphrey Carrasco Antiques, London; and Mark Jacoby, Philip Colleck, New York.

In the course of preparing the book for publication, a number of the people on the staff at Harry N. Abrams, Inc. have been extremely generous with their time and practical suggestions. I am especially grateful to Margaret Rennolds Chace, Vice President and Managing Editor, who first introduced the book to the firm's editorial board, and who has been supportive in myriad ways throughout the editorial and design process. I would like to thank Elaine Stainton, my editor, for her guidance, enthusiasm, and unerring editorial direction. Bernard Furnival, Walter de la Vega, and Hope Koturo helped with photo scanning and digital printing. Sarah England went well beyond the call of duty in copyediting and making final corrections to the manuscript. I would also like to thank Maria Miller for her handsome design of the book, and Catherine Cain for her unfailing good humor and courtesy.

Finally, I owe a special debt of gratitude to my parents, Robert and Catherine Brawer, and to my wife, Meredith, for their ongoing support and encouragement of my work on the book, and for their many practical contributions to it, large and small.

Nicholas A. Brawer
New York, June 2000

I.
British Campaign Furniture

"To unite elegance and utility,

and blend the useful with

the agreeable, has ever been

considered a difficult,

but an honourable task."

—A. Hepplewhite & Co.
The Cabinet-Maker and Upholsterer's Guide, 1787

1. Late George III Brass-Mounted Mahogany Two-Part *Secrétaire*-Military Chest, with three long drawers and a full *secrétaire* drawer above, containing a satinwood fitted interior. H: 3 ft. 6½ in.; W: 2 ft. 5 in.; D: 1 ft. 2½ in. Courtesy Phillips of Hitchin (Antiques) Ltd.

Most military chests to be seen today are of the Victorian period, but this is one of the few early examples, dating from the turn of the nineteenth century. The bracket feet are an unusual feature, and the chest is of a relatively small size.

Campaign Furniture as a Reflection of British Society

British officers of high social position in the Georgian and Victorian periods (1714–1901) took it for granted that when they set out on a military campaign in Africa or India they could enjoy the same standard of living as they did at home. While "under canvas," as life in camp was called, an officer and a gentleman assured himself a high degree of comfort by using specially designed pieces of campaign, or knockdown, furniture. The only real difference between fine household furniture and its campaign counterpart was that the latter could be quickly folded up, packed away in boxes, transported, and—without the use of nails, tacks, or tools—reassembled in "some corner of another foreign field that was forever elegantly furnished England."[1] The superb designs of these pieces reflected the strong sense of superiority of the gentleman-officer class, its rank in both society and in the army, and its attitudes toward travel, camp, and battle. Officers' campaign furniture included chests (plate 1), writing desks (plates 2–3), bookcases (plates 4–5), games tables (plates 6–8), chairs (plates 9–10), beds (plates 62–63), sofa-beds (plates 11–12), washstands (plates 13–14), and even bidets for their ladies (plates 15–17).

Below:
2. Late George III Mahogany Writing Desk, with lift-up top, fitted interior, and frieze drawer, raised on square tapering legs with stretcher, c. 1800. The table is shown here with its top raised and side drawers extended. H (with top closed): 2 ft. 9¾ in.; W: 1 ft. 11¾ in.; D: 1 ft. 5¾ in. Courtesy Phillips of Hitchin (Antiques) Ltd.

Right:
3. Because this piece was made for travel or campaigning, the legs fold up under the frame of the table. (The stretchers are replacements, but of correct design.)

4. Regency Brass-Mounted Mahogany Traveling Bookcase, with inset-brass grille doors, c. 1820. H: 2 ft. 6 in.; W (open): 3 ft.; W (closed): 1 ft. 6 in.; D: 1 ft. 6½ in. Courtesy Phillips of Hitchin (Antiques) Ltd.

This bookcase has removable wood panels that fit behind the grilles, in order to prevent the books from shifting during travel.

5. When folded for travel, the bookcase takes on the appearance of a chest with brass detailing.

6. Regency Mahogany Campaign Games Table, on four reeded tapering legs that unscrew, c. 1810. H: 2 ft. 7¼ in.; W: 5 ft. 5½ in.; D: 2 ft. 1¾ in. Courtesy Phillips of Hitchin (Antiques) Ltd.

This table is an unusual design in that, when the top is removed, it reveals an open games board with markers for scoring. A somewhat similar table, made by Gillow of Lancaster, is in Abbott Hall, Kendal.

7. The table with top removed.

8. The table with legs unscrewed.

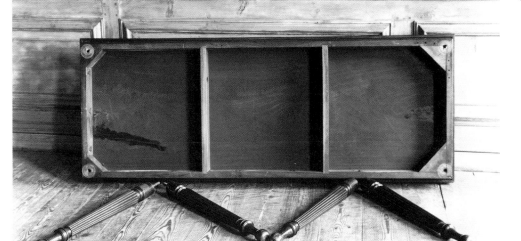

Left:
9. One from a Set of Four William IV Mahogany Dining Chairs, c. 1835. Courtesy Phillips of Hitchin (Antiques) Ltd.

This mahogany chair looks like a conventional William IV dining chair, but can be collapsed for traveling. Traveling chairs became increasingly in demand toward the end of the eighteenth century, due largely to the increasing population of Britain, the Napoleonic wars, and colonial expansion.

Below:
10. Set of Four William IV Dining Chairs, disassembled.

Opposite:
11. Regency Caned Mahogany Sofa-Bed, with out-scrolled arms, first quarter nineteenth century. H: 2 ft. 6 in.; H (to seat): 1 ft. 4½ in.; W: 6 ft. 2½ in.; D (of sofa): 2 ft. 1¼ in.; D (extended as bed): 5 ft. 10½ in. Courtesy Phillips of Hitchin (Antiques) Ltd.

12. The seat frame pulled out to form a bed, supported by four additional turned legs (replacements).

Opposite:
13. Victorian Officer's Mahogany Washbasin, mid-nineteenth century. H: 30¼ in.; W: 19½ in.; W (extended): 40½ in.; D: 29 in. Private collection.

This versatile piece of campaign furniture functions equally well as a washbasin, dining table, and writing desk. When used as a dining or writing table, the two D-shaped drop-leaves can be raised to form a large, smooth surface. If required as a washbasin, the top can be lifted to reveal a mirror, a metal wash bowl, a lead-lined hot water container, and a drain, which funnels the dirty water into a small copper basin stored in the body of the piece.

The washbasin contains a drawer in which to store its detachable, ring-turned legs when in transit, as well as flush brass handles so characteristic of military campaign furniture. Like most pieces of campaign furniture, this particular example is quite versatile, capable of being used for personal grooming, dining, writing, or storage.

On his trade card from c. 1847–1858, Gregory Kane, portmanteau maker to the Lord Lieutenant of Ireland, refers to designs of this type as a "Ship table."

14. When knocked down for travel, the ring-turned legs unscrew from the body of the table and can be stored inside a frieze drawer.

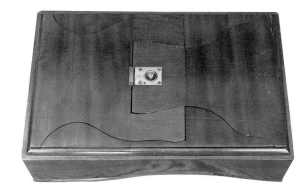

Above right:
15. Early Victorian Mahogany Traveling Bidet, with folding legs, possibly Continental, c. 1840. H: 1 ft. 6½ in.; W: 1 ft. 10 in.; D: 1 ft. 1½ in. Courtesy Phillips of Hitchin (Antiques) Ltd.

Middle right:
16. The bidet shown completely folded up into its own box measuring H: 6 in.; W: 1 ft. 10 in.; D: 1 ft. 1½ in.

Lower right:
17. The original leather carrying case, with sack handles.

CAMPAIGN FURNITURE / 27

18. Trade Card of William Pocock, c. 1810. Ink on paper. Public Record Office, London.

In January 1813, Rudolph Ackermann's *Repository of Arts* (p. 171) dubbed the designers at Pocock's firm "ingenious inventors."

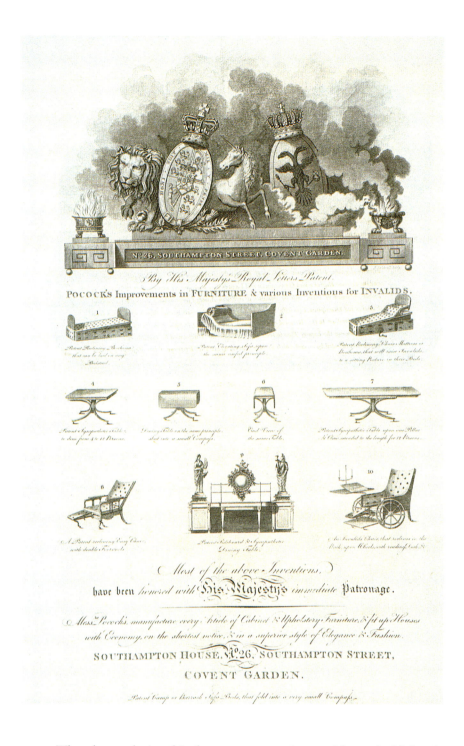

The close relationship between campaign and household furniture spanning nearly two centuries is illustrated by the comments of William Pocock (active c. 1802–1824), one of a small number of campaign furniture manufacturers operating near the Strand in London, and Edward Johnson (active c. 1839–1851), a manufacturer of camp, traveling equipage, and cabin furniture by appointment to the Honourable East India Company. In an advertisement from about 1810, (plate 18) Pocock describes the construction of one of his extending dining tables as "so astonishingly simple, and the Scale so variable as to suit either the Cottage Ornée, the festive Board of the hospitable Mansion, or the extensive Entertainments of the Nobility and Men of Fashion. [It] can . . . form an elegant Piece of Furniture for a Dining-Room . . . and yet can be made so portable as to go with the Baggage of a Regiment for the Officers' Mess."[2] Similarly, in 1839 Edward Johnson placed an advertisement for his "Newly Invented Metallic Folding Bedstead," which was designed for officers of the Army and the East India Company, emigrants to Canada and Australia, and those wishing to accommodate additional guests. By day, the bedstead was said to form "an elegant piece of drawing-room furniture," while at night it could be "converted into a bed in a few minutes." When not in use, it could be folded flat to take up "less than one-twelfth part of the room occupied by the common French bedstead."[3]

Pocock deliberately designed his table for use in a range of settings, knowing that gentlemen-officers in the Georgian period (1714–1820) would go to great expense to maintain their prestige, rank, and station in life, as well as the comforts of their permanent homes, while on military service abroad. It was precisely because issues of class and respectability were taken so seriously that makers of campaign furniture flourished. Commenting on a George IV period mahogany campaign dining table by Charles Stewart similar to that illustrated in plates 19–21, Peter Philp notes that the table was a "particularly ingenious example of campaign furniture, suitable for an officer's mess or governor's residence. Usable as a side table . . . it extends, with four leaves inserted, to a dining table about 11 ft. long . . . supported with the aid of a system of sliding bearers on only four legs which unscrew, so that the whole thing could be packed into a remarkably small space."[4]

In Georgian England, the need for high-quality campaign furniture was recognized by the preeminent cabinetmakers and furniture designers of the day. Thomas Chippendale (active c. 1747–1779), George Hepplewhite (d. 1786) Thomas Shearer (active c. 1788), William Ince (active c. 1758–1804), John Mayhew (active c. 1758–1804), and Thomas Sheraton (active 1751–1805) all bent their minds and genius to the task of portability. To these craftsmen, campaign furniture was as much in the mainstream of cabinet-making as domestic furniture. In his *Cabinet Dictionary* of 1803, for example, Thomas Sheraton displayed a keen awareness of how to wage war with elegant cabinetry in tow:

19. George IV Brass-Mounted Mahogany Concertina-Action Campaign Dining Table, with removable legs and brass plaque engraved, "*Stewart / INVENTOR / and Patentee / 115 St. Martin's Lane / Charing Cross / LONDON,*" c. 1810–1820. H: 57½ in.; L (fully extended): 109 in.; W: 21 in. Courtesy Christie's Images.

This campaign dining table by Charles Stewart (active c. 1810–1827) has the elegance and strength that would have made it ideal for an officers' mess about the time of the Battle of Waterloo. When the legs are removed and the two D-ends are folded together, it can fit in a space only several inches high, 47 inches long and 21 inches wide.

Right:
20. The table shown without its three middle leaves.

The four turned and tapering reeded legs can be unscrewed from the table for ease of transport.

21. Detail of maker's engraved brass label.

30 / CAMPAIGN FURNITURE

In encampments, persons of the highest distinction are obliged to accommodate themselves to such temporary circumstances, which encampments are ever subject to. Hence every article of an absolutely necessary kind, must be made very portable, both for package, and that such utensils should not retard rapid movement, either after or from the enemy. The articles of cabinet work used in such services, are, therefore, each of them required to be folded in the most compact manner that can be devised; yet this is to be done in such a way as, that when they are opened out, will answer their intended purpose. And it is to be observed, that most of the things which are of this nature, will also suit a cabin or sea voyage. . . . There are therefore camp or field bedsteads, camp chairs, desks, stools, and tables.[5]

Sheraton's design for a "Camp Bed" is illustrated in plate 22.

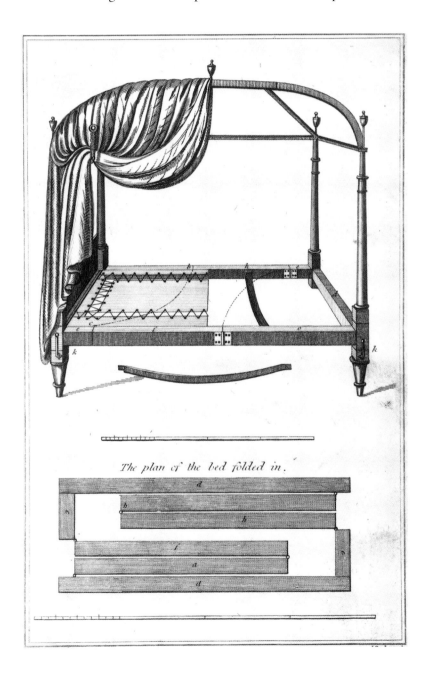

22. Thomas Sheraton (active c. 1751–1805). Design for a Camp Bed, and "The plan of the bed folded in," 1803, from *The Cabinet Dictionary*, pl. 15. Courtesy Victoria & Albert Museum; V & A Picture Library, London.

CAMPAIGN FURNITURE / 31

Chippendale's *The Gentleman and Cabinet-Maker's Director* (1762) illustrates six elaborate designs for "Tent, or Field Beds," as shown in plate 23. "The Furniture," Chippendale writes, with reference to his designs for campaign beds, "is made to take off [i.e., disassemble], and the Laths are hung with Hinges, for Convenience of folding up." A design for a collapsible field bed can also be seen in A. Hepplewhite & Co.'s *The Cabinet-Maker and Upholsterer's Guide* (1787) (plate 24). William Ince and John Mayhew's *The Universal System of Household Furniture* (1759–1762) illustrates an even more elaborate "Single Headed Couch or Field Bed," as well as a "Sofa Bed." This was "A Bed to appear as a Soffa [sic], with a fixed Canopy over it; the Curtains draws on a Rod; the Cheeks and Seat takes off to open the Bedstead."[6] A similar design for a "Sofa Bed" appears in Sheraton's *Cabinet Dictionary* (plate 25). Because space in camp and aboard ship was at such a premium, campaign furniture figured prominently in the gentleman officer's choice of

23. Thomas Chippendale (active c. 1747–1779). "Designs for Field Beds," 1762, from *The Gentleman & Cabinet Maker's Director*, pl. XLIX. Courtesy Victoria & Albert Museum; V & A Picture Library, London.

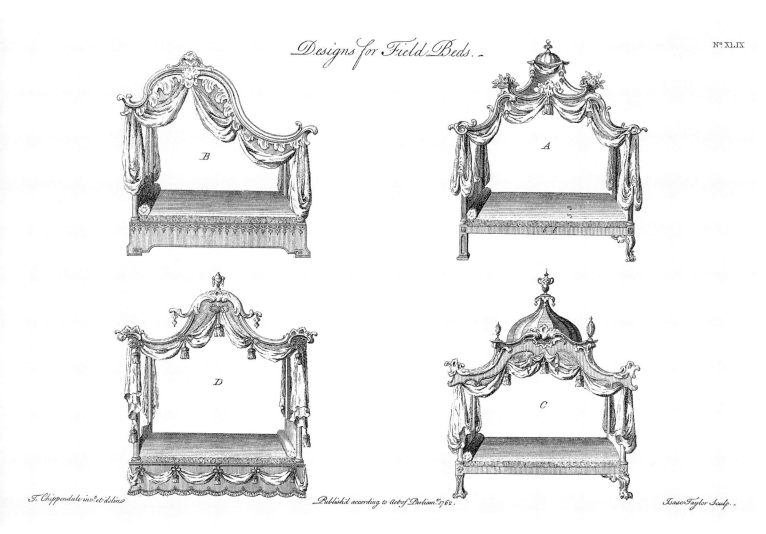

32 / CAMPAIGN FURNITURE

24. A. Hepplewhite & Co. "Design for a Field Bed," 1787, from *The Cabinet-Maker and Upholsterer's Guide*; pl. 103. The New York Public Library.

A field bed based on Hepplewhite's design is pictured in plates 62–63.

25. Thomas Sheraton (active c. 1751–1805). "Design for a Sofa Bed," 1803, from *The Cabinet Dictionary*, pl. 17. Courtesy Victoria & Albert Museum; V & A Picture Library, London.

CAMPAIGN FURNITURE /33

furnishings while serving overseas. The style and convenience of such pieces also appealed to Britons at home and abroad, who often used them for activities where space was *not* limited, such as camping, picnicking, or attending the races. According to Stanley Northcote-Bade:

In the eighteenth century, folding furniture became fashionable; and designers vied with each other to invent furniture with adjustable, movable, and retractable parts. Cabinets were often specially equipped with sliding, adjustable, or disappearing mirrors; folding or swiveling candle brackets; specially equipped drawers for the toilet or for shaving; writing slides; adjustable reading flaps, etc. Those designs produced at the turn of the century are noted for their neatness and compactness. . . .[7]

In the eighteenth and nineteenth centuries, many London cabinetmakers and travel outfitters catered especially to the needs of ships' officers and passengers, as well as to those of emigrants sailing from the British Isles. In an age when sea voyages could take months and military campaigns might last for many years, military officers, colonial administrators, tea planters, and other civilians equipped themselves with as many of the most comfortable furnishings as their servants could carry. Amin Jaffer of the Victoria and Albert Museum has noted that, because no tax was due on furniture carried from England as personal baggage to India in the eighteenth century, travelers had an added incentive to take along as much as possible.[8] Because campaign furniture could be packed flat, it was the ideal choice for most. In about 1810, firms such as Morgan & Sanders and Thomas Butler published broadsheets advertising dining tables that could be expanded to seat twenty, yet fold up into the floor space of a large Pembroke table, in a box only ten inches deep; one dozen portable dining-room chairs that could be packed in the space of two common chairs; and sofas that could easily be transformed into four-poster tented bedsteads, complete with drapery and bedding. Such pieces were designed specifically for "Captains [*sic*] Cabins & ladies or Gentlemen going to the East or West Indies." An example of one of Morgan & Sanders' broadsheets from this time is illustrated in plate 26.

Because travel in the eighteenth century was rugged and slow, campaign furniture was specifically designed to be folded and packed into manageable loads that could be stowed in the closed quarters of a ship before being carried across land by both man and beast. James Thornton, cook to the Duke of Wellington, recalled in an interview with Lord Frederick Fitzclarence that he required six mules to trans-

Opposite:
26. Trade Card of Morgan & Sanders, 16 & 17 Catherine Street, London, c. 1803. Ink on paper. British Museum, Banks Trade Card Collection.

In July 1809, upon beholding the "spacious and well-furnished warerooms of Messrs. Morgan and Sanders," Ackermann's *Repository of Arts* (p. 122) observed that "their patent sofa-beds, chair-beds, brass screw four-post and tent bedsteads, newly invented imperial dining-tables [and] portable chairs . . . evince to what perfection modern ingenuity and invention have arrived in these lines."

34 / CAMPAIGN FURNITURE

Morgan & Sanders's
Manufactory *for their New Invented* **Dining Tables**
AND **PORTABLE CHAIRS**,
The best & most approved SOFA BEDS, CHAIR BEDS, *handsome* FOUR POST *and* TENT BEDSTEADS, *with Furniture and Bedding complete, at their*
UPHOLSTERY & CABINET WARE-ROOMS
N.º 16 & 17, Catherine Street,
Three doors from the Strand.
L O N D O N.

MORGAN & SANDERS'S *NEW INVENTED*,

IMPERIAL DINING TABLE, forming an elegant Sett, to Dine from Four, to Twenty Persons, or any greater Number; the whole TABLE, shuts up into the space of a Large Pembroke Table, the Feet are completely out of the way & the whole may be packed in a Box only 10 Inches deep.
One of the above TABLES, T. MORGAN, had the Honour of shewing to Their MAJESTIES and the PRINCESSES at Buckingham House, who according to their accustomed Goodness, of encouraging Ingenuity, were most graciously pleased to express their highest Approbation and Sanction of the same.

PORTABLE CHAIRS, a Dozen of which packs in the space of 2 Common Chairs.

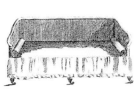 

The best & most approved SOFA BEDS, forming an elegant SOFA, and may be transformed with great ease into a compleat FOUR POST -BED, with Furniture, Bedding &c.

The best & most approved CHAIR BEDS, forming a handsome easy CHAIR, and is with great ease transformed into a TENT BED, with Furniture and Bedding compleat.

This elegant FOUR POST and TENT BEDSTEAD, with Lath or Sacking Bottom, made upon the best & most approved Principle, are fixed up or taken down in a few minutes, without the use of Tools &c.
The Furnitures are made upon a New Plan, of taking off or on, without Tools, Tacks &c.

A very convenient & highly approved of SOFA BED, contrived on purpose for Captains Cabins & Ladies or Gentlemen going to the East or West Indies with every other Article necessary for Voyages & use of Foreign Climates, Musquito Nett Furniture, Bedding &c. also Army & Navy Equipage, compleat.
The above Inventions and Improvements with every other Article in the UPHOLSTERY and CABINET BRANCHES, executed in the most Fashionable and best manner.
NB. for Exportation.

port himself, his assistant, and their luggage, "but when the whole of the establishment was on the March, we had seldom less than eighty."[9] When asked how he packed and carried his tables, Thornton replied, "The tables were folded boards with hinges, the legs were separated and when put up formed a sort of tressal [sic], and they were packed on the side of the Mule."[10] Interestingly, a functional piece of furniture such as a trestle table received the attention of no less a designer than Thomas Sheraton. In his *Cabinet Dictionary* (1803), Sheraton wrote that a "trussel" camp table should have a top made from "one entire piece, 30 inches long by 20 broad; and being hinged at one side with swan neck hinges . . . the top easily turns over upon the trussel, and may be fastened with hook and eye. . . ." He also noted that "These tables are both simple, and will bear any degree of hardship."

The elaborate accouterments of the navy matched those of the army. Just as high-ranking army officers tried to re-create the comforts of home while under canvas, many senior naval officers turned their cabins into floating extensions of their homes and clubs. As the furniture historian Treve Rosoman explains, "A captain fitted up his quarters as his fortune, or interests, permitted; for example, Captain Johnstone of the sloop *Hornet* had so many books in his cabin that it looked 'more like a bookseller's shop than the captain's apartment in a man of war.'"[11] Similarly, in a letter to his wife, Fanny, Rear Admiral Edward Boscawen (1711–1761) described a fellow admiral's quarters as "fitted up like a modern palace," in contrast to his own, which were "strong and plain like an old country hall."[12] Boscawen might very well have found a friend in Admiral Croft, one of Jane Austen's most likable individuals in *Persuasion* (1818), whose "simplicity of character" was "irresistible."[13] Other writings from the period suggest, however, that these men of simple tastes were exceptional. The anonymous author of *The Navy "At Home"* (1831) reveals an eye for pretension and a keen sense of the absurd. In the following passage, the author seems to be satirizing some of the more extravagant practices of the day:

[Captain George Oakheart] was reclining on a sofa in the after cabin, where was blended a strange medley of rough tokens of war with the softer attributes of peace; here ranged, well filled bookcases—there, double barreled pistols, and Turkish and French sabers—Here polished mahogany satin chairs, vases of flowers, and billets-doux [love letters]—there, stern cold iron, in the shape of eighteen pounders, taking their way through windows (the ports) hung with silk curtains—their icy touch and strained lashings told their scorn of the

painter's art to render them less ferocious, in white and green—in the fore cabin hung a beautiful or-molu [sic] lamp, over a festive board, where, when at sea, smoked eight silver covers at least (every day at 4 p.m.) with all the delicacies of all the world—now garnished with a fine green cloth, cut-glass decanters, different sorts of wine, and a luncheon on a tray, after the most approved modes of the fashionable world. In short, all was of the most refined elegance, of the most approved taste, of the most exquisite delicacy, and of the richest description, side by side, with the instruments of stern and instant destruction—In five minutes all would disappear, and the dogs of war let slip, fire, smoke, cartridges, bleeding bodies, recoiled guns; and fifty devils incarnate would turn this floating paradise into a hellish pandemonium! As it now appeared, not Cleopatra herself, in her gilded and silken galley, knew an equal luxury . . . And yet here was a man of war, polished, accomplished, soft as the zephyrs whisper'd through summer Cynthea's light, in peace—collected, fierce, and terrible in war,—and hard as the oak he trod.[14]

This passage suggests that there may well have been a serious sense of unreality among some of His Majesty's finest. The reader almost forgets that the captain's cabin was on a man-of-war and not a room in a fashionable London house. The captain's efforts to disguise the "instruments of stern and instant destruction" behind "all the delicacies of the world" reflect a strangely ambivalent mentality. It is as if his job—having to fight—were offensive to good taste. A similar attitude can still be glimpsed over sixty years later in a photograph of the captain's cabin on the H.M.S. *Powerful* (plate 28).

27. Victorian Oak Pedestal Campaign Desk, third quarter nineteenth century. H: 2 ft. 6 in.; W: 4 ft. 6 in.; D: 1 ft. 5¾ in. Collection of Peter Bronson.

This Victorian oak pedestal desk has three drawers in each pedestal, carved turned feet, and a top that lifts for reading and writing (top probably reversed or adapted at a later date). This piece has the sunken handles found on military chests, together with brass corner supports and brass fittings to secure the top to the pedestals.

28. The Captain's Cabin of the *Powerful*, c. 1898. Black and white photograph. Courtesy of the Director, National Army Museum, London.

In an effort to give his cabin a domestic feel, the captain has furnished it with a campaign pedestal desk similar to that illustrated in plate 28, slip-covered chairs, chintz curtains, potted plants, leather-bound books, oil paintings, and framed photographs.

The ability of the British to keep up appearances abroad was so compelling that, as sometimes happens where a ruling class exists, those whom they had subdued in the name of God and Empire tried to emulate them. In 1803, for instance, Lord Valentia observed firsthand how one of the most senior Indian princes, Saadat Ali, Nawab of Oudh, sought to affect the appurtenances of an English aristocrat: "An English apartment, a band in English regimentals playing English tunes, a room lighted by magnificent English girandoles, English tables, chairs and looking glasses, an English service of plates, English knives and forks, spoons, wineglasses, decanters and cut-glass vases—how could these convey any idea that we were seated in the court of an Asiatic Prince?"[15] Ironically, the celebrated Lord Clive ("Clive of India," 1725–1774), who became the first Governor of Bengal after defeating Siraj-ud-daula, the Nawab of Bengal, at the battle of Plassey in 1757, strove to emulate the trappings of his defeated Indian foe. He did so by appropriating the Nawab's elaborate palanquin, or passenger carriage,

38 / CAMPAIGN FURNITURE

which had been abandoned during the battle of Plassey. It took four to six bearers to lift the device, and one can imagine the imperious Clive being carried triumphantly from the battlefield on the backs of six Indians. Some years later, the second Lady Clive acquired the carved sandalwood traveling bed/throne that had belonged to Tipu, the Sultan of Mysore, whom British forces had defeated at the battle of Seringapatam in 1799. According to Veronica Murphy,[16] "Like the European campaign bed of the period, this one is easily dismantled for traveling. . . . A prince's traveling bed might well have doubled as a throne in camp."[17] Displaying the furniture of those whom he had vanquished helped Clive maintain the image of a triumphant general.

More than a century after Clive's victory at Plassey, many Victorian firms were carrying on the tradition of making elegant knock-down furniture. In 1879, for example, the cabinetmaker and upholsterer J. W. & M. Jarvis placed an advertisement for an adjustable easy chair, twelve of which could be packed in a case 4 feet 6 inches by 3 feet 8 inches by 1 foot 10 inches. In the same way, six of J. W. & M. Jarvis's "Colonial" dining tables could be packed in a space 3 feet 6 inches by 3 feet 8 inches by 3 feet, when their legs were unscrewed, as seen in a detail from their advertisement (plate 29).

29. Advertisement for J. W. & M. Jarvis, 1879. Ink on paper. Courtesy Victoria & Albert Museum; V & A Picture Library.

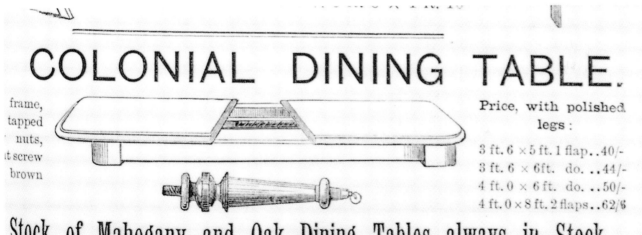

30. Victorian Walnut Campaign Chiffonier, third quarter nineteenth century. The maker's brass plaque is embossed, "*Ross & Co. / Manufacturers / 9, 10 & 11, Ellis's Quay / Dublin.*" H: 5 ft. 5 in.; H (of cabinet): 3 ft. 4½ in.; W: 3 ft. 8½ in.; D: 1 ft. 5 in. Courtesy Phillips of Hitchin (Antiques) Ltd.

This chiffonier was specifically designed to hold a suite of campaign furniture, including four chairs, a sofa, and a center table.

31. The superstructure of shelves on this walnut chiffonier unscrews and can be packed away into a drawer beneath. The overhanging moldings on each side of the cabinet come away so as to present a flush surface, thereby allowing it to be packed tightly against a similar piece.

Most traveling furniture of this period was made of mahogany or oak, but this chiffonier, once the property of W. S. Steel of the Scots Greys, has the relative rarity of being made of walnut. The arched panels on the cupboard doors are very similar to those on the pedestals of a sideboard made for Captain and Mrs. Simner in 1863 and illustrated in plates 34 and 35.

32. Ross & Co., "Printed Directions for Packing this Cabinet." Ink on paper label affixed to drawer of chiffonier.

Remarkably, an entire suite of furniture, including four dining chairs, a sofa, and a center table (not to mention the superstructure) could all be packed within the lower cabinet of the chiffonier.

33. Detail of the maker's embossed brass plaque.

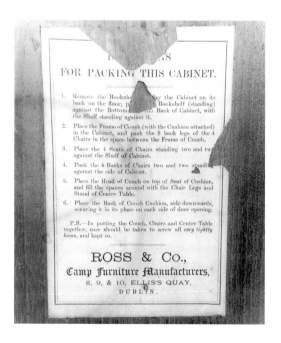

40 / CAMPAIGN FURNITURE

During the second half of the nineteenth century, the traditional efforts of the British to make their presence felt abroad are reflected in the popularity of entire parlor suites of campaign furniture among officers, travelers, and colonists, such as those emigrating to New Zealand. These suites were made in the style of the day and would not have looked out of place in an elegant drawing room. In 1865, for example, the campaign furniture manufacturers S.W. Silver, of Liverpool and London, exhibited their folding furniture at the New Zealand Exhibition. According to the *Reports and Awards of the Jurors*, "The only British exhibitor in the furniture section was the firm of S. W. Silver & Co., London, Exhibit No. 2978. . . . The judges took special note of their folding chairs. The suitability of some of the exhibits of furniture, where lightness, portability, and convenience are required, is particularly noticeable in some chairs, which, although fit for luxuriantly furnished apartments in point of appearance, can yet be folded and removed with all the readiness of a camp stool."[18] As Edward T. Joy has observed, "To the early Victorians comfort had to be seen as well as experienced, and this was achieved by lavish upholstery and multiplicity of gadgets."[19] A typical suite, such as that advertised by the Army & Navy Co-operative Society around 1875, consisted of a mahogany or walnut chiffonier designed to hold a knock-down couch, a folding round or oval dining table, two collapsible easy chairs (one for a lady, the other for a gentleman), and four portable dining chairs, each stuffed with horsehair and covered with wool, damask, or leather. The chiffonier from a suite similar to that described above, made by the eminent military furniture manufacturer Ross & Co. of Dublin in 1863, is illustrated in plates 30–31 together with its maker's embossed brass plaque (plate 33). A paper label entitled "DIRECTIONS FOR PACKING THIS CABINET," illustrated in plate 32, is affixed to the interior of one of its drawers. It explains how to pack inside the chiffonier four upholstered campaign chairs, a folding couch with its cushion, a collapsible bookshelf, and a folding center table.

An English officer named Captain Benjamin Simner (born in London in 1832) of the 76th Regiment took just such a set of carved campaign furniture with him while in India from 1865 until his return to Chatham in 1877. Nine pieces from the suite are shown assembled in plate 34 and broken down for travel in plate 35. The suite originally came with a sideboard and traveling bath, and may also have included

some traveling bedroom furniture as well.[20] According to information supplied by the Regimental Headquarters of the Duke of Wellington's Regiment at Halifax, Yorkshire, Captain Simner joined the 76th Regiment in Madras in 1865. He traveled with his regiment to Burma in 1869 and to Secunderabad in 1871, and from 1872 to 1875 he was Instructor of Musketry, most likely in India.[21] His suite, made by Ross & Co., was given to him and his wife, Frances Mary Bolton, as a wedding present on March 27, 1863. It consisted of a dining table, four dining chairs, a "lady's chair" with settee, and a two-part sideboard, all constructed from walnut taken from the family estate at Bective in Ireland. Remarkably, the entire suite folded neatly into the two pedestals of the sideboard, with each of the two resulting boxes measuring 2 feet 11 inches by 1 foot 10 inches by 2 feet 3 inches. Captain Simner and his bride were clearly accustomed to traveling in style, for they spent twelve years having their elegant suite of campaign furniture portered with them around India.

The "lady's chair" that formed part of Captain Simner's suite was a much appreciated piece of furniture, especially out in India. The Honourable Emily Eden, who accompanied her brother Lord Auckland, Governor-General of India from 1835 to 1842, on an official trip up-country from Calcutta, recorded just how comfortable an upholstered chair could be while under canvas. In a diary entry dated February 27, 1839 she wrote, "Captain Z. came into my tent this morning and flung himself into my arm-chair—Mr. D.'s chair, that sacred piece of furniture . . . and he began: 'I was just going to say—what a delicious chair this is! Such a spring! . . .'"[22] Like Captain Simner, Emily Eden also enjoyed home-style living standards in camp. On December 31, 1838 she wrote in her diary, "We went first to a little tent, where we left E. and the two aides-de-camp, and which was fitted up very like an English drawing-room, full of plate, and musical-boxes and china."[23]

In 1803 the English furniture designer Thomas Sheraton described a typical field officer's quarters when on campaign in terms that illustrate the military and social hierarchy of the day:

A captain's tent and marquee is generally 10½ feet broad, 14 feet deep, and 8 feet high. The subalterns' are one foot less; the major's and lieutenant colonel's a foot larger. The subalterns of foot [infantry] *lie two in a tent, and those of horse* [cavalry] *but one. The tents of private men are 6½ feet square and 5 feet high, and hold five soldiers each. The tents of horse are 7 feet broad and 9 feet*

Opposite:
34. Suite of Victorian Walnut Campaign Furniture, with brass plaques embossed, "*Ross & Co. / Manufacturers / 9, 10 & 11 Ellis's Quay / Dublin*," 1863. Courtesy Phillips Fine Art Auctioneers, London

This suite of walnut campaign furniture, consisting of four dining chairs, a center table, an easy chair, a day bed, and two packing cases that doubled as pedestals of a sideboard for which the center piece is now lost, was made in 1863 by E. Ross of Dublin as a wedding present for Captain Benjamin Simner, of the 76th Regiment, and his wife, Mary Bolton of Dublin, to take to India, where he served from 1865–1877. Sydney J. Maiden writes:

It is pleasant to think that Captain and Mrs. Simner, during some twelve years in the East, had their changing quarters furnished in a way that must have alleviated the discomforts of life in the East in the days before modern comforts such as electric fans and refrigerators. It is easy to picture the scene as the Simners sat under a punkah in a tent furnished with these pieces so reminiscent of Ireland. The walnut of which they are constructed came from the family estate in Bective. Mrs. Simner's thoughts must often have returned to the woods of Ireland as she entertained her husband's brother officers at little dinner parties, far from the home she left to go on service with her husband.[1]

1. Sydney J. Maiden, "A Wedding Present of 1863: An Officer's Travelling Furniture," *The Connoisseur* (May 1957), 168.

35. The entire suite collapses neatly into two crates, measuring 2 feet 11 inches by 1 foot 10 inches by 2 feet 3 inches, which double as pedestals for a sideboard, the center section of which is now lost.

36. Thomas Sheraton (active c. 1751–1805). Drawing of an Officer's Tent, from *The Cabinet Dictionary* (1803), pl. 79. Ink on paper. Courtesy Victoria & Albert Museum; V & A Picture Library, London.

deep; they likewise hold five men and their accoutrements. . . . The inside of the [captain's] tent is lined with cotton, and hung in draperies. The plan of the tent is semi-circular at each end; and where the circle commences, a curtain is hung extending the whole width of the tent, parting in the middle for easy admission of company to dine. Within the circular ends the servants wait, and are thus parted from the company. The circular room at the end of the tent, is the sleeping apartment, which has a passage to it leading straight from the body of the tent, in length about 12 feet, and 8 feet wide, having a curtain on each side, behind which they put trunks and other articles out of the way."[24] (plate 36)

An *Invoice of Camp Equipage* (plates 37–38) packed for Lieutenant Robert Ballard Long of the 1st Regiment of Dragoon Guards (plate 39) by Messrs. John Trotter & Co. of Soho Square, London on July 5th, 1793, in anticipation of the ill-fated Flanders Campaign (1793–1795), gives further insight into traditional British observance of caste and class. Of the sixty-two items of camp equipment available for purchase, only eight were intended for an officer's servant. Lieutenant Long selected forty-nine articles of camp equipment at a cost of £47 17s. 4d., which, for reference, was approximately three and a half times the annual salary of an English porter in 1792, and six times the annual salary of an English footman in 1787.[25] In preparation for active service he selected a "Captain's Marquee and Tent," together with a "Curtain

37–38. List of Camp Equipment, 1793. Ink on paper. Long Military Papers. Courtesy of the Director, National Army Museum, London.

List of sixty-two items of camp equipage available for purchase from Messrs. Trotter & Co. in 1793. On July 5th of that year, Lt. Robert Ballard Long of the 1st (or King's) Dragoons purchased forty-nine items for himself and a servant in anticipation of the ill-fated Flanders Campaign. Of note, Long chose to purchase a "Captain's Marquee and Tent," a table, two stools and, like a true gentleman, a bedside carpet. In an unusual show of restraint, he chose a folding cot in lieu of the Messrs. Trotter & Co.'s more substantial "Folding Field Bedstead."

39. W. Fowler. *Portrait of Lieutenant General Robert Ballard Long in the Uniform of a General Officer of Hussars*, 1821. Oil on canvas. Courtesy of David McAlpine.

CAMPAIGN FURNITURE /45

for the boot, of Ticking." For his servant he ordered a "Round Tent, which," the firm added parenthetically, "in cases of necessity may answer for the officer himself."[26]

The British military historian T. H. McGuffie, writing as late as 1948, admired Long's "fixed determination to campaign like a gentleman, even taking a bedside carpet,"[27] but makes no mention of his abilities as a fighting man. That a mere lieutenant on the field of battle felt it necessary to outfit himself with as many as forty-nine articles of camp equipment makes one wonder just how much these massive loads might have retarded "rapid movement, either after or from the enemy" (per Sheraton), and even contributed to the ultimate failure of the Flanders Campaign. It is ironic that the more portable the furniture became, the more of it the officers were able to take with them—hence, the *less* portable the Empire really became.

In a diary entry dated 1813, Lieutenant-Colonel William Tomkinson, a contemporary of Lieutenant Long, explained why he equipped himself with six hundred pounds of personal baggage while on military service in Spain during the Peninsular war:

[My equipment] *may appear a large fit-out for a person going on service, but experience taught us that campaign after campaign was not to be got through without the things I have stated; and the more an officer makes himself comfortable, the better will he do his duty, as well as secure his own health, and the comfort of those belonging to him.* [As if comfort were a virtue to be practiced, like courage or tenacity!]
 It does not follow, that because we attempt the best in every situation, that we cannot face the worst. The poorer the country the greater must be your baggage, from the length of time you are obliged to march without obtaining a fresh supply.[28]

In his diary Tomkinson writes that his baggage would be carried by two mules: one to balance a trunk of clothes and a canteen capable of dining six; the other, to carry two large baskets containing provisions, a tent, and a bed. His description of the contents of his canteens shows how fastidious he was, and reads more like that of a man setting off for a few leisurely days in the country rather than on a military expedition:

The canteen to be very complete should dine six people, though four is sufficient. Twelve plates—four or six out of which to be deep enough for soup—six dishes, two of which should be covered, and one of them deep enough for soup, with a cover making a dish of itself. Six silver cups for wine. The same, but larger, for water—Queen's metal, very good. Neither knives nor forks in the canteen, but in two leather rollers, and, if room, a place may be left in the canteen, though they will carry anywhere. The soup ladle to be in the canteen and to answer for punch ladle. The soup dish to answer for a punch bowl; decanters in the canteen. Four tea-cups and saucers. Independent of which a basket for picket [picknicking], *containing two plates, both deep enough for soup, a coffee-pot, kettle to boil meat in, frying pan, two tea-cups and saucers. Space for cold meat, tea, etc. . . .*

[The first basket contains] *a nest of kettles, with a smaller one for kitchen knife, spoon, etc., with the* prenrice spit. *In the nest of kettles two or three things for tarts, pies, etc. . . . Butter tub, oil can, kitchen lamp, pickle jar, lard, etc. . . . Tins for flour, rice, sugar. Tin for candles.*

The second basket contains a partition for meat, with a cover to separate salt from fresh; another for vegetables, and a third for hams. . . . A wine and brandy tub. A picket tent. Four or six table-cloths, knife cloths. . . .[29]

40. Selection of the Duke of Wellington's Campaign Plate, with fitted leather case, c. 1810. Collection of the Victoria & Albert Museum, London. Photo: Victoria & Albert Museum; V & A Picture Library.

This portable set of monogrammed silver dining utensils is a good example of what Clare LeCorbeiller describes as demonstrating "the harmony of function and design that made dining pleasant in unpleasant circumstances."[1]

1. Quoted in Paula Deitz, "Providing the Comforts of Home in War," *New York Times*, July 1, 1982, C10.

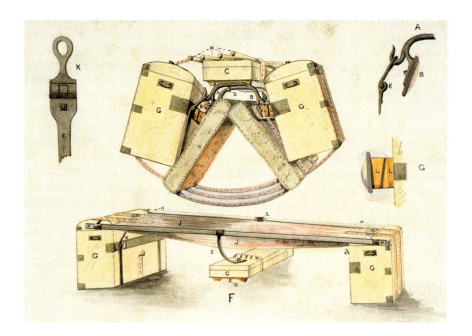

41. Combination "Pack Saddle" Boxes and Bedstead, registered by Bowring, Arundel & Co., Outfitters, Nos. 11 and 12 Fenchurch Street, London, between 1881 and 1884. Watercolor and ink on paper. Public Record Office, London.

An example of a pack saddle designed to balance two large trunks, patented between 1881 and 1884 by the London outfitters Bowring, Arundel & Co., is illustrated in plate 41.

In a remarkable display of the staying power of the imperial attitude, the Eton- and Oxford-educated Captain Julian Henry Francis Grenfell (1888–1915), 1st Royal Dragoon Guards, echoed Tomkinson's civilized approach to campaigning almost one hundred years later. In a letter to his mother during the First World War, Grenfell wrote, "I *adore* war. It is like a big picnic."[30] Grenfell, like many of his fellow gentleman-officers, would soon be shot down by German gunners.

The overriding insistence on precedence expressed by Sheraton and illustrated by Lieutenant Long and Lieutenant-Colonel Tomkinson lasted until the end of the nineteenth century, and extended to equipment and dress as well as to furnishings. There existed a fierce rivalry among the three regiments of Household Cavalry before they were amalgamated. Between 1854 and 1882, for example, officers in the 1st Life Guards carried swords that were exactly one-quarter inch longer than those carried by officers in both the 2nd Life Guards and Royal Horse Guards.[31] One does not have to stretch terribly far to know what Freud would have made of this. Their sword dimensions were apparently as precisely differentiated as the dimensions of their tents. Today, Guards officers all carry swords of the same length, but continue to wear plumed metal helmets, cuirasses (steel breastplates), white leather breeches, and thigh-length jackboots similar to those worn by their Victorian counterparts. They still provide mounted escorts for the Royal Family and visiting dignitaries traveling by coach on state occasions, as well as a guard of two mounted sentries outside the Horse Guards building in Whitehall.[32]

Throughout the Victorian era, gentleman-officers on campaign continued to live as sumptuously as their Georgian predecessors, particularly in India, where their tents tended to be larger than those of their fellow officers posted to the farther corners of the Empire. Writing in 1858, Captain George F. Atkinson of the Bengal Engineers described the proprieties of an encampment in India:

Commanding officers frequently have a large double-poled tent, measuring thirty feet by sixteen feet; besides one or two other smaller ones, usually single-poled, from fourteen to sixteen feet square; besides an awning and tents for the servants and horses. . . . The prevailing kind of tent . . . is a single-poled tent, about fourteen feet square, with an outer fly or covering, and an outer wall . . . which gives a verandah of from two to three feet in width. . . . Subalterns, however, are generally content with a smaller kind, commonly called a hill tent, such as is represented in the Drawing; it is usually ten feet square, with a double roof but only single walls, and therefore with no verandah; but a strip of canvas extends over the sides a few feet, as a protection from the sun for servants: such a tent can be carried by a single camel. . . .[33] (plate 42)

42. Captain George F. Atkinson. "Scenes in Camp," 1857, from *The Campaign in India*, pl. 4. Courtesy Victoria & Albert Museum; V & A Picture Library, London.

Clearly, there was more concern for observing social distinctions in the field than for such military exigencies as having to break camp rapidly. Pity these soldiers if their camels had run away.

The elaborate officers' quarters had a further practical liability: they afforded little protection against the *real* day-to-day enemy—the harsh Indian climate. "This is my second hot season in Tents, with the thermometer seldom below 120°, [even] with grass Tatties [screens] well watered," wrote John Brownrigg Bellasis (1806–1890), a young officer who arrived in Bombay as an ensign with the 10th Regiment of Native Infantry in 1822.[34] Captain Atkinson provides an even grimmer glimpse into the unbearable conditions found inside an officer's tent in India:

The heat is terrific; the tent is pitched on a sandy piece of ground, and the sun beats right through the thick double roof; the thermometer stands at 118° of heat. The only resource is to wrap the head in a towel and keep it saturated; and incessantly had the attendant . . . to be summoned to provide a fresh supply of water, as the heat soon makes the towel as dry as chalk. Then, as an additional refuge, the bed is hoisted up on to the camel-trunks, and beneath its thick mattress there is some slight modification of the direct rays of the sun; but still the heat is prodigious. In vain letters are attempted to be written—the ink has dried up—the pens have split; and then there goes the alarm—again it sounds—no time to be lost; the sword is seized from its sheath, which is left behind—the revolver is laid hold of—the turbaned helmet is clapped on, and away, right under the burning sun, rushes forth the gallant hero, regardless of heat, or aught that could impede him in his duty.[35]

Atkinson's description of the furnace that was the interior of a Victorian officer's tent shows that under such conditions no furniture, portable or otherwise, could provide relief from the blistering sun. It is interesting to consider whether any of these men thought to pitch a more modest establishment, perhaps in the shade. The impression is unmistakable that campaigning in India would have been more bearable with a (quite literally) less buttoned-up lifestyle. The journalist Hugh Boyd, writing in *The Indian Observer* on December 10, 1793, proved to be a sharp, dispassionate commentator on the imperial attitude of his fellow Englishmen: "Of all the people under the sun our countrymen alone, as if insensible to cold or heat, affect to brave all vicissitudes of climate and obstinately to wear the same dress in every part of the world."[36] Arthur William Devis's portrait of the Honourable William Monson and his wife Ann Debonnaire, painted in India about 1786 shows them in attire that would have been perfectly acceptable in London society (plate 43).

43. Arthur William Devis (1762–1822). *The Honorable William Monson and his wife, Ann Debonnaire*, c. 1786. Oil on canvas. H: 40½ in.; W: 51½ in. Los Angeles County Museum of Art, William Randolph Hearst Collection.

The extent to which British officers were willing to suffer for the sake of appearances is remarkable.

Throughout the Empire, British nationals could be found steadfastly, if not obstinately, asserting their Britishness by wearing tight-fitting, European clothes ill-suited to foreign climates; hunting not foxes, but jackals, boars, and tigers; establishing exclusive social clubs such as The Bengal Club and The Bombay Yacht Club, modeled after their English counterparts along Pall Mall; writing letters on carved elm or mahogany desks; sitting in upholstered leather armchairs; and sleeping in cushioned beds. Regardless of which corner of the globe they found themselves, the officers of the British Empire and their ladies acted with almost complete disregard for the culture, geography, and climate in which they were stationed. In their furniture as well as in their architecture, dress, social customs, and mannerisms, they simply carried on as though in England. Their determination to do so is well illustrated in a watercolor from 1824 of the sumptuously appointed summer room in Charles D'Oyly's house in Patna (plate 44).

There is no better example of this frame of mind than Lord Wellesley's decision in 1798 to build a magnificent new Government House in Calcutta to represent British authority in India (plate 45). The design he chose was based upon one of Robert Adam's greatest neo-classical residences, Kedleston Hall in Derbyshire, and therefore bore no relation to

CAMPAIGN FURNITURE / 51

44. Charles D'Oyly (1781–1845). *The Summer Room in the Artist's House At Patna*, September 11, 1824. Watercolor over graphite on paper. H: 6⅞ in.; W: 13½ in. Yale Center for British Art, Paul Mellon Collection.

CAMPAIGN FURNITURE /53

45. South Front, Government House, Calcutta. Black and white photograph. The British Library, Oriental and India Office Collections.

The New Government House was built between 1798 and 1803 for the Earl of Mornington, Governor General of India and elder brother of the Duke of Wellington. The architect was Captain Charles Wyatt, who based his design on Lord Curzon's Kedleston Hall in Derbyshire.

India's architectural past. Wellesley's aristocratic philosophy for building such a quintessentially English, even Roman, building is summarized by Lord Valentia, who witnessed its inaugural ceremony:

The Esplanade leaves a grand opening, on the edge of which is placed the new Government House erected by Lord Wellesley, a noble structure, although not without faults in the architecture; and, upon the whole, not unworthy of its destination. The sums expended upon it have been considered as extravagant by those who carry European ideas and European economy into Asia, but they ought to remember that India is a country of splendour, of extravagance and of outward appearances; that the Head of a mighty Empire [Wellesley] ought to conform himself to the prejudices of the country he rules over. . . . In short, I wish India to be ruled from a palace, not from a counting-house; with the ideas of a Prince, not with those of a retail-dealer in muslins and indigo.[37]

It is interesting that Lord Valentia justifies the construction of Wellesley's palace by citing the need to conform to *India's* passion for splendor, extravagance, and outward appearances. Indeed, in the eighteenth century India's ruling princes maintained vast personal fortunes that were the envy of the British. Thomas Babington Macaulay, the famous biographer of Robert, Lord Clive, recounts how Clive, who had been called to account by Parliament for his purported plundering of Bengal after his victory at the Battle of Plassey, eloquently refuted the charges against him. According to Macaulay, "Great princes [were] dependent on his pleasure; an opulent city [was] afraid of being given up to plunder; wealthy bankers [bid] against each other for his smiles; vaults piled with gold and jewels [were] thrown open to him alone. 'By God, Mr. Chairman,' [Clive] exclaimed, 'at this moment I stand astonished at my own moderation!'"[38]

In a diary entry dated October 22, 1856, Lady Charlotte Canning, wife of a Victorian Governor-General, describes her sitting-room at another Government House, this one in Barrackpore: "I am getting so fond of this place . . . I believe it would look rather nice even as an English country-house, so marvelously is it improved by 450 yards of rose-chintz, a great many arm-chairs, small round tables, framed drawings etc."[39] In a letter to Queen Victoria, Lady Canning writes that even the "park is carefully planted with round headed trees to look as English as possible. . . . The luxuriant growth in the jungly ground outside . . . is more beautiful than I can describe & I always think of the Palm House at Kew which gives a faint idea of it."[40]

It seems that the farther from England they found themselves, the more the British tried to maintain the illusion that they were back in Britain. In 1859 a force of Royal Marines was sent halfway around the world to fight a company of American infantrymen over the jurisdiction of San Juan Island, between Vancouver Island, B.C. and the United States, in what was to become known as the "Pig War." With both Britain and America claiming jurisdiction over San Juan Island, the conflict developed into a stalemate that lasted until 1872, when Kaiser Wilhelm I, the arbiter in the matter, decided in favor of America's claim of ownership. In the intervening years, however, the Royal Marines attempted as best they could to secure the comforts of home:

. . . the [British] encampment had a comfortable, almost a domestic look. Two rows of Douglas firs were planted, in honour of the Governor. Little flower gardens were lovingly tended. The steep wooded hill behind was hacked into limestone terraces for tennis courts and croquet lawns. There was a white clapboard barrack for the men, and the officers did themselves very well with seven-roomed houses among the trees. The commander's house had a ballroom and a billiard room, and in old pictures of the establishment everybody looks very contented in this improbable outpost of imperial arms—the soldiers spanking and muscular in immaculate uniforms, the officers lounging about on verandahs in sporting gear, with gun-dogs at their feet.[41]

This self-conscious tableau suggests that there was even more at stake than keeping up appearances. Whether in India or Vancouver, these gentlemen-officers were bent on preserving their identity as British subjects living abroad. Their empire was portable, and they took Britain with them wherever they went.

Throughout the Empire, maintaining the British image was ever of the utmost importance. One man who embodied British ideals, and whose imperial attitudes filtered down through the rank and file, was Lord George Nathaniel Curzon, Viceroy of India from 1899 to 1905. The most flamboyant of all the viceroys, Curzon scorned "the sordid policy of self-effacement"[42] of his predecessor. He epitomized British respectability—and not just because he wore a metal back brace that forced him to sit and stand ramrod straight. In 1889 he wrote, "I should never think of travelling either to Timbuctoo or even the North Pole without a dress suit—for in anxious circumstances this is a recognised hall-mark of respectability throughout the world, and will procure an audience of almost any living potentate."[43]

Image was everything. For Curzon, it was paramount that the British must *appear* to be respectable. His sense of respectability was only bolstered by the fact that the seat of British government in India, Government House in Calcutta, had been designed after Kedleston Hall, his ancestral estate. Upon his appointment as viceroy, Curzon was to remark, "when I left the doors of Government House in Calcutta on the first and only occasion on which I have visited it, in 1887, it made me feel that some day, if fate were propitious and I were held deserving of the task I should like to exchange Kedleston in England for Kedleston in India."[44]

Thus ensconced in a replica of his English country house, decorated no doubt with fine examples of English furniture, and given his exalted position as the ruler of India, Curzon had an immense influence on his men. In keeping with this attitude, as Scott Hughes Myerly writes, "Some colonels insisted that their corps maintain the pristine peacetime appearance to as great an extent as possible; some believed that wearing a buttoned-up scarlet coat and white gloves in combat was necessary for the proper image, because scarlet symbolized British power to the 'natives.'"[45]

For members of the officer class, maintaining decorum abroad socially as well as militarily became merely an extension of observing standards of behavior in England. As Byron Farwell writes:

Manners included an observance of taboos, and General George Younghusband warned young officers that "to smoke a pipe in uniform in Pall Mall or Hyde Park is a more grievous offence than to elope with the colonel's mother." Guards officers never carried their own suitcases or parcels, never smoked Virginian cigarettes, and never reversed [direction] in waltzing.[46]

One regiment whose officers could never be accused of waltzing against the line of dance was the 10th "Prince of Wales's Own" Hussars. The former regiment of that celebrated arbiter of taste, George "Beau" Brummell, these Hussars were also known as "The Don't Dance Tenth." Even junior officers felt the need to maintain a manly image, whether at war or at play:

> ... *at hunt balls and other glittering functions embracing the ecstasy of dance, the officers of the 10th resolutely refused to take the floor: many theories for this social idiosyncrasy were advanced—dancing was considered to be effeminate; their overalls were too tight; dancing interfered with drinking. Their more malicious rivals contended that it wasn't that the officers of the 10th wouldn't dance, it was that they couldn't. Whatever the real reason, demure young ladies at balls looked hopefully in the direction of superbly uniformed young officers of the 10th and looked in vain.*[47]

A sporting disregard for official dress regulations was the prerogative of gentlemen-officers, especially while serving abroad. Francis Grose, author of the military satire *Advice to the Officers of the British Army*, insisted that "The fashion of your clothes must depend on that ordered in the corps; that is to say, must be in direct opposition to it: for it would shew [*sic*] a deplorable poverty of genius, if you had not some ideas of your own in dress." Grose further advised these officers, "Never wear your uniform in quarters, when you can avoid it. A green or brown coat shews you have other clothes beside your regimentals, and likewise that you have courage to disobey a standing order."[48] The spirit of Grose's remarks is illustrated in the following picture of a hunting party at breakfast in India in 1829 (plate 46). As Scott Hughes Myerly explains, "Whereas Prussians or other continental officers might consider any deviation in dress to be a crime, British officers saw it as a sign of their political status as free-born Britons, and in the design of their uniforms many defied not only the adjutant-general's regulations but also the regimental ones."[49] In the eighteenth and early nineteenth centuries, high-ranking officers spent inordinate amounts of money competing with each other to design the most elegant uniforms for their regiments. As the anonymous author of "Aesthetics of Dress. Military Costume" (1846) observed, "Nothing is so short-lived as a good uniform; it varies with the taste of a commander-in-chief, or a commander-in-chief's toady; or the fancy of some royal favorite."[50]

46. John Brownrigg Bellasis (1806–1890). *Hunting Party Breakfast*, 1829. Pencil, pen and ink, and watercolor on paper. H: 6 in.; W: 9 in. Inscribed and dated "Candeish / 29," and (from left to right) "Graham C. S.," "Dr. Tawsi," and "Outram." Courtesy Martyn Gregory Gallery, London.

In Georgian England, where the pay of a cavalry trooper had been fixed at 2 shillings 6 pence per day since the end of the seventeenth century, an independent income was necessary for these officers to outfit their regiments in custom-made, gold-and-silver-embroidered tunics, finely crafted silver helmets, and the requisite boots, spurs, gauntlets, swords, and pouches. How the enlisted men felt about their officers' desire to dress them in uniforms that made them an easy target for the enemy is another matter. As Douglas Sutherland wryly observes, "It is very difficult for a non-gentleman to behave like a gentleman in battle because non-gents do not have the same belief that all foreigners are bad shots."[51] During the Battle of Waterloo, Captain Rees Howell Gronow witnessed just such a display of aristocratic sangfroid, which he recorded in his *Reminiscences*:

The road was ankle-deep in mud and slough; and we had not proceeded a quarter of a mile when we heard the trampling of horses' feet, and on looking round perceived a large cavalcade of officers coming at full speed. In a moment we recognized the Duke [of Wellington] *himself at the head. He was accompanied by the Duke of Richmond, and his son, Lord William Lennox. The entire staff of the army was close at hand. They all seemed as gay and unconcerned as if they were riding to meet the hounds in some quiet English county.*[52]

From the Georgian through the Edwardian periods, gentlemen-officers lavished time and money on both their full dress uniforms and their campaign furniture. In 1813, Charles James, author of *The Regimental Companion*, wrote, "It is expected from the soldier, that his arms and accoutrements [including furniture] are at all times in the highest order, that they be not only clean but highly polished."[53] Officers were expected to outfit themselves in style.

The vast majority of campaign furniture was purchased privately. Desks, chairs, beds, game tables, and other luxuries of travel were manufactured for any person of means—civilian, naval, or military—who had need of it while traveling. Few, if any, of these pieces were supplied by the British Board of Ordnance; these rarities would have been marked with the initials *BO* or (after 1856) *WD*, for War Department, and accompanied by the Broad Arrow stamp.[54] Plate 47 shows Pioneers of the King's Own (Royal Lancaster) Regiment in 1898 with examples of campaign furniture that may very well have been stamped with the Broad Arrow. Occasionally the army recommended certain models and manufacturers of campaign furniture, as it did in *The Report of the Kabul Committee on Equipment* (Calcutta, 1882; p.22):

> *. . . the committee now considers the question of camp furniture for officers. . . . The majority of the committee consider it to be necessary for the comfort of an officer, that he should have a bed, and they find that the pattern . . . made by Ross of Dublin is the most suitable. It weighs under 20 lbs. . . . They also consider that each officer should have a chair, and they recommend the pattern shown in the sketch . . . which weighs 3 lbs. . . . They also consider a table . . . for each officer is necessary. These for all officers should be of one uniform size and pattern, viz. 24" x 18" x 30". Trestle legs, joined by a cross bar which is connected by a leather thong to a D riveted in centre of table. These tables being joined together make an excellent mess table. . . .*

Brass-bound military chests were among the most popular pieces of campaign furniture for both colonists and military officers in the late eighteenth and nineteenth centuries. An example of a mid-Victorian campaign chest made by Ross & Co. of Dublin is illustrated in plate 48. These chests, which were often contained within their own wooden packing cases, split into two sections of equal size for ease of storage

47. Pioneers of the King's Own (Royal Lancaster) Regiment, with their campaign furniture, 1898. Black and white photograph reproduced in *The Army and Navy Illustrated*, May 28, 1898, p. 237. Courtesy of the Director, National Army Museum, London.

This fascinating image shows men of the Royal Lancaster Regiment making their own campaign furniture. Of particular interest are the two campaign chests on the far left and far right of the picture.

48. Victorian Brass-Mounted Mahogany Two-Part Campaign Chest of Drawers, second half nineteenth century. The sunken brass handles are engraved, "*Ross & Co. / Manufacturer / 8, 9, 10 Ellis's Quay / Dublin.*" H: 3 ft. 8 in.; W: 3 ft. 3 in.; D: 1 ft. 7½ in. Courtesy Phillips of Hitchin (Antiques) Ltd.

This mahogany military chest of drawers is made in two sections, with feet that unscrew. The top of the lower section of the chest is stenciled "*Ross & Co. / Camp Furniture / Manufacturer / 8, 9, 10 / Ellis's Quay / Dublin.*"

and transportation. For example, the two halves of a chest formed a balanced load when hung over a mule's back (cf. p. 182, plate D.40). They were used both on the outward sea voyage, forming a necessary part of the traveler's cabin furniture, as well as on land upon arrival, where they served as a chest of drawers in a tent or bungalow. Emigrants to New Zealand in the mid-nineteenth century took many such chests with them, and some can still be seen there at the Canterbury Museum in Christchurch and the Otago Museum in Dunedin. The furniture manufacturer Benjamin Taylor and Sons, of Southwark, England, exhibited a particularly interesting and amusing line of "furniture in cork" for a steamship or yacht's cabin at the Great Exhibition at the Crystal Palace in 1851, receiving honorable mention for the firm's enterprise. According to the official catalogue of the Great Exhibition, their line of cork furniture consisted of a "walnut-wood couch, forming a bed when required, stuffed with the exhibitor's patent cork fibre, to make it buoyant when placed in the water. Each part being made portable, is immediately convertible into a floating life-preserver; and the whole forms a floating surface of 50 feet, or life-raft, in the case of danger at sea. . . ."[55]

Army General Orders 13 (7) from 1879 specified that all packing cases for campaign furniture must have the owner's name and regiment marked on it. The late Victorian, iron-clamped box designed to hold a portable "Douro" pattern campaign chair (named after the Douro River in Spain and Portugal, which became well known to the British during the Peninsular War (1808–1814), illustrated in plates 49–51, is painted with the words "The Master of Sinclair / Royal Scots Greys." Army General Order 131 (d) from 1871 specified a maximum size for campaign chests of drawers of 3 feet 6 inches by 2 feet 2 inches by 2 feet, although there were always exceptions to the rule, especially among wealthy officers. These officers frequently commissioned large, elaborate chests with a *secrétaire* drawer for writing, a back that raised to become bookshelves, and a looking-glass, as illustrated in plate 52. In the 1880s one such chest, offered for sale through the *Army & Navy Catalogue*, measured 3 feet 9 inches when closed and over 5 feet when the back was raised to form a set of shelves.

49. English Birch Douro Pattern Chair, with leather-strap arms and horsehair cushions covered in red tufted Moroccan leather, c. 1865–1895. Courtesy Christopher Howe.

This pattern of chair was advertised in 1867 by both W. Day & Son, and J.W. Allen, as well as by the Army & Navy Co-Operative Society and Allen's in the 1880s and '90s. The chair disassembles and folds neatly into a black painted box, which itself becomes a dressing or dining table with the addition of four turned legs.

50. Iron-Clamped, Black-Painted Box for Chair with Four Removable Legs, shown assembled for use as a dressing or dining table. It is painted with the name "The Master of Sinclair / Royal Scots Greys," for whom the chair would have been made.

51. Box with the chair enclosed.

A remarkably complete example of a cavalry officer's outfit of campaign or "barrack room" furniture was advertised by the trunk and camp equipage maker J. W. Allen of 37 West Strand, in the firm's *Illustrated Catalogue of Portable Military Furniture* of October 1860. It included such apparent necessities as:

Portable Brass Sofa Bedstead with cushions and damask covers in strong chest, one best horsehair mattress, two ditto bolsters, one feather Pillow, three Blankets, one white Counterpane, in patent waterproof valise, lined and name printed . . . £20.0.0

Portable Mahogany Recumbent Easy Chair with Leg Rest in maroon or green leather, in strong chest, to form a Dressing Table with Castors. £11.10.0.

Mahogany reading board £1.8.0.

A strong oak Canteen containing Breakfast Service for Three Persons. Electro-plated fittings. 26½ inches long, 16 inches wide, 15 inches deep. £24.10s. complete. Containing: 1 large dish, 2 10-inch dishes, 6 breakfast plates, 3 cups and saucers, 1 butter cooler, 3 egg cups, 1 slop basin in white china with gold edges. 2 pint decanters, 1 vinegar cruet, two tumblers in cut glass. 1 pair candlesticks, 1 chamber candlestick, 1 pepper cruet, 1 mustard pot, 1 sugar basin, 1 cream jug, 2 salt cellars. 1 candle box, 1 sugar canister, 1 coffee canister, 1 spice box, 1 Lucifer box. Tea caddy, toast fork, corkscrew, spirit flask and cutlery;

A portable mahogany Swing Looking Glass with Drawer and Bramah Lock. 25 inches by 19 inches . . . £4.10.

A Portable Mahogany Wash Hand Table on castors, 3 feet 6 inches long, with fittings complete in strong chest, to form a large dressing table and cupboard . . . £12.10.0

A large leather brush case, and space for boot trees with best shoe, cloth, and hat brushes, boot-top and breeches ditto, two metal bottles, large boot jack and button stick, brass plate, name engraved . . . £3.15.6.

52. Victorian Brass-Mounted Mahogany Campaign Chest, with central *secrétaire* drawer, first half nineteenth century. Courtesy W. R. Harvey & Co. (Antiques) Ltd.

Like the majority of campaign chests, the present example has inset-brass drawer handles and can be split in two parts for ease of transport. This example differs from most in that it is surmounted by a removable superstructure with scrolled cornice headed by a brass finial. The superstructure consists of four hinged shelves with brass supports and finials centering a small cheval mirror. Beneath is an arrangement of two short and four long drawers, one fitted with an adjustable writing slope, a stationery rack, and two lidded compartments.

CAMPAIGN FURNITURE /63

> *A set of damask window curtains, with brass extending rods . . . £3.10.0*
> *A pair of glove trees . . . 7s.*

The total cost of such an outfit was the princely sum of £161.5s.[56] By comparison, in 1865 at Holkham Hall in Norfolk, a grand neo-Palladian house begun in 1734 by the 1st Earl of Leicester, a valet might earn £60 per *year*.[57] H.E. Malet's watercolor of the interior of his tent in Bangalore in 1865 shows a number of pieces of campaign furniture similar to those described by J.W. Allen. These include a portable "Douro Chair," four-post camp bedstead, and set of campaign shelves complete with books resting on top of a campaign chest (pages 2–3).

Allen's also offered a slightly less elaborate "Barrack Room or Aldershot Camp Outfit," which might have been purchased by a junior officer. This consisted of "a portable iron bedstead with mattress, feather pillow, blankets and counterpaine, portable dressing table, and wash stand, the whole in one chest 2 ft 6 in long, 2 ft wide and 3 ft high, plus a portable mahogany half set of drawers in chest to form a wardrobe." The whole ensemble cost £20, or roughly the yearly salary of a lady's maid at Holkham Hall in 1865.[58] Plate 53 illustrates a similar ensemble from 1862.

Until the reforms carried out by Secretary of War Edward Cardwell following the Franco-Prussian War of 1870–1871, a private income was also necessary for a gentleman to purchase his commission as an officer.[59] According to *The Army List* for 1857, for example, the expected price for the post of lieutenant-colonel in Foot Guards regiments was £9,000; Life Guards, £7,250; Dragoons, £6,175; and Regiments of the Line, £4,500. As Christopher Hibbert notes, these prices were only rough guides, and were quite regularly exceeded. In 1826, for example, the Earl of Lucan paid £25,000 for the lieutenant-colonelcy of the 17th Lancers.[60] To put that figure in perspective, G. M. Young, editor of *Early Victorian England 1830–1865*, writes, ". . . beginning with an income of £150 per annum, the man becomes a gentleman, and when his income rises [to] £250 per annum, his 'wife' becomes his 'Lady.'" Young also notes that about 1830 a man with an income of £1,000 per year could afford a footman, three female servants, a coachman, two horses, and a carriage.[61]

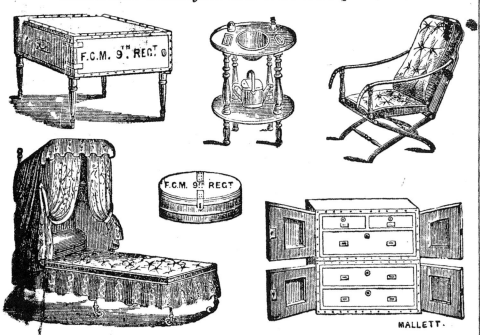

53. Advertisement for J. W. Allen, 37 West Strand, London, in *The Army List Advertiser*, 1867. Ink on paper. Collection of Peter Bronson.

54. Major General R. Pole-Carew Seated in a Roorkhee Chair, right, with members of his staff, Modder, 1900. Black and white photograph. Courtesy of the Director, National Army Museum, London.

The End of An Era

The idea of portability was as important to the Edwardians (1901–1910) as it had been to the Georgians and Victorians, though with an important difference. The years after the Boer War (in which the British fought against the Transvaal and Orange Free State in South Africa from 1899–1902) witnessed the transition from the domestic furniture styles of the eighteenth and early nineteenth centuries to the more familiar camp furniture seen just before the outbreak of World War I in 1914. The Boer War was a watershed in the history of the British Empire. As James Morris writes, "nothing would be quite the same after the Boer War, and even Queen Victoria, as if recognizing it to be the end of her era, died when it was half-way through."[62] Morris continues:

The Boer War came to be called "the last of the gentlemen's wars". . . . Never again did the British go to war with the old imperial éclat, or greet their victories with their frank Victorian gusto. . . . The British had never suffered such terrible casualties before, while the run of defeats in South Africa came as a terrible psychological shock, the first of a series which progressively whittled away the British taste for glory, and even perhaps for honour.[63]

What did not change, however, was a respect for the old social and military hierarchy, as illustrated by the story of two officers who, during the First World War, accidentally collided in a dark, narrow trench:

"Who the devil are you?" one of them demanded angrily.

"And who might you be?" asked the other.

"I am Major Sir Frank Swinnerton Dyer, Coldstream Guards," retorted the first.

"Oh, are you indeed?" said the second. "Well, I am Lieutenant-Colonel Lord Henry Seymour, Grenadier Guards. I beat you on all three counts. Get out of the way."[64]

Tradition dies hard. An early twentieth-century cartoon hanging in the Cavalry and Guards Club in London shows how Georgian and Victorian attitudes prevailed even after radical changes in military campaigns. It depicts an infantry officer outfitted in a simple khaki uniform asking an elaborately dressed cavalry officer of the Life Guards, bedecked in silver helmet and cuirass over his gold-embroidered scarlet tunic, what possible purpose the cavalry could have in the modern army. "The purpose of the cavalry," the elegantly dressed Guards officer replies, "is to give panache to what would otherwise be a vulgar brawl."

As late as World War I, Norman Watney, a young officer living in India, described his experience getting outfitted for duty:

We were recommended to go to an emporium called Whiteaway and Laidlaw . . . [which] had acquired the distinction of being solely for those with small purses and had a large clientele of junior officers such as ourselves . . . we were directed to a counter where we obtained all the necessities required by the junior officer during his first tour of duty. The assistant was able to tell us that it was not expected of people in our position to buy indigenous articles; it would not look good for us to be seen to have inferior equipment and for this reason only the best would do.[65]

In the nineteenth and even into the early twentieth centuries, British India was the kind of place where even a solitary young Englishman isolated in the countryside would still dress for dinner. Kenneth Warren, who worked as a tea planter before joining the army and serving in World War I, was just such a man. From 1906 to 1913 he worked on a remote tea garden in Assam, where he always went out of his way to look and act his best:

If you lost your self-respect you were not looked upon in a respectful and proper manner. So in order to maintain my self-respect I put on a dinner jacket and dressed for dinner and I said to my servants, who were quite likely to get a bit slack just looking after a man by himself in the middle of the jungle, "Now this is a dinner party and you will serve my dinner as though there are other people at the dinner table."[66]

In the officers' mess, it was expected that gentlemen would sit in comfortable armchairs around a massive mahogany dining table set with the mess silver and china, the walls decorated with big-game trophies and regimental colors. After dinner they could write letters on elegant mahogany and brass traveling desks, and then retire to comfortable beds. Lieutenant-Colonel Kenneth Mason, who joined the Survey of India Department in 1909, approved of this refinement and formality: "The British reputation in India was extraordinarily high," he wrote. "I would have been the first to have told a man off if I thought he was lowering our prestige. We had to rule by prestige; there's no question about it. It wasn't conceit. We were there to rule, and we did our best."[67] Furniture, dress, discipline, and lavish military display all worked together to forge the imperial image. Lord Curzon concurs when he writes:

Nothing is more remarkable than the character and spirit of the young men, British Subalterns as a rule, who on the outskirts of our Indian Dominions are upholding the fabric and sustaining the prestige of the British Raj. . . . In remote mountain fastnesses, amid wild tribes, far from civilisation, in a climate sometimes savagely hot, at others piercingly cold, with no comforts or luxuries, often amid cruel hardships, they face their task with unflinching and patriotic ardor, dispensing justice among alien populations, training and disciplining native forces, and setting a model of manly and uncomplaining devotion to duty, which reflects undying credit on the British name.[68]

That the members of the Indian Civil Service to whom Curzon refers, otherwise known as the "Heaven Born," really lived without "comforts or luxuries" is, of course, highly unlikely. In fact, the one thousand Englishmen of the Indian Civil Service who formed the administrative brain of the Indian Empire frequently used campaign furniture and often employed servants to work in their bungalows. The years of fighting in the Boer War took a toll on the British government's finances, and officers were no longer willing to spend great sums of money on their campaign furniture. What is more, the guerrilla-warfare tactics employed by the Boers led to the need for lighter, more mobile equipment. It is not surprising, therefore, that perhaps the largest and most popular manufacturer of campaign furniture, Ross of Dublin, went out of business by 1907, to be replaced in large part by the Army & Navy Co-Operative Society, whose simple, lightweight, and inexpensive designs were bought by officers and enlisted men alike.

55. English Mahogany Roorkhee Campaign Chair, with leather strap arms, and canvas back and seat, c. 1900. H: 30½ in.; H (to seat): 10 in.; W: 22½ in.; D: 22½ in. Private collection.

56. The chair shown disassembled.

The Roorkhee chair, for example, typifies this transition from the domestic furnishings of the Victorian army to the more utilitarian camp chairs of the Edwardians. A typical Roorkhee chair is shown assembled in plate 55 and disassembled in plate 56. In plate 54 Major General R. Pole-Carew is shown relaxing in one of these chairs near Modder River Village, during the Boer War, in 1899. Named in honor of the headquarters of the Indian Army Corps of Engineers at Roorkhee, United Provinces, India, it was among the most popular models of campaign chair used by British officers from approximately 1898 to the start of World War II. As Clement Meadmore writes:

This chair was originally designed to be used by British army officers in India. They needed a chair that was light in weight, could be folded up and carried around easily, could be used on uneven terrain without breaking and was reasonably comfortable. This was achieved by constructing the chair from a series of turned oak parts which were fitted into each other loosely and were not

57. English Mahogany Roorkhee Campaign Chair, leather strap arms, and canvas back and seat, c. 1900. H: 35¾ in.; H (to seat): 17½ in.; W: 22 in.; D: 21¾ in. Private collection.

These chairs typify the transition from the domestic furnishings of the Victorian army to the more utilitarian camp chairs of the Edwardians. Named in honor of the headquarters of the Indian Army Corps of Engineers at Roorkhee, United Provinces, India, and a mainstay of the Army and Navy Stores catalogues, the Roorkhee chair was among the most popular models of campaign chair used by British officers from approximately 1898 to the start of World War II.

The excellence of the Roorkhee chair's design influenced the work of such well-known modernists as Marcel Breuer, Le Corbusier, and the Danish designer Kaare Klint, all of whom made variations of it. Its influence is clearly shown in Breuer's "Wassily" chair of 1925, Le Corbusier's "Basculant" chair of 1928, and Klint's "Safari" chair of 1933.

CAMPAIGN FURNITURE /71

58. Lieutenant-Colonel Jim Corbett in Dhikala, India, c. 1937. Black and white photograph. The British Library, Oriental and India Office Collections.

Lieutenant-Colonel Jim Corbett (1875–1955) was, according to the *Times* of London, "one of the most expert big game hunters in his day in India, and won to an unexampled degree for a European the confidence and affection of the simple village folk of the north by his patient understanding and helpfulness."[1] Known for his famous quip, "A tiger is a large-hearted gentleman," and author of such ripping yarns as *Man-Eaters of Kumaon*, *The Temple Tiger*, and *The Man-Eating Leopard of Rudraprayag*, Corbett was born in 1875 at Naini Tal, in what is now Uttar Pradesh. He fought in both world wars, eventually moving to Nairobi, Kenya, where he died in 1955.

This picture depicts Corbett sitting in a Roorkhee chair in Dhikala, at the foothills of the Himalayas, approximately 300 kilometers from New Delhi, in Corbett National Park, which was designated India's first national park in 1936.

1. *London Times*, 22 April, 1955.

glued, being held together by a combination of leather straps and leather or canvas seat and back. The straps, arms, seat and back all acted under tension to keep the structure in place, while allowing it to adjust to uneven ground.[69] (plate 57)

Weighing between ten and one-half and thirteen pounds, the chairs proved highly portable on campaign, as well as on hunting and camping expeditions. Meadmore explains:

The [Roorkhee] *chair looks what it is, a strong, functional, work-horse of a chair, capable of roughing it out of doors and virtually lasting forever. All its elements express their function perfectly—they are simple and direct. All parts are constructed at right angles, the angle of the seats made by stretching the canvas or leather from front to back on two bars which are mounted at different heights, and the backrest is arranged on two pivoted strips of wood.*[70]

In plate 58, the famous tiger hunter-turned-conservationist Lieutenant-Colonel Jim Corbett is shown seated in his Roorkhee chair in Dhikala, India, about 1937.

The excellence of the chair's simple, functional design was acknowledged in the work of Marcel Breuer's tubular-steel and leather

"Wassily" chair of 1925 (plate 59); Le Corbusier's chrome-plated, tubular-steel "Basculant" chair of 1928; Kaare Klint's popular "Safari" chair of 1933; Wilhelm Bofinger's "Farmer Chair" of 1966; and Vico Magistretti's "Armchair 905" of 1964. As such, the Roorkhee chair was a model of how to unite what the Georgian firm of A. Hepplewhite & Co. called "elegance and utility."

From the end of the Boer War through 1914, portability, lightness, and ease of assembly, all characteristics of the Roorkhee chair, became more important than elegance and comfort. The elaborate and heavy Victorian furnishings slowly gave way to a more austere camp or barrack type of campaign furniture, characterized by "X" folding legs, canvas seating, and a lack of upholstery. Such pieces lacked all individuality, were designed to be utilitarian, and were mass-produced according to prescribed designs. As a result, they lack the character and sense of romance found among the often unique, custom-made designs of the eighteenth and early nineteenth centuries.

59. "Wassily" Chair, in tubular steel and leather by Marcel Breuer (1902–1981), 1925. Courtesy Victoria & Albert Museum; V & A Picture Library, London.

Marcel Breuer, the Hungarian-born architect and furniture designer of the Bauhaus School in Germany, was directly influenced by the British Roorkhee chair in his design of the "Wassily" chair. The Bauhaus sought not only to blend simplicity of design with functionality, but also strove to incorporate modern materials that could be mass-produced and therefore made more accessible to the public.

CAMPAIGN FURNITURE /73

60. Victorian Mahogany Traveling Open Bookcase, made in four sections, second half nineteenth century. H: 6 ft. 8½ in.; W: 3 ft. 11½ in.; D: 1 ft. 3 in. Courtesy Phillips of Hitchin (Antiques) Ltd.

61. Because the bookcase is made in four sections, it can be taken down and packed up as two trunks. The various facings and arches can also be packed away.

Characteristics of British Campaign Furniture

Campaign furniture was extremely versatile. It was particularly popular among officers in the army and navy, as well as among explorers and travelers, who appreciated its elegance, strength, and ease of assembly. It appealed to invalids and home owners, who found collapsible chairs and beds useful for solving the problem of the extra guest. Campaign furniture made from iron and brass was also designed to be vermin-resistant. John Thomas Thompson, military bed-and-camp equipage maker to Their Majesties and patentee of the light military traveling bed, placed an advertisement in the *Times* on January 1, 1816, in which he built every possible benefit into his "Patent East and West India Wellington Bed":

This elegant and portable BEADSTEAD *is made of Wrought Iron Tubes, plated with brass, thereby rendering it extremely light, not liable to rust, or harbour vermin, by its ingenious and simple construction being only one piece, it forms in two minutes into a most complete bed, weighing only 56 lb, with the bedding complete; and by its portability and very small size into which it folds, will fix to any part of a carriage; to the invalid in particular traveling for health it has been invaluable, as by the elasticity of the sacking turning in bed is rendered less painful and when in a warm climate its use will enable them to enjoy the blessing of sleep, often denied to them in the beds of the country which cannot be kept from vermin. As a spare bed in a house it has been found to be extremely useful, it being soon put up, and also forming an elegant couch; a very extensive assortment of different sizes, fitted up with an entire new pattern of Mosquito-Nets are now on show at the warerooms of the patentee J. T. Thompson 116 Longacre.*

Ease of Assembly

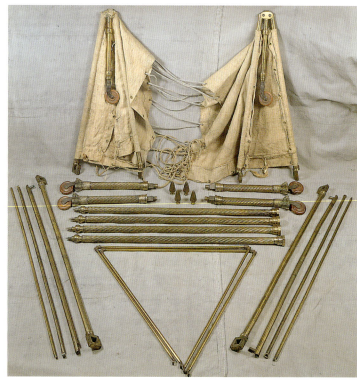

62. Regency Gilt-Brass Officer's Campaign Field Bed, with four rope-twist posts, each of which is numbered one through four, surmounted by conforming finials and terminating in gilt-brass lion-paw feet and wooden wheels, c. 1815. H: 6 ft. 9½ in.; L: 6 ft. 2¼ in.; W: 3 ft. 11¼ in. Collection of Professor and Mrs. John Ralph Willis.

Beds of this type are described by Hepplewhite in *The Cabinet-Maker and Upholsterer's Guide* of 1787 as "field beds," [pl. 24] and the demand for them grew especially in the early nineteenth century. This example would have been suitable for a Georgian officer of very high rank.

63. The bed shown fully dismantled for transportation, showing the canvas sacking bottom that doubles as a case for the gilt-brass tubes.

CAMPAIGN FURNITURE FOR BOTH NAVAL OPERATIONS AND OVERLAND EXPEditions is distinguished most clearly by its simplicity of design and the ease with which it could be assembled and disassembled. Both Morgan & Sanders and Thomas Butler, in broadsheets dating from about 1810, advertised four-post bedsteads that could be set up or taken down in a few minutes, without the use of tools, tacks, or nails.[71] An example of a high-ranking Regency period officer's four-post bedstead that can be assembled and disassembled in such a manner is illustrated in plates 62 and 63. By the middle of the nineteenth century some pieces of campaign furniture were being designed with legs and arms that could be folded by means of a trigger mechanism (plates 64–66). Most pieces are generally free from moldings, and if they do have them, the moldings can be easily removed. Two early portable bookcases are shown fully

Top:

64. Detail of Trigger Mechanism, which, when activated, enables the arms to fold inward and the cane splat to fold flat against the seat.

Lower left:

65. Victorian Caned Satin-Birch Traveling or Invalid's Chair, third quarter nineteenth century. The maker's brass plaque is engraved "J. ALDERMAN / Inventor, / Patentee and Manufacturer, / 16 Soho Square, LONDON," c. 1870. H (to top rail): 23 in.; W: 19 in.; D (extended): 51½ in.; D (to seat): 20 in. Private Collection.

Lower right:

66. The invalid chair folded, showing front and rear carrying handles and massive iron rings in place of legs, perhaps designed to lash it to a wagon or elephant howdah.

assembled with their cornices in plates 60 and 67, and disassembled with these embellishments removed in plates 61 and 68. Campaign furniture often has distinctive brass or silver hardware, though in India the brass was sometimes plated with nickel to prevent corrosion. Particularly characteristic are flush brass corner straps, handles, and escutcheons, all of which made it easier to slip the pieces into square or rectangular traveling crates and store them side by side. A detail of a sunken brass handle from a chest dated 1858 is illustrated in plate 69.

As Thomas Sheraton, the London furniture designer, observed in his *Cabinet Dictionary* (1803), the portable, compact furniture required by army officers was also suitable for use by naval officers aboard ship. In 1804, for example, when Captain John P. Beresford took command of the frigate H.M.S. *Cambrian*, he took with him a 38-inch-high

67. George IV Mahogany Campaign Bookcase, in two sections, with detachable cornice, inset-brass grille doors, and removable feet. H (set up): 5 ft. 9 in.; W: 3 ft. 2 in.; D: 1 ft. 2 in. Courtesy Phillips of Hitchin (Antiques) Ltd.

68. The bookcase shown disassembled, forming its own packing cases.

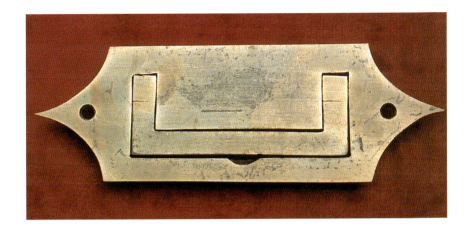

69. Sunken Brass Handle, from a campaign chest owned by J. Briggs, Jr. and dated 1859. Private collection.

mahogany sea chest that was designed specifically for use on board a man-of-war, and that illustrates the flexibility and ingenuity of knock-down furniture. It was mounted with two heavy brass rings on either side that enabled the chest to be lashed to the floor of his cabin in stormy weather, and each drawer was fitted with a touch lock to enable them to be secured with ease. Beresford's chest was uniquely designed to serve him at sea, whether working, dressing, or entertaining. For work, one of the chest's ten drawers served as a *secrétaire*; for dressing, the top opened to reveal a retractable shaving mirror that could be raised on an adjustable stand; and for entertaining, bottles of wine or liquor could be removed from a deep drawer adjacent to a slide-out serving shelf.[72] An example of a mahogany two-part traveling bureau, about 1760 and almost certainly of naval origin,[73] is illustrated in plates 70–72. This piece may be considered the forerunner of the standard military chests with *secrétaire* drawers so popular in the Victorian period, such as the example illustrated in plate 73.

Even Admiral Lord Nelson, of Trafalgar fame, equipped his cabin on the *Victory* with knock-down furniture that was comparable in quality and elegance (if not in size) to that of the furniture designed by Morgan & Sanders for Merton Place, his house in Surrey, in the years immediately before the Battle of Trafalgar (1805). One such piece might have been their popular "Chair Bed," illustrated in plates 74–75, which, like their "Sofa Bed," of the type illustrated in plates 76–78, was "contrived on purpose for Captains Cabins." An example of a chair-bed in the manner of Morgan & Sanders can be seen aboard the ship today. One of Morgan & Sanders's competitors, William Pocock of 26 Southampton Street, London, claimed that his sofa-beds "Make a comfortable and convenient Sofa and Bed, suitable either for Camp or Barracks, or

CAMPAIGN FURNITURE /79

Right:
70. George III Mahogany Campaign Slant-Front Desk, third quarter eighteenth century. H: 36½ in.; W: 30¾ in.; D: 18 in. Courtesy W. R. Harvey & Co. (Antiques) Ltd.

This bureau, almost certainly of naval origin, is of outwardly conventional form but actually made for traveling. It separates into two parts, the top containing a fall-front, which opens to an arrangement of drawers and pigeon-holes above one long and two short frieze drawers, the latter secured with brass pins from inside the bureau section. The base has a polished top (so that it might be used as a chest on its own), and retains lugs for the top section above three full-width drawers. The lower section is raised on bracket feet and has the brass carrying handles and waist molding usually found on pieces from this period.

Treve Rosoman has noted the similarity between this style of bureau and a mahogany desk used by Admiral Earl Howe aboard the *Queen Charlotte* in 1794, and now housed in the regimental museum of The Queen's Royal Surrey Regiment in Clandon Park, Surrey.[2]

Of note, this piece may be considered the forerunner of the standard military chest with *secrétaire* drawer that was produced in the nineteenth century for officers serving abroad.

1. Treve Rosoman, "Some Aspects of Eighteenth-Century Naval Furniture," *Furniture History*, vol. 33, 1997: 123–24.
2. "Some Aspects of Eighteenth-Century Naval Furniture," 123.

Above:
71. The slant-front upper section shown alone, removed from the chest.

Left:
72. The chest of drawers shown alone.

80 / CAMPAIGN FURNITURE

73. Victorian Brass-Mounted Mahogany Two-Part Campaign Chest, third quarter nineteenth century, with a removable panel covering the satinwood fitted interior of the *secrétaire* drawer, all above three long drawers on square flat feet. Courtesy Patrick Adam, Galerie Le Scalaphré, Paris.

74. Regency Mahogany Metamorphic Chair-Bed, with the brass maker's plaque engraved *"(Patent) / Morgan & Sanders / Manufacturers / 16 & 17 / Catherine Street, Strand / London,"* c. 1810. H: 6 ft. 6½ in.; W: 3 ft. ½ in.; L (as chair): 2 ft. 3¼ in.; L (extended as bed): 6 ft. Courtesy Phillips of Hitchin (Antiques) Ltd.

75. The chair set up as a bed, with the under-frame pulled out and the seat cushions forming the mattress.

76. Regency Mahogany Sofa-Bed, with rectangular-shaped back and reeded seat rail on turned legs, c. 1815. H: 2 ft. 11½ in.; W: 5 ft. 11 in.; D (as sofa): 1 ft. 11¾ in.; D (as bed): 5 ft. 10¾ in. Courtesy Phillips of Hitchin (Antiques) Ltd.

This Regency period sofa-bed illustrates that fold-away beds are not a modern concept, as is sometimes thought. Such sofas were featured in the first quarter of the nineteenth century in the advertisements of Thomas Butler, Morgan & Sanders, and Samuel Oxenham.

J. C. Loudon in his *Encyclopaedia of Cottage, Farm, and Villa Architecture and Furniture* observed that "Sofas which may be converted into beds are most convenient articles of furniture for cottages and other small dwellings." [1]

1. (1833; London: Longman, Brown, Green, and Longmans, 1853), 325.

77. Although it looks like an elegant sofa in daytime, the piece converts easily to a bed, as the under-frame pulls out and four additional (replacement) legs are screwed into the frame for support.

Right:
78. The sofa fully disassembled, with back, arms, and additional legs removed for traveling.

on Board a Ship, or even for an elegant Drawing-Room; and yet are very portable by folding into a very small Compass for the Convenience of Carriage."[74]

Because it could be easily and quickly folded up, campaign furniture also had the benefit of allowing the decks of a man-of-war to be cleared quickly and easily for music, dancing, or battle. As Treve Rosoman writes:

A wooden fighting ship was essentially a floating gun platform and the main gun deck was totally clear of obstructions from bow to stern gallery when cleared for action. The captain or admiral had his living quarters on the main gun-deck, indeed he shared his great cabin with four 24-pounder cannon. Thus it followed that all his furniture had to be easily movable, as a large 74 or 100-gun ship like HMS Victory *would clear for action in about 15 minutes or less if required, a considerable feat with a crew of over 1000 men. The chairs folded flat, sofas dismantled, tables collapsed and all was quickly carried down to the orlop deck below water-level.*[75]

In the event that the crew could not clear the decks in time for an engagement, many pieces of furniture were simply thrown overboard.[76]

We can get a sense of just how cramped it was on board an eighteenth-century wooden man-of-war from a letter written by Lieutenant James Trevenen, a junior officer on the 24-gun frigate *Crocodile*, on August 17, 1781:

My habitation . . . is six feet square, which six feet is now completely filled up as an egg. My cot in which I sleep is two feet broad and five and a half long, allowing half a foot on each side for swinging (and this is too little when it blows hard). . . . Allowing half a foot then for swinging, my cot will take up just half my cabin and there will be left six feet by three feet. A very small bureau will take up three feet square, and my chair and myself will pretty well complete the rest of the space.[77]

Commercial ships put the same premium on space as warships. The 8 feet by 7 feet 6 inches cabin of the sixteen-year-old Ensign John Brownrigg Bellasis on the East-Indiaman *Euphrates* was even tighter than Lieutenant Trevenen's cabin, considering that he shared it with another traveler while en route to Bombay from England in 1822. Other cabins on the *Euphrates* were of similarly small proportions and made for extremely cramped living conditions.[78] Because campaign furniture was designed to be packed compactly in cases, and could therefore be transported without difficulty, it became a much-appreciated part of

the traveler's equipage. When not required by passengers during a voyage, for example, the cases could be grouped closely together in the ship's hold, or underneath the passengers' cots, thereby making the most efficient use of available space. Ensign Bellasis's watercolor of his cabin on the ship *Malabar* (c. 1842) shows his campaign chests fitted tightly together under his cot (plate 79). Two early examples of folding furniture are illustrated by a Georgian folding chair (plates 80–81) and a collapsible Regency dining table (plates 82–84).

79. John Brownrigg Bellasis (1806–1890). *The Artist's Cabin on the Malabar*, c. 1842. Pen and ink and watercolor on paper. H: 7¼ in.; W: 9½ in. Inscribed on *verso* in pencil "Our Cabin / 'Malabar' / wrecked nr. Cape 1842 all saved DG." Private collection. Photo courtesy Martyn Gregory Gallery, London.

80. George III Caned Mahogany Folding Chair, possibly naval, with iron hinges, last quarter eighteenth century. H: 37⅜ in.; W: 20¾ in. D: 19⅛ in. Courtesy of Christopher Clarke.

This campaign chair is fairly provincial, with a simplified, elongated, pierced vasiform splat.

Commenting on a set of five folding chairs of similar design ascribed to Rear Admiral Edward Boscawen, who died at sea in 1761, Treve Rosoman writes:

To have belonged to Boscawen the chairs must have been made before his last voyage to Canada in 1758. . . . a similar set is believed to have belonged to Admiral Paulet in the 1750s. The set [of Admiral Boscawen's] at Cotehele [Cornwall] have the same folding action but have solid backs and seats upholstered in leather and plain chamfered legs. They appear to date from the 1740s, but their precise origin is . . . not known. . . . On board the Victory in Portsmouth is another set of folding chairs like those of Admiral Boscawen . . .[1]

1. "Some Aspects of Eighteenth-Century Naval Furniture," *Furniture History*, vol. 33, 1997: 124.

81. The chair folded concertina-style.

82. Regency Brass-Mounted Mahogany Campaign Draw-Leaf Dining Table, first quarter nineteenth century. H: 28½ in.; L (fully extended): 10 ft. Courtesy W. R. Harvey & Co. (Antiques) Ltd.

The two D-shaped end sections pull apart with a telescopic draw-action to accommodate two leaves above the ebony-inlaid frieze. The table is raised on four rope-twist legs that terminate in brass caps and casters. When the legs are unscrewed and the intermediary leaves are removed, the entire table folds down into the space of a box only several inches high, 51 inches long and 47 inches wide.

The favored symbol of naval power used on furniture in the early nineteenth century was the rope or cable twist, which can be seen on the legs of this table.[1]

1. I am grateful to David Harvey for this information.

83. The dining table shown with its legs removed and placed inside the table.

84. The dining table with its extra leaves removed and folded up into a box for travel.

Ease of Transport

BECAUSE THE BRITISH INSISTED ON TAKING ALL OF THE COMFORTS OF home with them when they traveled, furniture designers used their ingenuity in trying to make the loads as easy to transport as possible. In the eighteenth and early nineteenth centuries, the British traveled throughout their colonies with servants, boats, bullock carts, mules, camels, and elephants. Plate 85 shows Beatrice and John Holmes being carried by two bearers in Naini-Tal, India, in 1899. As late as 1910, Harrods's *Supplementary Export Price List* advertised equipment for explorers, surveyors, prospectors, miners, and sportsmen that could be packed in cases suitable for "Camel Loads, Mule Loads, Pony Loads, and Native Head Loads." Furniture would be transported to home, camp, or barrack, where it furnished the bungalow, tent, or officers' mess. The illustration on pages 6 and 7, for example, shows a small assemblage of campaign furniture inside a double-pole tent in India in 1867. Thomas Butler advertised that his "sofa bed" was an elegant sofa that could be transformed with great ease into a complete four-post bed. He sold it complete with goose-feather bedding. Due to the large

85. Beatrice and John Holmes, Naini-Tal, India, September 1899. Black and white photograph. Private collection.

86. *Tom Raw Carried up the Country*, illustration from *Tom Raw: The Griffin, a Burlesque Poem* . . . (London: R. Ackermann), p. 257. The Anne S. K. Brown Military Collection, Brown University, Rhode Island.

amount of camp equipage carried by the Regency and Victorian traveler, local people were almost always hired by the British to help them move, as seen in the accompanying caricature of a young British officer falling through his palanquin while traveling up country (plate 86).

As the Victorian travel writer Francis Galton wrote, "The luxuries and elegances practicable in tent-life, are only limited by the means of transport. Julius Caesar, who was a great campaigner, carried parquets of wooden mosaic for his floors!"[79] When Emily Eden traveled "up the country" with her sister and brother from Calcutta in November, 1837, for example, the party had at its disposal 60 horses, 140 elephants, "two or three hundred baggage camels," and "bullock carts without end."[80] They also had twelve thousand camp followers, "with their tents, elephants, camels, horses, trunks, etc." to help them along.[81]

In the mid-eighteenth and nineteenth centuries, such displays of extravagance by the elite of British India appear to have been the rule rather than the exception, as seen in the following illustration of Her Excellency Mary Curzon being carried across a stream in India in 1904 (plate 87). Even a mere captain in the 16th Lancers had numerous men, beasts, and carts at his disposal; for in 1845, while on campaign in India, one such captain wrote:

CAMPAIGN FURNITURE /89

87. Her Excellency Lady Curzon, crossing a Nullah, India, 1904. Black and white photograph. The British Library, Oriental and India Office Collections.

Mary Victoria Leiter Curzon was born in Chicago on May 27, 1870, the daughter of Levi Z. Leiter, who was an early partner of department store magnate Marshall Field. In 1895 she married George Nathaniel Curzon, about whom the following doggerel was written: "My name is George Nathaniel Curzon, I am a most superior person. My cheek is pink, my hair is sleek, I dine at Blenheim once a week."

Upon her husband's appointment as viceroy of India in 1898, Mary Curzon, as vicereine, occupied the highest position that any American had ever held in the British Empire. Tragically, she died at the age of thirty-six.

I can quite understand now how Xerxes and Darius had such multitudes with them when they took the field. Each fighting man with us has more than one follower, and a large bazaar accompanies the camp besides. We carry the men's tents on elephants, and each elephant has two men; four water carriers to each troop; a cook to every sixteen men; every horse has a man to cut grass for it; the men have six camels and two men per troop to carry their beds. Then come the grain grinders, tailors, bakers, butchers . . . men for pitching tents, and many others. . . . I should say that for 560 officers and men we must have 5,600 followers. . . . I have in my own service 40 men, 10 camels, and a hackery, five horses and two ponies![82]

The captain's comments make it clear that portability in the Georgian and Victorian periods was dependent on the manpower of innumerable servants. When Captain Hope Grant of the 9th Lancers, an avid violinist and composer, was posted to Simla around 1845, he required the help of ninety-three men to carry his military *and* musical equipment into the hills.[83] Similarly, in 1890 Flora Annie Steel advised English

90 / CAMPAIGN FURNITURE

women living in India that "a piano must be carried by coolies, of whom fourteen or sixteen will be needed."[84] Plate 88 shows *Punch* magazine's humorous view of an officer and his lady's life in India, compared with their more modest circumstances at home on retirement.

An example of what the British called a "native head load" was the "Bellamy West African Carrier," which was advertised, remarkably, as late as 1926 in the *General Price List* of the Army and Navy Co-Operative Society (plate 89). As Peter Johnson explains in his article "Camp Comforts: A Roll-Call of Campaign Furniture," "Perhaps to order 'the Bellamy West African Carrier' was to carry the quest for comfort too far in modern eyes. Remember, however, that in the early days of the [twentieth] century, when this bizarre piece of campaign furniture was avail-

88. Wallis Mills. *East Is East And West Is West*, signed and dated 1913. Black and white drawing in *Punch* magazine's *Almanac*, 1914. Private collection.

In the first picture we see "Colonel and Mrs. Clive-Smythe's Christmas in India." In the second we see "The Same at Home on Retirement." During the years of the Raj, British subjects were able to live much more luxuriously than they could otherwise afford to do at home.

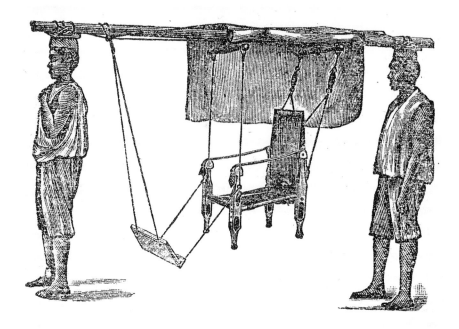

Top:
89. *The "Bellamy" West African Carrier,* line drawing from the Army & Navy Co-Operative Society's *General Price List 1923–24*. Private Collection.

According to the Army & Navy Co-Operative Society's *General Price List 1923–24*, this carrier "Consists of a Roorkhee chair, suspended from a bar with cords and springs, leg rest and awning. Head pieces are provided for either 2 or 4 bearers. Invaluable for traveling in the bush. Each . . . £10 10 0."

Bottom:
90. Mrs. Holmes in her Dandy, Bhim Tāl, India, October 1916. Black and white photograph. Private collection.

Opposite:
91. John Brownrigg Bellasis (1806–1890). *The Artist's Ascent of Ram Ghat, Belgaum,* third quarter, nineteenth century. Inscribed in ink "Ram Ghat Belgaum." Pencil, pen and ink, and watercolor on paper. H: 9¼ in.; W: 6¼ in.; signed and inscribed in pencil on the reverse, "My / Ascent of 'Ram-ghat' / to Belgaum / East Indies / JBB." Courtesy Martyn Gregory Gallery, London.

able, notions of the white man's superiority and the gentleman's born right to servile respect had hardly been challenged."[85] The Carrier consisted of a Roorkhee chair, suspended from a bar with cords and springs, a leg rest, and even an awning. Head-pieces were provided for either two or four bearers. At £10, the *General Price List* deemed it "invaluable for travelling in the bush." A photograph of Mrs. Holmes in her dandy, taken in Bhim Tāl, India, in 1916, captures the essence of the Bellamy West African Carrier (plate 90). The Empire was indeed portable, so long as it was borne on the backs and heads of men (plate 91).

Durability and Comfort

DURABILITY AND COMFORT IN CAMPAIGN FURNITURE WERE OFTEN JUST AS important as portability. As *The Complete Indian Housekeeper and Cook*, first published in England in 1890, advised, "the first axiom for camp is not to do without comfort . . . do not make yourself uncomfortable for want of things to which you are accustomed. That is the great secret of camp life."[86] Campaign furniture maintained as many of the creature comforts and materials of the best civilian furniture as possible. It was usually constructed from fine woods carved into fashionable designs. Most pieces even came with their own outer box or canvas cover to protect the fine wood while in transit, as illustrated by the mid-Victorian military chest of drawers from around 1860 in plates 92–94. In a letter to a friend dated 1843, Honoria Lawrence, wife of Sir Henry Lawrence, later the Chief Commissioner of the Kingdom of Oudh,

92. Victorian Brass-Mounted Mahogany Chest of Aldershot or Hut Drawers, with painted doors of deal, c. 1880. H: 3 ft. 9 in.; H (of lower section only): 2 ft. 3 in.; W: 3 ft. 6 in.; D: 1 ft. 9 in. Courtesy Phillips of Hitchin (Antiques) Ltd.

This military chest of drawers is interesting in that the lower section is in effect its original packing case. When set up, it forms a chest of drawers on top with cupboard (including a movable shelf) below, which is a relatively rare combination. Two of the locks are conventional, although one drawer has a Bramah-type lock, perhaps for extra security.

Chests of this type were advertised by the Army & Navy Co-Operative Society, which recommended them as particularly suitable for officers of militia regiments.

93. The chest with lower cupboard shown open.

94. The lower section, which doubles as the packing case, with the upper section inside.

95. Early Victorian Caned Mahogany Campaign Armchair, with Moroccan leather armrests, and legs ending in brass caps and casters, c. 1840–1850, the seat rail stamped, "*Johnstone & Jeanes / 67 New Bond Street*" and numbered "6572." H: 38¼ in.; H (to seat): 17⅜ in.; W: 19 in.; D: 18¾ in. Private collection.

Johnstone & Jeanes, cabinetmakers and upholsterers, were established at 67 New Bond Street in 1842 and were the successors to Johnstone Jupe & Co. The firm exhibited at the 1862 London Exhibition, where *The Art Journal's Illustrated Catalogue of the Exhibition* described (p. 207) the firm as "one of the oldest in London, having been established in New Bond Street for upwards of a century; its renown has been obtained not only by a good and substantial manufacture, but by continual study to introduce Art into all their works."

96. Chair, folded concertina-style for packing. The chair can be quickly knocked down for travel by means of two trigger mechanisms that release the arms. The seat can then be raised up against the cane splat, and the front legs can be folded flat against the rear legs by means of a concertinalike action. Chairs such as this example were particularly popular aboard ship, where they took up a minimal amount of space when not in use.

96 / CAMPAIGN FURNITURE

makes it clear why protective cases and covers were necessary. Lawrence complained about "trying to carry some few household goods, the vexation of their arriving smashed, cracked, rubbed, bruised, drenched after jolting on miserable *hackeries* over unutterably bad roads, being dragged through streams of all imaginable depths and regaled with alternate showers of dust and rain."[87]

Teak, which had the advantage of only minimally expanding and contracting when exposed to extremes in temperature and humidity, was probably the most commonly used wood. It was resistant to woodworm, termites, and the occasional splash of seawater. Mahogany, beechwood (stained to look like mahogany), rosewood, cedar, camphorwood, oak, walnut, English satin birch, and occasionally cypress were also employed. Veneers were seldom used, though burr walnut was probably the most popular for some of the larger campaign chests.

One particularly influential development in the design of campaign furniture in the early nineteenth century was an increase in the use of caning.[88] In 1819, Thomas Martin, author of *The New Circle of the Mechanical Arts*, observed that "Cane work is now more in practise than it was ever known to be at any former period . . . indeed, canes are very properly used in anything where lightness, elasticity, cleanness, and durability are desired."[89] This material also allowed increased air circulation for comfort in hot temperatures. The campaign armchair from about 1845 illustrated in plates 95–97, for example, employs caning in both the seat and back. Some chairs were manufactured with

97. Detail of Moroccan leather arm pad.

CAMPAIGN FURNITURE /97

98. "Design for an Adjusting Arm for Reclining Chairs," registered by Henry Hill and Richard Millard of No. 7 Duncannon Street, London, January 5, 1854. Watercolor and ink on paper. Public Record Office, London.

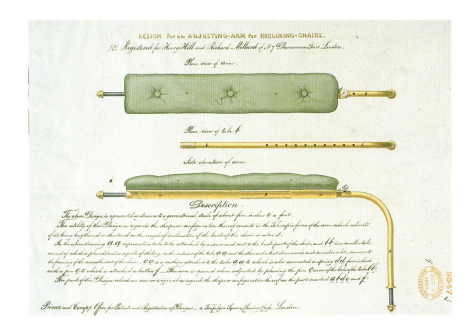

cushions that were leather on one side, for colder climates, and caned on the other for use in the tropics. A traveler could simply flip the chair seat over when he or she entered the equatorial regions.

For greater comfort still, caned chairs often had leather-padded arms. Two examples of padded arms on early Victorian chairs are illustrated in plates 97 and 98. Elaborate upholstery and elegant bed hangings were also common, as seen in the advertisements from 1867 of both W. Day & Son (plate 99) and J. W. Allen (plate 53). In his article *Campaigning in Style*, Peter Philp writes, "As well as providing an elegant appearance, the drapes served to ensure a measure of privacy and to keep the temperature up in a cold climate, or the mosquitoes out in a humid one—the latter an advantage of great benefit to the servants of the Crown and other civilians, as well as the military, in India during the long years of the British Raj."[90] Examples of elaborate bed hangings from the first quarter of the nineteenth century can be seen in the illustrated broadsheets of Thomas Butler (plate 100) and Morgan & Sanders (plate 26), who draped their sofa-beds and four-post beds with elegant damasks. Several weeks after the Battle of Waterloo, General Cavalié Mercer, who had commanded the 9th Brigade Royal Artillery, found lodging in a stately home in Colombes, just outside of Paris, that was filled with elegant French Empire furniture. In describing his bedroom, Mercer observed, "The bedstead is of mahogany, highly varnished, sculptured, and enriched with gilt ornaments, but looks unfinished to an English eye not yet accustomed to the absence of posts and cur-

THE ARMY LIST ADVERTISER. 12

PRIZE MEDAL 1862,
FOR
"EXCELLENCE & ECONOMY."

W. DAY & SON,

Manufacturers of every variety of

PORTABLE MILITARY FURNITURE
FOR
BARRACK ROOM, CAMP OR FIELD.

ILLUSTRATED **CATALOGUES.** POST FREE.

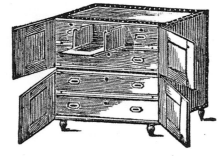

PATENTEES OF THE

"Eclipse" and Railway Compendium Portmanteaus.

W. DAY & SON,
353 & 378, STRAND, LONDON.
16 *Established 1812.*

99. Advertisement for W. Day & Son, 353 & 378 Strand, London, in *The Army List Advertiser*, 1867. Ink on paper. Collection of Peter Bronson.

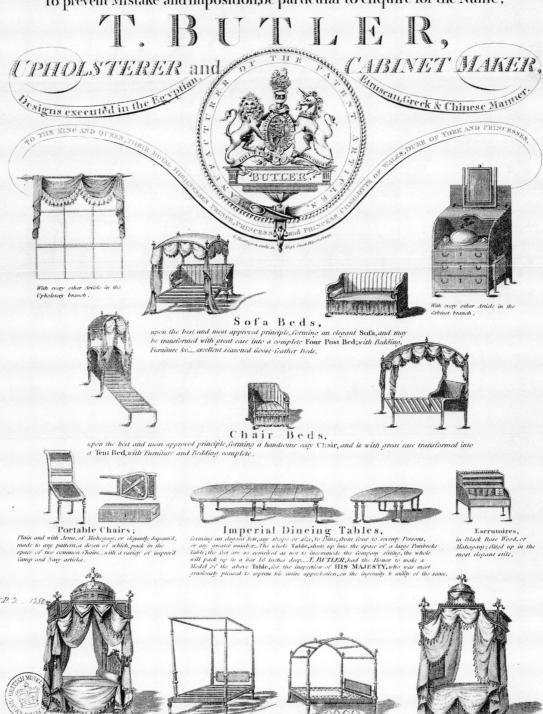

tains."[91] Thus the portable nature of early campaign furniture was well hidden, and only upon close inspection could it be distinguished from Georgian household furniture. The elegance and comfort of patent campaign beds such as those made by Thomas Butler or Morgan & Sanders is documented in the writing of Thomas Smith, an acquaintance of Lord Byron, who happened to be staying with the poet at the monastery on Samos Hill in Cephalonia, Greece, during Byron's self-imposed exile in 1823. Smith recalled how, after one of Byron's violent fits, he was finally pacified, "and had lain down on my mattress and bedding, prepared for him by my servant, the only regular bed in the company, the others being trunks and portable tressels [sic], with such softening as might be procured for the occasion. Lord Byron's beautiful and most commodious patent portmanteau bed, with every appliance that profusion of money could provide, was mine for the night."[92] It has been suggested that the bed in which Thomas Smith spent the night was made by Thomas Butler.[93] (*See* plate 101).

In January 1800 Thomas Butler was declaring that his patent bedsteads were "highly approved of and strongly recommended by officers and gentlemen of the first distinction for the West and East Indies, Gibraltar, and all parts of the globe troubled with vermin." His bedsteads were advertised as having "Sacking or Lath Bottoms" which prevented the harboring of parasites. Describing her drawing room at Government House in Barrackpore to Queen Victoria in 1856, Lady Charlotte Canning writes that the ceiling beams were painted white so that "the ravages of white ants may be instantly discovered."[94] British officers serving in India would frequently place the feet of their furniture in small bowls of water or oil to prevent insects, particularly the ubiquitous white ants of the East, from eating the wood. In the watercolor illustrated on pages 8 and 9, painted in India about 1825, the legs of the officer's bed are placed in ceramic bowls. The deterioration caused by such practices would account for the occasionally "reduced" or cut-down legs on pieces of furniture that have survived from the period.

Another innovation in nineteenth-century design that made for more durable campaign furniture was hollow metal tubing, which also helped contribute to the development of the metal bedstead industry in Birmingham.[95] Hollow metal tubing was stronger than wood and, most important, insect-resistant. A fine example of a Regency officer's brass bed is illustrated in plates 62–63. According to Edward T. Joy:

Opposite:
100. Trade Card of Thomas Butler, Nos. 13 & 14 Catherine Street, London, c. 1806. Ink on paper. British Museum, Banks Trade Card Collection.

The problem of beds . . . was tackled first by introducing metal joints to the wooden frames, then discarding wood altogether in favour of metal. The best method was to use hollow tubes of brass, iron or steel, and between 1812 and 1831 seven patents for such frames were taken out. These tubes were light and cheap as well as clean ("will not harbour vermin" is a recurrent phrase in their specifications). John Thompson twice patented metal tubes for beds, in 1812 and 1826; Samuel Pratt, later to be famous for his metal springs, patented metal rods in 1825 for bed hangings; and in 1826 William Day went a stage further by patenting extending tubes for altering the size of beds (and also couches and chair backs).[96]

According to the early-nineteenth-century satirist William Heath, the Duke of Wellington was extremely fond of his brass campaign bed, and preferred it to all others, even after he had retired from active service. In 1829 Heath wrote: "During the Duke's temporary sojourn at Walmer Castle he invariable [sic] reposes on the Camp bedstead which form'd his Grace's couch throught [sic] the Peninsular Campaigns—the highly prized article of furniture being regularly convey'd from Downing Street to Walmer Castle when ever the Duke visits the later [sic] place."[97] (plate 102)

During the Napoleonic Wars (1793–1815), a lucrative market developed for campaign furniture designed specifically for the large numbers of wounded and disabled British soldiers. Not surprisingly, a four-page advertising card for metamorphic and invalid furniture from the Georgian inventor William Pocock is still to be found among the records of the British Embassy in Spain during the Peninsular War from 1814.[98] One of Pocock's signature pieces, which he advertised on the front of his trade card, was his "Boethema, or Rising mattress." This was a bed that contained a lever mechanism operated by a handle for raising invalids up in their beds (plate 18). Such "boethema" beds were also advertised in the broadsheets of Morgan & Sanders. Joy has noted the large increase in the number of patents granted for invalids' beds and sofas from the 1790s to the 1830s.[99]

With all their fighting, many officers and men were badly wounded, and many became permanently disabled. As one would expect, however, the British took their injuries on the chin. During the Sikh wars J. J. Cole, a British surgeon, decried the use of chloroform on the battlefield when he wrote, "But what is pain? It is one of the most powerful, one of the most salutary *stimulants* known."[100] The following exchange between the Duke of Wellington and Lord Uxbridge during the Battle of Waterloo

Opposite:
101. George III Brass-Mounted Mahogany Campaign Four-Poster Bedstead, with the maker's brass plaque engraved "BUTLER'S PATENT Nos. 13 & 14 Catherine Street, The Strand, London," c. 1805. H: 76 in.; W: 48 in. Courtesy Bonham's, London.

Although no evidence exists, it has been suggested that the present bed was once the property of Lord Byron. According to an entry in *Medora Leigh: A History and Biography* (1869), and summarized by Bonham's, "In 1823 Byron and his companions were staying at the monastery on Samos Hill in Cephalonia. Byron was seized by a violent fit and barricaded himself into his room. He was eventually pacified by Mr. Hamilton Brown and went to sleep on Thomas Smith's mattress. Smith recalls how he spent the night on Lord Byron's beautiful and most commodious patent portmanteau bed; with every appliance that profusion of money can provide."

102. Edward Heath, Doyle, and others. *"TAKE UP YOUR BED - AND WALK!!!"* Dated October 1st, 1829. Ink on paper. Courtesy Victoria & Albert Museum; V & A Picture Library, London.

This caricature of the Duke of Wellington is one of fifty-eight of the duke drawn by Edward Heath, Doyle, and others for the Wellington Museum Picture Book.

illustrates Dr. Cole's point by revealing the stiff upper lip and indifference to pain so characteristic of British officers on campaign. As the two gentlemen were sitting side by side on their horses, a cannon ball whistled past. A moment later, Uxbridge casually remarked, "By God, Sir, I've lost my leg." At this, Wellington replied, "By God, Sir, so you have," and supported him until help could arrive to carry him away.[101] One can imagine Lord Uxbridge retiring from the field of battle to one of Pocock's Boethema mattresses, or finding comfort in one of his elegant and comfortable sofa-beds, which Pocock claimed were "highly approved by distinguished Officers of the Army and Navy."[102]

By the 1850s and '60s firms such as John Ward of Leicester Square and John Alderman of Soho Square were specializing in self-propelling and self-acting chairs and beds of every description for the use and comfort of the disabled. An example of a wheelchair made about 1860–1875 by John Alderman is illustrated in plate 103. Alderman billed himself as an inventor and manufacturer of general invalid couches, chairs, carriages, and every other description of article required by the infirm. Many of these pieces were completely collapsible and designed for ease of transportation as well.

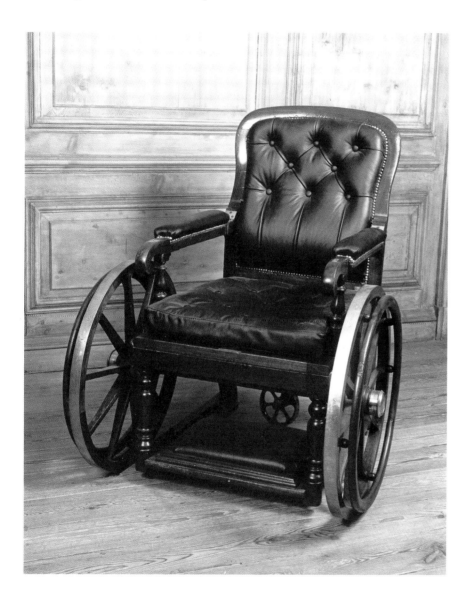

103. Victorian Brass and Mahogany Invalid's Armchair, upholstered in close-nailed leather, and with brass maker's plaque on back seat rail engraved, "*J. Alderman, / Inventor, / Patentee & Manufacturer. / 16, Soho Square, / London*," c. 1875. H: 3 ft. 5¼ in.; H (to seat): 1 ft. 8 in.; W: 1 ft. 11½ in.; D: 1 ft. 9 in. Courtesy Phillips of Hitchin (Antiques) Ltd.

This invalid's armchair has collapsible arms and large wheels. The wheels also have hoops for the occupant to grasp (thus avoiding the necessity of having to touch the dirty tires), a feature thought to have been devised by John Joseph Merlin, the famous late-eighteenth-century inventor.

A chair similar to the present example was exhibited at "John Joseph Merlin . . . The Ingenious Mechanick [*sic*]" at Kenwood House, London, 1985, bearing the label "T. Chapman, 22 Edwards Street, Portman Square and 8 Denmark Street, Soho." John Alderman appears to have joined Chapman, trading as "Chapman and Alderman," at 8 Denmark Street, Soho, from 1852–1856. John Alderman first appears on his own at 16 Soho Square in 1860. He appears to have continued to make furniture of this type, especially small invalid's chairs with carrying handles and cane backs and seats, possibly used in India.

Secret Compartments

Because travel in the eighteenth and nineteenth centuries could be extremely dangerous, especially for men and women of means, campaign furniture often contains secret storage compartments designed to hide its owner's personal effects. As Paul Fussell writes, "In the early nineteenth century, luggage had to be both numerous and copious not just because you carried so many obligatory changes of costume. You also had to carry things either not provided by inns or hotels, or necessitated by flagrant threats to your possessions and person."[103] In an age when pirates were a serious menace at sea, and bands of brigands roamed the countryside, gentlemen regularly carried sword-sticks for protection. The travel writer Mariana Starke, author of *Information and Directions for Travellers on the Continent* (1824), strongly urged her readers to take not one, but two pistols with them when traveling to major European cities.[104] One wonders what she might have advised for travelers to India or Africa. Under such circumstances it is hardly surprising that secret compartments were thought an essential element in the construction of campaign furniture. There was recently on the market in London a campaign chest of drawers by

104–107. Regency Brass-Mounted Mahogany Campaign Dispatch Box, with iron crank handle for making copies of correspondence (Watts Patent) and sunken brass handles, c. 1805. H: 8¼ in.; W: 20 in.; D: 11⅞ in. Private collection.

This box was once in the possession of the Trappes family of Nidd. According to the National Army Museum, a "Charles Trapps served as a Lieutenant with the 5th (Northumberland) Regiment of Foot with effect from 1801 and later as Captain, perhaps by purchase, with the 72nd (Highland) Regiment of Foot. He retired in 1822. The spelling of his name is corrected to Trappes in the later *Army Lists* . . . A John Trapps joined the 2nd (Queen's Royal) Regiment in 1799 and later transferred to the 5th West India Regiment. He died in 1811. The variations in spelling were common at the time."

President Thomas Jefferson (1801–1809) thought highly of such dispatch boxes, which he referred to as "polygraph" desk copying presses. On June 9, 1805, for example, Jefferson sent a letter to Charles Wilson Peale in which he asked Peale to build one:

Having determined never while in office to accept presents beyond a book or things of mere trifling value, I am sometimes placed in an embarrassing dilemma by persons whom a rejection would offend. In these cases I resort to counter presents. Your polygraph, from its rarity and utility offers a handsome instrument of retribution to certain characters. I have now such a case on hand, and must therefore ask you to make me one immediately of the box (not desk) form, but not larger than the desk-ones you made for me. . . . Let it be of fine wood and completely finished and furnished, and send it by the stage. . . .[1]

1. The Library of Congress. Thomas Jefferson Papers Series 1. General Correspondence, 1651–1827. Thomas Jefferson to Charles Wilson Peale, June 9, 1805.

Opposite bottom:
105. The box shown with sand drawer and blotter extended.

Top:
109. The box shown open to reveal a baize-lined fitted interior with a pen and ink tray.

Bottom:
110. The box shown with internal compartment open. The panel at the back of the compartment conceals three secret drawers.

CAMPAIGN FURNITURE / 107

the military outfitters Hill & Millard, dated 1873, with an escritoire containing over one dozen hidden drawers. By the turn of the twentieth century, security was still an issue, and the Army & Navy Co-Operative Society advertised military chests that were "fitted with [a] secret drawer." Dispatch boxes, or traveling desks, of the Georgian and Victorian periods also contained one or more secret drawers. One such box, dating from about 1800 and now in a private collection, contains three drawers with tiny, turned-ivory knobs hidden behind a removable length of wood (plates 104–107). Secret drawers remained popular right up through the 1920s. For example, a dispatch box from an officer of the 19th Bengal Lancers, now in a private collection, contains a locked compartment in which were discovered two envelopes containing perfectly preserved locks of blond and brunette hair.

The Accelerating Demand for Campaign Furniture in Eighteenth- and Nineteenth-Century Britain

The demand for campaign furniture in Georgian Britain was stimulated to a large extent by wars with the French in North America, India, and Europe, as well as with the rebellious American colonists. The campaign furniture required by an officer of the period had to be made to withstand a wide variety of climatic conditions, from freezing North American winters to the blistering heat of the Indian plains. In North America, British troops had been dispatched to fight in the French and Indian War (1756–1763), where they remained and eventually fought in the American War for Independence (1775–1783). In the mid-eighteenth century, the British army was also actively involved in a struggle for ascendancy in India against the French, whom they defeated in 1760; and from 1808 to 1814, British troops fought in Spain and Portugal during the Peninsular War.

The various conflicts in which the British were engaged, which required the dispersal of thousands of troops on three continents and which lasted for years on end, led to a great increase in travel by members of the army, navy, and government, as well as their families. Campaign furniture, which could easily be dismantled for packing and shipping, and which often contained hiding places for booty acquired in battle, proved invaluable during these times of war.

The demand for campaign furniture did not end, however, with Wellington's victory at Waterloo. After 1815, campaign furniture became particularly popular among explorers, travelers, and emigrants, in addition to officers in the army and navy. As Paul Fussell explains, "The Napoleonic Wars meant that for some years European travel was restricted or impossible. It revived with a vengeance after the peace...."[105] Indeed, there remained a tremendous demand for portable furniture throughout the nineteenth century with the ongoing development of British colonies, particularly in India, South Africa, New Zealand, and North America.

108. C. I. Fry. *His Excellency the Viceroy's Bodyguard*, 1890. Signed lower right. Watercolor on paper. H: 14½ in.; W: 10 in. The Anne S. K. Brown Military Collection, Brown University, Rhode Island.

Domestic Demand for Campaign Furniture in Eighteenth- and Nineteenth-Century Britain

Demographic changes within the British Isles also helped to stimulate the demand for campaign furniture. Most significant was the lack of urban living space as the population in England and Wales doubled between 1751 and 1821, with a fifty percent increase in the population between 1801 and 1821.[106] It was not until the arrival of the railways in the 1830s and the subsequent growth of suburbs that the pressure on living space in the cities was eased. In the interim there arose a need for adaptable, dual-purpose furniture, which, in order to maximize space, could be folded flat and packed away when not in use, such as the Victorian butler's tray illustrated in plates 109–110. Writing in 1819, Thomas Martin, author of *The New Circle of the Mechanical Arts*, observed "it is the fashion of the present day, to resort to a number of contrivances for making one piece of furniture serve many purposes, 'a bed by night, a chest of drawers by day.'"[107] One such bureau-bedstead is illustrated in the Gillow Estimate Sketch Book from 1788 (plate 111). A similar example is illustrated in plates 112–113. According to Joy:

Only four patents under the heading of furniture and upholstery were granted before 1760, all in the seventeenth century. By the end of 1800 the total was thirty-seven, and by the end of 1810, fifty. The total of 100 was reached by the end of 1829, fifty registrations occurring between 1811 and 1829. The 200th

109. Victorian Mahogany Collapsible Butler's Tray-on-Stand, second quarter nineteenth century. The tray is shown extended from the X-frame stand and supported on a single ring-turned leg. Courtesy Phillips of Hitchin (Antiques) Ltd.

J. C. Loudon in his *Encyclopaedia of Cottage, Farm, and Villa Architecture and Furniture* (1833) observed that this pattern represents "a very useful article, called a camp table, from its going into little bulk, being light, and being used by officers in camps.... In families, accustomed to give large dinner parties, these tables are found useful, as forming additions to the sideboard: they are also brought in requisition when parties are given in the open air, or when a meal is taken in any room deficient in tables" (p. 310).

110. The Camp Table, shown folded.

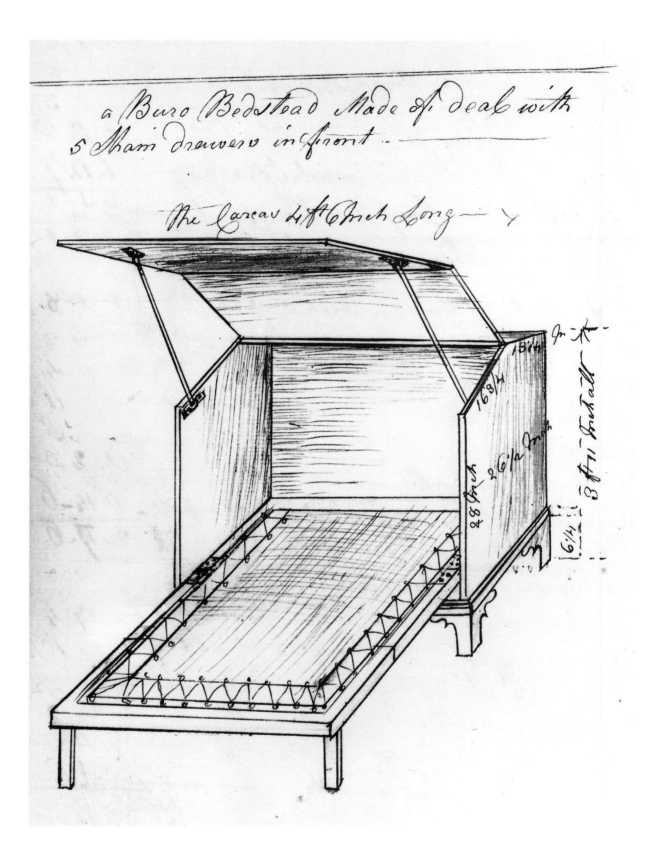

111. Design for "a Buro [*sic*] Bedstead Made of deal with 5 Sham drawers in front." Gillow Estimate Sketch Book 344/94, p. 310, 1788. Courtesy Westminster City Archives, London.

112. George III Mahogany Bureau-Bedstead, c. 1790. H: 3 ft. 7½ in.; W: 3ft. 7½ in.; D: 1 ft. 11 in.; D (as bed): 6 ft. 2 in. Courtesy Phillips of Hitchin (Antiques) Ltd.

This bureau-bedstead is an interesting example of the type of furniture made toward the end of the eighteenth century, where one piece could appear to have a dual function. Although it appears to be an ordinary slant-front desk, it actually functions as a bed, usually for use in a spare room. In March 1811, Ackermann's *Repository of the Arts* (p. 222) states that a "military couch-bed" in two parts could also be suitable "for a second drawing-room, dressing-room, etc." The front of this bureau-bedstead is made from mahogany, while the hidden bed section is fashioned from deal, a relatively inexpensive secondary wood.

According to Wallace Nutting, author of "Double-Purpose Furniture" in *The Magazine Antiques* (October 1940, p. 160), "In 1770 Oliver Goldsmith wrote of a piece of furniture that was 'a bed by night, a chest of drawers by day.'" Gillow of Lancaster recorded two designs for bureau-beds. The first is illustrated in plate 113, while the second, described as a "press bed in the form of a desk" was recorded in 1789, and is illustrated in *Sheraton Furniture* by Ralph Fastenedge (p. 81).

By the early 1830s, such bureau-bedsteads went out of fashion and were replaced by metal bedsteads, which had the advantage of not harboring vermin. J. C. Loudon observed in his *Encyclopaedia of Cottage, Farm, and Villa Architecture and Furniture* (1833) that these older bureau-bedsteads were now "very common in kitchens, and, sometimes, in parlours [of cottages] where there is a deficiency of bedrooms . . . [they] are sometimes made to imitate a chest of drawers, or a secretary, in front; in order, if possible, to prevent the real use of the article from being discovered: a proof that beds of this kind are not held in much repute; because they indicate a deficiency of bedrooms" (pp. 329–30).

113. The bureau extended to form a bed.

114. George III Mahogany Traveling Rent Table, the octagonal top with a tooled leather surface, the frieze fitted with drawers, on square legs that fold up for ease of transportation, c. 1790. Courtesy of Mallett.

115. The rent table shown folded.

CAMPAIGN FURNITURE / 115

registration took place in 1848, and by the end of 1850 the number was 220. A graph would show a steady rise between 1800 and 1825, then a progressively steeper one to 1850.[108]

Clive Edwards lends further insight into the demand for campaign furniture when he writes, "Patents taken out in England for both *folding and portable* furniture during the period of 246 years between 1620 and 1866 equaled just 28. In the space of only 33 years between 1867 and 1900 there were 305 patents relating *just to folding chairs.*"[109] Because of its space-saving convenience and ready portability, campaign furniture was the perfect solution for city dwellers, travelers, and officers who were all faced with cramped living quarters. The following description of a campaign chair from a catalogue of 1880 highlights the attributes that made such furniture so useful: "The compactness of the chair when folded is a special merit for use in small quarters—office, cottage, cabin, 'French flat,' small lodging room etc. . . . for when out of use it folds to a trifle over the thickness of a board . . . and will stand behind a door or sofa, lie under a bed, or hang on a nail in the wall."[110]

Campaign furniture eventually became so popular that it found a market with the landed gentry in Britain, who required, much like military officers on campaign, elegant yet portable rent tables (plates 114–115), bureaus, chairs, chests, and the like.

Conclusion

The creation of campaign furniture is more than a quaint chapter of British history. Rather, it is a good example of how cultural characteristics, combined with the exigencies governing war, gave rise to a unique type of portable furniture. Today the imperial attitude characteristic of the late eighteenth and nineteenth centuries is generally considered anachronistic. Yet even though we may decry it, we should remember that this mind-set gave rise to some of the most carefully wrought furniture of the period. The most renowned furniture makers of the Georgian and Victorian periods, including Chippendale, Ince & Mayhew, Seddon, and Gillow were all engaged in its manufacture. It is ironic that the outmoded viewpoints espoused by Clive, Curzon, and their officers should find their expression in a unique style of furniture that is of enduring interest to us today. The ingenuity, aesthetic appeal, and historical value of the pieces described here are prized by collectors of furniture and connoisseurs of the decorative arts. Although the cultural attitudes and assumptions that inspired the most respected furniture makers of the day to create ingenious pieces of campaign furniture have long since vanished, the work these masters created stands as a testament to the long tradition of outstanding British craftsmanship.

Notes

1. Peter Johnson, "Camp Following," *Country Homes and Interiors* (Jan. 1991), 26.
2. Broadsheet. Public Record Office, Kew. Foreign Office, 185/50, Spain 1814.
3. James Pigot & Co., *Royal National and Commercial Directory* (London, 1839), 97.
4. Peter Philp, "Campaigning in Style," *Antique Dealer and Collector's Guide* (Aug. 1990), 36–40.
5. Thomas Sheraton, *The Cabinet Dictionary*, vol. 1 (London, 1803), 123.
6. Plates XXVIII and XXVII.
7. *Colonial Furniture in New Zealand* (Auckland, A. H. & A. W. Reed, 1971), 102–3.
8. "How Shall We Get Beds: Furniture in Early British India," from *A Nabob's Collection*, conference, Shropshire, England, 25 Sept., 1999.
9. James Thornton, *Your Most Obedient Servant: James Thornton, Cook to the Duke of Wellington* (Exeter: Webb & Bower, 1985), 61.
10. James Thornton, 58.
11. Treve Rosoman, "Some Aspects of Eighteenth-Century Naval Furniture," *Furniture History* (1997), 122.
12. Rosoman, 122.
13. Jane Austen, *Persuasion* (1818; Oxford, Oxford University Press, 1988), 127.
14. Anonymous, *The Navy "At Home,"* vol. 1 (London: William Marsh, 1831), 75–77.
15. George Annesley (Lord Valentia), *Voyages and Travels to India, Ceylon, the Red Sea, Abyssinia and Egypt in 1802–1806*, vol. 1 (London, 1809), 144.
16. Formerly of the Indian Department, Victoria and Albert Museum, London.
17. "Furniture and Boxes," *Treasures from India: The Clive Collection at Powis Castle* (London: The Herbert Press in association with The National Trust, 1987), 80.
18. *Reports and Awards of the Jurors*, New Zealand Exhibition, 1865. (Dunedin, New Zealand: Mills, Dick & Co., 1866), 290.
19. "Early Nineteenth-Century Invalid Etc. Furniture," *Furniture History* (1974), 76.
20. Sydney J. Maiden, "A Wedding Present of 1863: An Officer's Travelling Furniture." *The Connoisseur* (May 1957), 168.
21. Maiden, 168.
22. Emily Eden, *Up The Country: Letters Written to her Sister from the Upper Provinces of India* (1866; Oxford: Oxford University Press, 1930), 266.
23. Eden, 236.
24. *The Cabinet Dictionary*, vol. 2 (London, 1803), 317.
25. Christopher Hibbert, *The English: A Social History 1066–1945* (New York: W. W. Norton, 1987), 503.
26. Long Military Papers (ex. Royal United Services Institution, M. M. 219, 31–34). National Army Museum, London.
27. "Camp Equipage 1793," *Journal of the Society for Army Historical Research* 26 (1948), 39.
28. *The Diary of a Cavalry Officer in the Peninsular and Waterloo Campaigns 1809–1815*, ed. William Tomkinson (New York: Macmillan & Co., 1894), 329–30.
29. *The Diary of a Cavalry Officer*, 329–30.
30. Byron Farwell, *Mr. Kipling's Army* (New York: W. W. Norton, 1981), 116.
31. Farwell, 35.
32. I am grateful to Mr. Charles Webb for providing me with information on the Household Cavalry.
33. George F. Atkinson, *The Campaign in India 1857-58* (London: Day & Son, 1859), plate 4.
34. Quoted in Patrick Conner, *100° In The Shade: Military and Domestic Life in India, 1800–1860* (London: Martyn Gregory Gallery, 1999), 6.
35. *The Campaign in India 1857-58*, plate 13.
36. Hugh Boyd, "Fashion in Men's Clothes," *The Indian Observer*, 10 Dec. 1793.
37. George Annesley (Lord Valentia), *Voyages and Travels to India, Ceylon, the Red Sea, Abyssinia and Egypt in 1802–1806*, 235.
38. *Critical and Historical Essays*, vol. 2 (Boston and New York, Houghton, Mifflin and Company, 1901), 754.
39. Charles Allen, *A Glimpse of the Burning Plain* (London: Michael Joseph, 1986), 35.
40. Allen, 41.
41. James Morris, *Heaven's Command* (New York: Harcourt Brace & Company, 1973), 373–74.
42. Lance Morrow, "Lighting Out for the Territory," *Civilization* (Nov./Dec. 1994), 32.
43. *Tales of Travel* (1923; London: Century, 1988), 228.
44. Nayana Goradia, *Lord Curzon: The Last of the British Moghuls* (Delhi: Oxford University Press, 1993), 25.

45. *British Military Spectacle* (Cambridge, Massachusetts: Harvard University Press, 1996), 110.
46. *Mr. Kipling's Army* (New York: W. W. Norton, 1981), 72.
47. Tim Carew, *How the Regiments Got Their Nicknames* (London: Leo Cooper, 1974), 29.
48. Francis Grose, *The Mirror's Image: Advice to the Officers of the British Army*, sixth edition, (London, 1867), 53–54.
49. *British Military Spectacle*, 69.
50. *Blackwood's* 59 (1846), 115.
51. *Debrett's The English Gentleman*. (London: Debrett's Peerage, 1978), 39.
52. Christopher Hibbert, ed. *Captain Gronow: His Reminiscences of Regency and Victorian Life 1810–60.* (London: Kyle Cathie, 1991), 134.
53. Seventh ed., vol. 3 (London, 1813), 13.
54. Information kindly provided by the National Army Museum, London.
55. *Great Exhibition of the Works of Industry of all Nations, 1851: Official Descriptive and Illustrated Catalogue*, vol. 2 (London: Spicer Brothers, 1851), 730.
56. "Equipping an Officer and a Gentleman," *The Armourer* (May–June 1995), 10.
57. Christopher Hibbert, *The English: A Social History 1066–1945* (New York: W.W. Norton, 1987), 503.
58. Hibbert, 503.
59. Hibbert, 673.
60. Hibbert, 609.
61. G.M. Young, ed. *Early Victorian England 1830–1865*, vol. 2, (London: Oxford University Press, 1934), 104–5.
62. *Farewell the Trumpets* (New York: Harcourt Brace Jovanovich, 1978), 65.
63. *Farewell the Trumpets*, 72, 89, 99.
64. Douglas Sutherland, *Debrett's The English Gentleman*, 38.
65. Charles Allen, ed., *Plain Tales from the Raj* (London: André Deutsch, 1975), 50.
66. Allen, 69.
67. Allen, 69.
68. *Tales of Travel*, 225.
69. Clement Meadmore, *The Modern Chair: Classics in Production* (New York: Van Nostrand Reinhold & Co.), 16.
70. Meadmore, 16.
71. Which is true, though moving them without the help of at least one other person is a difficult task.
72. The chest is illustrated in Paula Deitz, "Providing the Comforts of Home in War," *New York Times*, July 1, 1982: C10.
73. Treve Rosoman, "Some Aspects of Eighteenth-Century Naval Furniture," *Furniture History* (1997), 123–24.
74. Broadsheet. Public Record Office, Kew. Foreign Office, 185/50, Spain 1814.
75. "Field Furniture," *Traditional Homes* (Feb. 1985), 38.
76. Rosoman, "Some Aspects of Eighteenth-Century Naval Furniture," 120.
77. Christopher Lloyd and R.C. Anderson, eds., "A Memoir of James Trevenen," *Navy Records Society*, 101 (1959), 44–45.
78. Conner, *100° in the Shade*, 5.
79. *The Art of Travel*, eighth ed. (London: John Murray, 1893) 168–69.
80. Eden, *Up the Country*, 21.
81. Eden, 31.
82. Col. Henry Graham, *History of the Sixteenth, The Queen's, Light Dragoons (Lancers), 1912–1925* (Devizes, Wiltshire: George Simpson & Co., 1926), 85.
83. James Morris, *Heaven's Command*, 201.
84. Flora Annie Steel, *The Complete Indian Housekeeper and Cook* (London: William Heinemann, 1909), 201.
85. *Art & Antiques* (Feb. 8, 1975), 23.
86. Steel, 152.
87. Margaret MacMillan, *Women of the Raj* (New York: Thames and Hudson, 1988), 44–45.
88. William Rieder, "Campaign Furniture," *Architectural Digest* (July 1995), 140.
89. London: J. Bumpus, 116.
90. *Antique Dealer and Collector's Guide* (August 1990), 38.
91. General Cavalié Mercer, *Journal of the Waterloo Campaign* (Edinburgh; London: William Blackwood and Sons, 1870), 258.
92. Charles Mackay, ed. *Medora Leigh: A History and an Autobiography* (London, 1869), 61.
93. A patent portmanteau bed manufactured by Thomas Butler and possibly owned by Lord Byron was sold at Bonham's, Knightsbridge, Fine English and Continental Furniture, July 14, 1999, lot 405.
94. Charles Allen, *A Glimpse of the Burning Plain: Leaves from the Indian Journals of Charlotte Canning* (London: Michael Joseph, 1986), 41.
95. William Rieder, "Campaign Furniture," 140.
96. "Early Nineteenth-Century Invalid Etc. Furniture," *Furniture History* (1974), 75.
97. V & A Picture Library, Z 305.
98. Public Record Office, Kew. Foreign Office, 185/50, Spain 1814.
99. "Early Nineteenth-Century Invalid Etc. Furniture," 74–75.
100. Morris, *Heaven's Command*, 213.
101. *The Duke of Wellington: What They Said, What He Said*, (Northamptonshire: J. L. Carr: n.d.), n.p.
102. Broadsheet. Public Record Office, Kew. Foreign Office, 185/50, Spain 1814.
103. Deborah Sampson Shinn, J. G. Links, Paul Fussell, and Ralph Caplan. *Bon Voyage: Designs for Travel* (New York: Cooper-Hewitt Museum, The Smithsonian Institution's National Museum of Design, 1986), 77.
104. London: John Murray, 324.
105. Shinn, 56.
106. Edward T. Joy, *English Furniture 1800–1851* (London: Sotheby Parke Bernet, 1977), 200.
107. London: J. Bumpus, 111.
108. Joy, 199.
109. "Folding Chairs," *Antique Collecting* (Aug. 24, 1990), 5–8.
110. Quoted in Edwards, "Folding Chairs," 5–8.

II.
Elegance Abroad: A Portfolio

116. An Assemblage of Georgian and Early Victorian Campaign Furniture.
Courtesy W. R. Harvey & Co. (Antiques) Ltd. Photo: Simon Wheeler.

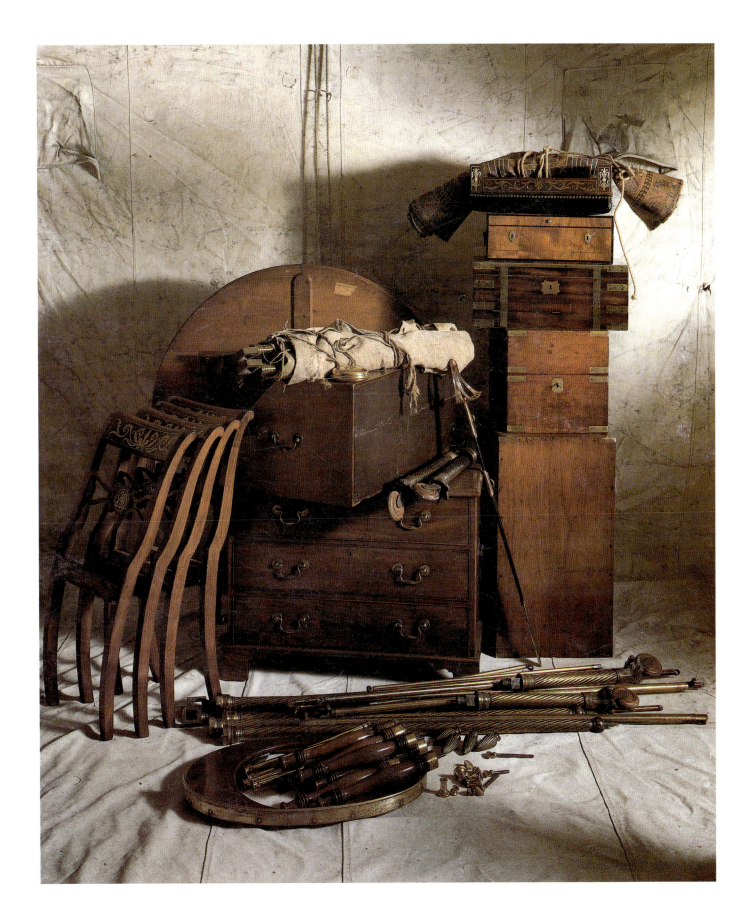

117. The same furniture shown knocked down and ready for travel.

Life Under Canvas

118. One from a Set of Four Regency Brass-Inlaid Mahogany Campaign Chairs, c. 1810. H: 2 ft. 9 in.; W: 1 ft. 7¼ in.; D (of seat): 1 ft. 3 in. Courtesy W. R. Harvey & Co. (Antiques) Ltd.

These chairs are of surprisingly sophisticated design, as illustrated by the monogram "G. M. D." in brass inlay on the middle rail of each back splat. To dismantle the chairs one unscrews the front legs and unbolts the seats from the backs before packing all the components into a case.

Contemporary makers of this type of furniture, such as Morgan & Sanders of Catherine Street, London, advertised sets of such chairs, which folded up into boxes.

119. The chairs shown disassembled and ready for travel.

120. Regency Mahogany Campaign Center Table, c. 1810. Courtesy Phillips of Hitchin (Antiques) Ltd.

This table might have been used as a small tea table or a card table and illustrates how campaign furniture developed to embrace "civilian" traveling furniture. This table is typical of the rather sturdy character of campaign furniture, as illustrated by the unusual feature of the fifth leg in the middle, which provides extra strength.

121. The five legs unscrew from five metal disks in the top, allowing the table to be folded over, thus making it portable.

PORTFOLIO / 123

122. Regency Teak Two-Part Military Chest (perhaps of colonial manufacture), with *secrétaire* drawer, iron carrying handles at the sides, and brass inset handles on the drawers, c. 1825. H: 3 ft. 8¾ in.; W: 2 ft. 11 in.; D: 1 ft. 6½ in. Courtesy Phillips of Hitchin (Antiques) Ltd.

123. The top drawer opens to reveal a *secrétaire* interior fitted with a central cupboard, pigeon-holes, small drawers, and a writing surface. The small central cupboard has a sliding tambour door.

124. Georgian Officer's Mahogany Campaign Armchair, upholstered in tan, close-nailed leather, c. 1790. H: 35 in.; W: 19 in.; D: 20 in. Collection of Professor and Mrs. John Ralph Willis.

125. The chair, which was built expressly for campaigning, can be quickly and easily disassembled without the use of tools by means of a drop-in seat, hinged back, and concertina-style folding action.

126. Regency Oak Chair-Bed, c. 1805, with the maker's engraved brass plaque of "*Morgan & Sanders, 16 & 17 Catherine Street, London.*" H (as chair or bed): 3 ft. 5 in.; H (packed up): 1 ft. 4 in.; W: 3 ft.; D (as chair): 2 ft. 2 in.; D (as bed): 6 ft. 4 in. Courtesy Christopher Howe.

When it is used as a bed, the underframe pulls out and is supported by additional legs. When the chair is not being used as a bed, these additional legs are unscrewed and held underneath the frame of the chair by special catches. These unusual devices probably explain why this chair-bed, unlike many others, has retained its original legs.

127. Chair-bed shown folded down like a box for transportation.

128. Regency Brass-Mounted Campaign Bookcase, c. 1820. Courtesy Phillips of Hitchin (Antiques) Ltd.
When folded up for transport, the bookcase (as shown) takes the form of a box.

129. The bookcase open, revealing glazed doors and "Gothic" tracery. Such a bookcase would have been used by military officers, university students, and travelers alike.

130. Late Regency Mahogany Campaign Occasional Table, second quarter nineteenth century. H: 9¾ in.; W: 1 ft. 6½ in.; D: 9¾ in. Courtesy Phillips of Hitchin (Antiques) Ltd.

131. The legs, which have brass caps typical of traveling furniture from this period, shown unscrewed and with the top folded up.

132. Late George III Mahogany Occasional Table, raised on square tapering legs with box casters and joined by stretchers. H: 2 ft. 4¾ in.; W: 2 ft. 1 in.; D: 1 ft. 5¾ in. Courtesy Phillips of Hitchin (Antiques) Ltd.

133. The legs fold up under the frame of the table, indicating that this piece was made for travel or campaigning.

134. Victorian Mahogany Apothecary's Traveling Compendium, the doors with three shelves, flanking the middle section with an upper drawer and lower drawer fitted with compartments, centering a case with various drawers and compartments. Courtesy W. R. Harvey & Co. (Antiques) Ltd.

In offering the following words of advice to surgeons employing such compendiums in the field, the satirist Francis Grose makes light of the strict social hierarchy of the early Victorian army: "Keep two lancets; a blunt one for the soldiers, and a sharp one for the officers: this will be making a proper distinction between them."[1]

[1]. Francis Grose, *Advice to the Officers of the British Army* (1783; 6th edition. New York: Agathynian Club, 1867), 57–60.

Above:
135. Traveling Rostrum, folded and disassembled for travel.

Left:
136. Regency Inlaid Mahogany Traveling Rostrum, with reeded bowed ledge and bowed oval veneered panel front, flanked by reeded columns headed by paterae, and raised on ring-turned tapered legs with a detachable ledge seat, c. 1805. H: 4 ft. 1 in. Courtesy Phillips Fine Art Auctioneers, London.

As early as 1783 the satirist Francis Grose offered the following advice to regimental chaplains:

Never preach any practical morality to the regiment. That would be only throwing away your time. To a man they all know, as well as you do, that they ought not to get drunk or commit adultery: but preach to them on the Trinity, the attributes of the Deity, and other mystical and abstruse subjects, which they may never before have thought or heard of. This will give them a high idea of your learning: besides, your life might otherwise give the lie to your preaching.[1]

1. Francis Grose, *Advice to the Officers of the British Army* (1783; 6th edition. New York: Agathynian Club, 1867), 64.

PORTFOLIO /131

Writing the Evening Dispatches

137. Victorian Brass-Bound Mahogany Campaign Traveling Desk, third quarter nineteenth century. H: 7 in.; W: 18 in.; D: 10½ in. Collection of Peter Bronson.

138. The desk open to show writing slope, inkwell and various compartments.

139. Late Victorian Brass-Bound Coromandel Traveling Desk, opening to a green baize-lined writing surface and fitted interior, above a single frieze drawer, last quarter nineteenth century. This traveling desk bears the engraved brass plaque with the inscription, *"Presented to Sergeant A. J. Brawley on receiving his commission by the N.C.O.'s & Men of A. Troop—19th P.W.O. Hussars."* H: 9 in.; W: 20 in.; D: 11 in. Collection of Peter Bronson.

According to the National Army Museum, London, the 19th Princess of Wales's Own Hussars held this title from 1881 to 1902 during which period Brawley could have been sergeant.

140. Detail of engraved brass presentation plaque.

141. The desk closed, showing the relatively exotic Coromandel exterior.

PORTFOLIO /133

142. One Nickel-Plated and Two Brass Traveling Reading Lamps, for use with candles (shown together with a pair of "Brighton Bun" Candlesticks), c. 1900. H (of double-tube lamp): 26 in.; H (of single brass lamp): 12¾ in.; H (of nickel-plated lamp): 16½ in. Private collection.

This photograph shows what the Army & Navy Co-Operative Society's *General Price List 1923–24* describes as a brass-plated "Double Tube Candlestick for Reading, &c., corrugated hood," a nickel-plated "Candle Reading Lamp with telescopic small hood," a "Candle Reading Lamp with large hood," and a pair of "Brass Folding Candlesticks." While these lights were convenient for traveling, they were also used domestically. A silver-plated "Candle Reading Lamp with corrugated hood" can be seen today at Chatsworth, in Derbyshire, the ancestral home of the dukes of Devonshire.

Above:
143. One of a pair of Victorian Folding Brass "Brighton Bun" Candlesticks, closed together to form case, c. 1870. H (assembled): 2¼ in.; D: 4 in. Private collection.

These folding brass candlesticks were specifically designed for travelers and first appeared in the late eighteenth century. They were retailed by both Harrods and the Army & Navy Co-Operative Society in the late nineteenth century (and, in the case of the Army & Navy Society, at least until 1924). Commonly referred to as "Brighton Buns," they were usually constructed from brass or silver and occasionally wood. Some even include snuffers.

Left:
144. The candlesticks shown open.

145. Victorian Brass Traveling Candle Holder, engraved with an officer's crest above the letter "E.", third quarter nineteenth century. The reverse is engraved with the Prince of Wales's feathers above "3. D. G.," for the 3rd Dragoon Guards. H: 2 in.; W: 2 in. Collection of Peter Bronson.

PORTFOLIO /135

Gentlemen at Ease

146. A. Hepplewhite & Co. Design for a "Gentleman's Social Table," pl. 22 in *The Cabinet Maker's London Book of Prices*, 2nd edition, 1793. Courtesy Victoria & Albert Museum; V & A Picture Library, London.

Opposite:
147. Late Regency Mahogany Campaign Wine Table, c. 1820. H: 29¼ in.; W: 103 in.; D: 64 in. Private Collection.

This unusually large mahogany campaign wine or "social" table of D-shaped outline was intended for fireside drinking. The table would have been placed in front of the fireplace, with the guests seated around the outside of the table. The origin of such tables can be traced to the "Gentleman's Social Table" illustrated in A. Hepplewhite & Co.'s *The Cabinet-Maker and Upholsterer's Guide*, London, 2nd ed., 1788.

Significant to its function, especially in the officer's mess, is the semi-circular shape of the table. Port, that old stalwart of British civilization drunk by officers throughout the Empire, always circulates in a clockwise direction. N. M. Penzer offers several possible explanations for why the British customarily pass their port clockwise following the path of the sun:

Simply expressed, the answer to the question is that otherwise one would be transgressing against the laws of cosmical rotation and the primitive belief that to follow the sun's course strengthens its continuance and is beneficial and health-giving to mortals. A sun-wise direction, therefore, brings good luck . . . For its origin we can look to ancient Greece. Greek augurs looked to the north, so that lucky omens came from the east, and were on the right side. From the Greek preference for the right hand everything had to be done "towards the right hand," as Homer (Iliad. I, 597) called it. In fact, all things which went round in a circle —drinking and toasting at table, casting lots (Iliad. VII, 184), begging at table (Odyssey. XVII, 365) —had to be carried out clockwise or sun-wise, with the right hand and shoulder towards the centre, or from the left towards the right.

According to Percy McQuoid and Ralph Edwards, "The care bestowed upon the design of these tables serves to recall the habits of an age when 'intoxication was expected, as a matter of course, to conclude the evening's entertainment.'"[1] Examples of wine tables are illustrated in Christopher Gilbert, *Furniture at Temple Newsam House and Lotherton Hall*, Leeds: NACF and Leeds Art Collections Fund, 1978, vol. II, pp. 377–78, fig. 494; and N. M. Penzer, "Thoughts on Coasters," *Apollo*, June 1954, pp. 197–98.

1. *The Dictionary of English Furniture* (London, 1954), p.320.

148. The wine table shown disassembled.

PORTFOLIO /137

149. Victorian Mahogany Portable Games Table, with removable reversible top that doubles as gaming surface and table top, c. 1860. Courtesy Phillips of Hitchin (Antiques) Ltd.

150. Games table with green baize-lined top and ivory markers.

151. The table disassembled for travel.

Upper left:
152. George IV Traveling Games Table, c. 1830. H: 28 in.; W: 15½ in.; D: 13 in. Private collection.

The top of the table comes off and forms the box within which the telescopic-extending base and legs can be stored for travel.

Upper right:
153. The games table disassembled.

Left:
154. The games table disassembled and packed inside folded table top, which doubles as case.

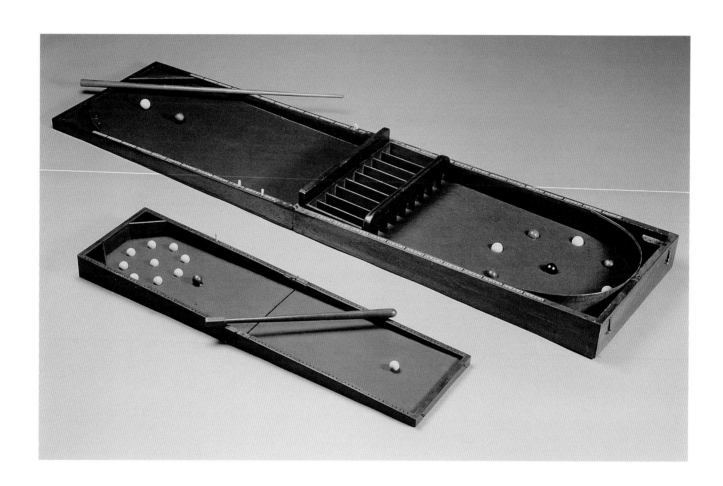

155. Regency Mahogany Folding Billiards Table (the larger) and a Regency Portable Bagatelle Table (the smaller). Courtesy Phillips Fine Art Auctioneers, London.

Personal Kit

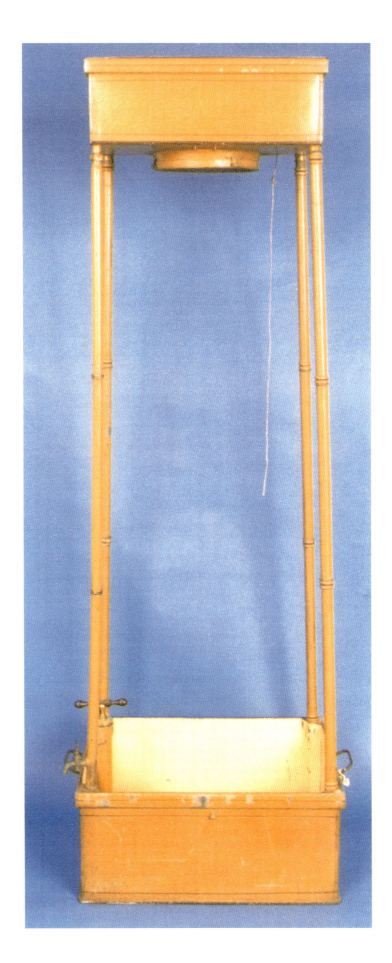

156. Victorian Campaign Shower.
W: 29 in. Courtesy Boulton & Cooper, Yorkshire.

The shower consists of interlocking metal and wood poles, shower head, pump, and curtain. When knocked down for travel, the entire shower fits within the lower section.

157. The Duke of Wellington's Brass-Mounted Mahogany Campaign Dressing-Table Box, c. 1810. Collection of the Victoria & Albert Museum, London. Photo: Victoria & Albert Museum; V & A Picture Library.

This box, designed for travel with flush brass handles and sturdy lock, contains a surprising number of supplies in a variety of sizes, including glass bottles and jars, combs, brushes, scissors, keys, razors, and pliers.

According to George Augustus Smythe, seventh Viscount Strangford (1818–57), the Duke of Wellington once remarked:

The man who always sharpens my razors has sharpened them for many years: I would not trust them with anyone else.... So you see, Strangford, every man has a weak point, and my weak point is about the sharpening of my razors. Perhaps you are not aware that I shave myself, and brush my own clothes: I regret that I cannot clean my own boots; for menservants bore me, and the presence of a crowd of idle fellows annoys me more than I can tell you.[1]

1. Christopher Hibbert, ed., *Captain Gronow: His Reminiscences of Regency and Victorian Life 1810–60*. London: Kyle Cathie, 1991, 214–15.

158. Victorian Brass-Bound and Inlaid Mahogany Campaign Shaving Kit, shown open, with two horn-handled razors, an ivory-handled brush, a space for scissors and various other implements, third quarter nineteenth century. L: 8½ in.; D: 2½ in. Collection of Peter Bronson.

159. Shaving kit shown closed for transport.

PORTFOLIO / 143

Upper left:
160. Victorian Brass-Bound Oak Campaign Razor Case, third quarter nineteenth century. H: 1½ in.; W: 7 in. Collection of Peter Bronson.

Upper right:
161. Razor case shown open with ivory-handled razors enclosed.

Right:
162. Razor case shown with one razor displayed open.

144 / PORTFOLIO

163. Late Victorian Teak Pivot-Folding Camp Mirror, last quarter nineteenth century. H: 1½ in.; W (closed): 10½ in.; W (open): 30 in.; D: 8 in. Collection of Peter Bronson.

 The three-part mirror folds together to form a protective case. Similar examples were retailed by the Army & Navy Co-Operative Society in the 1880s.

164. Mirror shown unfolded.

165. Victorian Campaign Knife and Fork, shown separately and stamped *"Williamson / Sheffield."* L: 8 in.; W: 1 in. Collection of Peter Bronson.

166. Knife and fork fitted into one another so that the handles form a case.

PORTFOLIO /145

Outfitting the Barracks

167. An Officer's Quarters At Newry, Northern Ireland, c. 1870. Watercolor on paper. Courtesy Phillips of Hitchin (Antiques) Ltd.

With all the comforts of home, this interior is equipped not only with campaign furniture, such as the *secrétaire-*military chest, book tray, boot rack, Douro chair, and brass bedstead, but it also includes several rugs and carpets, all of which are mingled with swords, guns placed on gun racks, and the officer's cap and gloves.

168. Victorian Brass-Mounted Mahogany Military Chest, with *secrétaire* drawer, third quarter nineteenth century. Courtesy W. R. Harvey & Co. (Antiques) Ltd.

This two-part, brass-mounted campaign chest with inset handles has a superstructure that encloses two hinged shelves with brass supports, above an arrangement of three short and three long drawers.

169. Victorian Mahogany Two-Part Traveling Chest, third quarter nineteenth century. H: 3 ft. 3½ in.; W: 2ft. 8½ in.; D: 1 ft. 5¼ in. Courtesy Phillips of Hitchin (Antiques) Ltd.

This traveling chest is in many ways similar to the traditional "military" chest, but with sunken knob handles instead of the more common brass fixtures, as well as two holes on each side to hold ropes.

170. Victorian Mahogany Campaign Writing Table, with inset brass handles and turned legs terminating in brass caps and casters, third quarter nineteenth century. Courtesy Phillips of Hitchin (Antiques) Ltd.

171. The table shown with the legs unscrewed.

172. Edwardian Mahogany and Brass-Mounted Coaching Table, c. 1905. H: 29 in.; W: 31¾ in.; D: 22¼ in. Private collection.

173. The coaching table shown folded.

174. Victorian Mahogany Campaign Armchair, with buttoned back and sprung seat. H: 40½ in.; W: 24¾ in.; D: 30½ in. Courtesy Christopher Clarke.

175. Armchair shown folded. On removal of the "slot in" buttoned back it becomes possible to lower the back framework and arm supports, which are hinged at the front. The front and back legs fold under the seat frame once the hidden locking rails have folded under the seat.

176. Set of Four Victorian Mahogany Campaign Dining Chairs, c. 1845. Courtesy Phillips of Hitchin (Antiques) Ltd.

These chairs are similar to a set of knock-down mahogany dining chairs stamped "MILES KINGTON & CO, / SOLE AGENTS FOR THE / AUSTRALIAN / COLONIES" and imported by the government of New Zealand for its House of Representatives in the mid-nineteenth century (illustrated in *Colonial Furniture in New Zealand* by S. Northcote-Bade, p. 105, fig. 72).

177. The chairs shown dismantled. This particular set of chairs is unusual in that the legs do not unscrew. Instead, the legs, together with the seat frame, fold up along the siderails.

178. Detail of Unusual Folding Action. The front legs and rail fold up alongside the siderail, the tenon of which slides into the backrail.

Solving the Problem of the Extra Guest

179. George III Brass-Bound Mahogany and Caned Child's Campaign Bed, with brass plaque engraved: "(Patent) / Morgan & Sanders / Manufacturers / 16 & 17 / Catherine Street, Strand / London," c. 1805. H: 70½ in.; W: 26½ in.; L: 53½ in. Courtesy Philip Colleck, Ltd., New York, NY.

180. The bed shown disassembled

PORTFOLIO / 153

Left:
181. Mid-Eighteenth Century Mahogany Campaign Chair, upholstered in close-nailed black leather. Courtesy Phillips of Hitchin (Antiques) Ltd.

Below left:
182. The chair folded up concertina-style.

Opposite:
183. George II Metamorphic Mahogany Sofa-Bed, c. 1740. H: 52 in.; W: 46½ in.; D: 29¾ in. Collection of Professor and Mrs. John Ralph Willis.

This sofa-bed, possibly military, but more likely domestic, has a tapestry cover signed and inscribed on the *verso*, "T. Hancock / January 3, 1779." Thomas Hancock of Tetbury, Gloucestershire, was active from 1778 to 1798.[1] When set up as a bed, the back of the sofa-bed raises to form a canopy. Of interest, the back bears a brass plaque with the crown of Czar Alexander I, emperor of Russia from 1801–1825.

An almost identical ribbon-back settee, c. 1740, but with curtains that run beneath the canopy, can be seen today in the Crimson Bedchamber at Nostell Priory in Yorkshire. It is also illustrated in R. W. Symonds' article "Pre-Chippendale Furniture at Nostell Priory" from the April 25, 1952 issue of *Country Life* (p. 1249). According to Symonds, "The fact that a put-up bed for the extra guest or his manservant should be enclosed by curtains shows to what a degree our ancestors thought it necessary to keep out the 'poisonous' night air." A similar example also exists in Gunston Hall, the colonial plantation home of George Mason, "Father of America's Bill of Rights," in Lorton, Virginia. A third and almost identical example was advertised by dealers Tiller & King in the January 1985 issue of *Antiques*.

A similar example, referred to as a "chair couch in Chippendale style" or "settle bed" is illustrated in Wallace Nutting's article "Double-Purpose Furniture," on pages 160–62 of the October 1940 issue of *The Magazine Antiques*. Nutting writes,

When closed it gives the effect of a double-width chair. Its molded legs and block feet are in the Chippendale tradition . . . When the piece is opened, it becomes a couch or bed, fully as wide as an ordinary single bed. The front section of the chair then serves as the foot. The mattress unfolds from within the seat, where it has been covered by a slip seat . . . A feature of special interest is the adjustable canopy which swings out and is supported by brackets from the back. When the canopy frame is raised it reveals a tufted back . . . In some respects the piece reminds one of the canopied "sophas" shown by Chippendale in his Director, *although the latter are much more ornate and do not open out in this fashion.*

Another example, referred to as a "convertible daybed" or "settle bed," is illustrated on pages 128 to 129 of the February 1953 issue of *The Magazine Antiques*.[2]

1. Geoffrey Beard and Christopher Gilbert, eds., *Dictionary of English Furniture Makers 1660–1840*. London: Furniture History Society and W. S. Maney & Son, Ltd., 1986, 393.
2. I am grateful to Professor John Ralph Willis for sharing his research into this sofa-bed.

184. The metamorphic bed extended.

PORTFOLIO / 155

185. English Iron-Bound Leather Trunk, c. 1910. H: 17 in.;
W: 27 in.; D: 17⅝ in. Private collection.

The hinges on the back of this trunk have holes
through which rope could be passed to lash the trunk to
a mule for transportation.

III.

Directory of British Campaign Furniture Designers, Makers, Outfitters, and Patentees

The following directory of designers, makers, outfitters, and patentees reveals the quality, variety, and ingenuity of the British campaign furniture available to military officers from the last quarter of the eighteenth century to the early twentieth. These pieces were also used by civilians traveling abroad, including civil servants, explorers, and emigrants.

The majority of manufacturers of such knock-down furniture made a concerted effort to broaden the possible uses of their wares, so that their designs were suitable for both military and domestic use. Thus, the phrase "campaign furniture" is somewhat limiting. The furniture could be used not only to outfit a ship's cabin, barrack room, or tent, but it could also accommodate an unexpected guest, or make a trip to the races a more civilized affair.

The advertisements placed by the manufacturers and outfitters of this furniture show how they successfully adapted their designs to the changing needs of their customers throughout the course of the nineteenth century. In 1861 the firms of James Clifton, S. W. Silver, R. W. Winfield, Angelo Sedley, John Ward, and J. W. Allen each placed an advertisement in the commercial pages of *Kelly's Post Office London Directory*. These advertisements reveal the many outfitting options available to anyone preparing to travel abroad. Each advertiser offered a breadth of products at competitive prices. J. W. Allen, for example, advertised over 500 articles for home or continental traveling, while S. W. Silver dealt in "furniture for camp, barrack, cabin, and Colonial use," as well as "every variety of Cabinet Work, Canteens, Trunks, Portmanteaus, etc."

Early- to mid-nineteenth-century advertisements for British campaign furniture offer many unique and often humorous insights into contemporary English society. As early as 1800, William Gaimes noted how difficult it was to get merchants to buy his portable letter copying machines and desks because their design rendered the jobs of two copying clerks obsolete—presumably because of the objections of the clerks themselves! In 1826 Samuel Pratt patented a bed to prevent sea-sickness, which was certainly outdone by Benjamin Taylor & Sons in 1851, when that firm made a "patent cork floating bed" that could also help save a passenger from drowning in case of shipwreck. And in 1839 Edward Johnson claimed that his newly invented metal folding bedsteads, couches, and chairs overcame all prior objections to the "weight, expensiveness and inelegance" of metal furniture, since his designs were light, durable, elegant, and inhospitable to insects and other vermin.

Newspaper advertisements can reveal telling information about the attitudes and practices of their times. For example, the often amusing skirmishes between Thomas Butler and Morgan & Sanders played out in the newspapers of their day give us the flavor of the intense competition among portable furniture manufacturers in the early nineteenth century. Likewise, by reading about the Bristol firm of Miles & Kington, we gain a sense of the global reach of a major shipping company operating at the height of Great Britain's imperial power. One very interesting revelation that results from tracking these firms through the annual post office directories is that among the successful makers and marketers of campaign furniture in nineteenth-century Britain are a number of women—including Fanny Heal, Elizabeth Powell, and Margaret Tait.

Unfortunately, the vast majority of company records for nineteenth-century furniture manufacturers and patentees have not survived to the present day. Thus, the information presented here was taken primarily from trade labels, patents, and trade and commercial pages in the annual post office directories held in libraries and various public record offices throughout England. As we follow the firms' changing addresses over the years, we can often observe their expansion and, in most cases, their eventual decline.

It was not always possible to find definitive information for each person or firm listed here. In some instances, this directory includes the names of patentees about whom very little is known, other than the purpose and date of their designs. Owing to the existence of very few primary sources, this compilation cannot be completely comprehensive. It is the author's hope, however, that it will serve as a useful reference tool for collectors, curators, and historians of the arts, and in addition provide a foundation for further study of British campaign furniture.

JOHN ALDERMAN
(c. 1860–1902)

In 1860 John Alderman established an independent business at 16 Soho Square, London and proceeded to identify his furniture with a brass plaque engraved "J. Alderman / Inventor, / Patentee and Manufacturer, / 16 Soho Square, London." In the commercial directories from 1865 to 1885, Alderman is recorded as "invalid chair, couch and carriage manufacturer, 16 Soho Square, Soho, and 50 Tottenham Court Road," with his factory at 8 Denmark Street in Soho. He is listed in the 1875 London commercial directory as a manufacturer of "invalid, bath, Brighton, self-propelling and every other description of chair, couch, bed and carriage for invalids," with offices at 16 Soho Square and workshops at 8 Denmark Street.

Prior to establishing his own firm, John Alderman worked for Thomas Chapman, a manufacturer of invalid chairs, at 6 Denmark Street in Soho. Chapman had moved his furniture works to Denmark Street in 1838, possibly from 9 New Bond Street. By 1848 he had offices in both Denmark Street and 22 Edward Street in Portman Square.

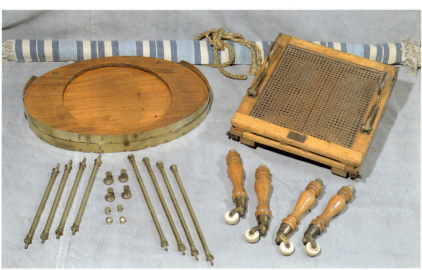

D.1: Victorian Brass-Mounted Washstand, c. 1850 (H: 33¾ in.; W: 27 in.; D: 19¾ in.) and Victorian Satin-Birch Armchair, with turned legs and ceramic casters, c. 1870, with maker's brass plaque engraved "J. Alderman / Inventor, / Patentee and Manufacturer, / 16 Soho Square, London," (H: 35 in.; W: 19 in.; D: 20 in.). Collection of Professor and Mrs. John Ralph Willis.

Professor Willis has suggested to the author that this mahogany and brass-bound military washstand is likely to have evolved from the three-tiered cake stands popular in France under the reign of Louis XVI (reigned 1774–1792).

Similar examples can be seen in the advertisements of W. Day & Son and Hill & Millard from 1867 (plates 101 and D.39).

D.2: The superstructure of the washbasin collapses to fold into a brass-wrapped tub which, when closed, forms a table. The armchair is also collapsible.

D.3: Detail of maker's engraved brass plaque, on back seat rail of chair.

D.4: Detail showing "J. ALDERMAN, MANUFACTURER, 16, SOHO SQUARE, LONDON" *engraved into the brass hubcaps of the invalid's armchair illustrated in plate 103.*

Even before he went into business for himself, Alderman's name appears in the London commercial directories when he became Chapman's partner in 1855 and the firm changed its name to Chapman & Alderman. They billed themselves as "inventors and manufacturers of the graduating spinal fracture and general invalid couches, chairs, carriages, and every other description of article required by invalids." The firm traded at 8 Denmark Street until about 1856.

In 1890 the firm was renamed Alderman, Johnson & Co. Limited, and moved to new premises at Charing Cross Road, as well as 87 and 453 New Oxford Street. From 1897 to 1902, Alderman, Johnson & Co., "invalid carriage, couch, chair and perambulator manufacturers," was located at 138 and 140 Charing Cross Road. Alderman & Johnson Co. Limited was transferred into John Ward Ltd. in 1903 (*see* John Ward).

JOHN ALLEN
(C. 1831–1913)

John Allen, trunk and camp equipage maker, is recorded at 22 Strand in the London commercial directories from 1831 to 1842. A maker's paper label affixed to a packing case for a campaign chest of this period reads, "JOHN ALLEN, / Trunk Portmanteau & Canteen Manufacturer, / No. 22, / STRAND, LONDON. / Hungerford House, corner of Hungerford Street. / PORTABLE BEDS, SEA COTS, and all sorts of FURNITURE / for Cabins, Barracks, &c. / SEA Chests, Imperials & Carriage Trunks. / Carpet-Bags & Brush Cases / in great variety / Writing Desks & Dressing Cases, Marquees and Tents" (plate D.5). By 1849 the firm had expanded to 18 and 22 Strand, where, from 1851 to 1855, it traded under the name of John, William, and Thomas Allen. In October 1860 the firm issued a two-page illustrated catalogue of portable military furniture, in which a Cavalry Officer's Outfit of Barrack Room Furniture was advertised for £161.5s. Several of these items are reproduced in *The Armourer*[1] and include such apparent necessities as:

Portable Brass Sofa Bedstead with cushions and damask covers in strong chest, one best horsehair mattress, two ditto bolsters, one feather Pillow, three Blankets, one white Counterpane, in patent waterproof valise, lined and name printed . . . £20.0.0

Portable Mahogany Recumbent Easy Chair with Leg Rest in maroon or green leather, in strong chest, to form a Dressing Table with Castors. £11.10s

Strong oak Canteen containing Breakfast Service for Three Persons. Electro-plated fittings. 26½ inches long, 16 inches wide, 15 inches deep. £24.10s. Complete. Containing: 1 large dish, 2 10-inch dishes, 6 breakfast plates, 3 cups and saucers, 1 butter cooler, 3 egg cups, 1 slop basin in white china with gold edges. 2 pint decanters, 1 vinegar cruet, 2 tumblers in cut glass. 1 pair candlesticks, 1 chamber candlestick, 1 pepper cruet, 1 mustard pot, 1 sugar basin, 1 cream jug, 2 salt cellars. 1 candle box, 1 sugar canister, 1 coffee canister, 1 spice box, 1 lucifer box. Tea caddy, toast fork, corkscrew, spirit flask and cutlery.

Portable Mahogany Swing Looking Glass with Drawer and Bramah Lock. 25 inches by 19 inches . . . £4.10.0

Portable Mahogany Wash Hand Table on castors, 3 feet 6 inches long, with fittings complete in strong chest, to form a large dressing table and cupboard . . . £12.10.0

A large leather brush case, and space for boot trees with best shoe, cloth, and hat brushes, boot-top and breeches ditto, two metal bottles, large boot jack and button stick, brass plate, name engraved . . . £3.15.6.

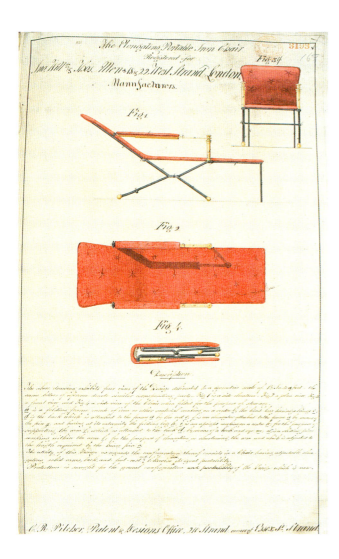

Above:
D.5: *Trade Label of John Allen, No. 22 Strand, London, c. 1831–1842. Ink on paper, second quarter nineteenth century. Private collection.*

Left:
D.6: *The "Elongated Portable Chair," registered by John, William and Thomas Allen of 18 & 22 West Strand, London, Manufacturers, March 24, 1852. Watercolor and ink on paper. Public Record Office, London.*

Other sundry requisites include "a set of damask window curtains, with brass extending rods . . . £3.10.0" and "a pair of glove trees . . . 7s."

For the less affluent enlisted man, Allen's offered a suite of campaign furniture it called a "Barrack Room or Aldershott Camp Outfit," which, in 1860, consisted of "a portable iron bedstead with mattress feather pillow, blankets and counterpaine, portable dressing table, and wash stand, the whole in one chest 2 ft 6 in long, 2 ft high and 3 ft high, plus a portable mahogany half set of drawers in chest to form a wardrobe . . . £20.0.0."

An advertisement in the 1861 London commercial directory for J. W. Allen, "MANUFACTURER OF OFFICERS' BARRACK FURNITURE AND MILITARY OUTFITTER," describes the firm's additional range of offerings: "ALLEN'S PATENT PORTMANTEAUS AND TRAVELLING BAGS, WITH SQUARE OPENING; LADIES' DRESS TRUNKS, DRESSING BAGS, WITH SILVER FITTINGS; DESPATCH [sic] BOXES, WRITING AND DRESSING CASES, AND 500 OTHER ARTICLES FOR HOME OR CONTINENTAL TRAVELLING."

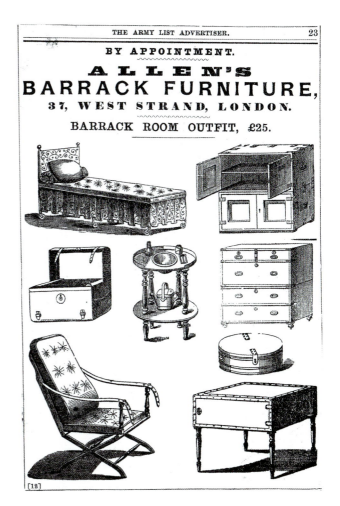

D.7: *Advertisement for Allen's, 37 West Strand, London, in* The Army List Advertiser, *1891. Ink on paper. Collection of Peter Bronson.*

DIRECTORY /161

In 1862 the firm was awarded a Prize Medal for General Excellence, and by 1865 John William Allen had moved to 37 West Strand, where the company remained for at least the next thirty years. The firm is described in the London commercial directory for 1865 as a military outfitter and manufacturer of barrack room furniture, dressing cases, and patent dispatch boxes. By 1867 J. W. Allen was a Royal Warrant holder to H. R. H. The Prince of Wales and had placed advertisements describing the firm as a manufacturer of barrack room furniture, portmanteaus, and trunks. In an advertisement in *The Army List Advertiser* of 1867, J. W. Allen once again offered a "Barrack Room or Aldershott Camp Outfit." In this instance the outfit consisted of a "Bedstead and Bedding, in Chest and Valise. Mahogany Drawers, Bramah Lock, in Chests to form a Wardrobe. Easy Chair in Chest to form a Dressing Table. Mahogany Wash-hand Stand and Fittings, in Oak Tub. £26:10s." J. W. Allen registered designs for patents in 1869 and 1873, describing the firm as a "Dressing Case Manufacturer."

J. W. Allen is entered in the London commercial directory for 1875 as a "manufacturer of barrack room furniture and military outfitter; patent despatch [*sic*] box and dressing case manufacturer" and that year ran an advertisement for its "Solid Leather Portmanteaus." These included designs for dressing bags and cases, lady's wardrobes, and dispatch boxes. An advertisement from 1885 reveals a variation on its "Barrack Room Outfit." J. W. Allen now offered "Barrack Furniture and India Outfits" consisting of "Stump Bedstead and Bedding, in Chest and Valise. Mahogany Drawers, in Chests, to form a Wardrobe. Easy Chair, in Chest, to form a Dressing Table. Mahogany Wash-hand Stand and Fittings, in Oak Tub. £25." In addition J. W. Allen offered such leather items as portmanteaus, overland trunks, and patent dispatch-box desks. By 1885 the firm was manufacturing almost one hundred different styles of chests of drawers, but by the late 1890s J. W. Allen was entered in the London commercial directories solely as a manufacturer of portmanteaus. In 1901 the firm is recorded as "John William Allen, portmanteau manufacturer, 37 Strand." The firm is listed at this address through 1913.[2]

Right:
D.8. *Regency Mahogany Caned Chair-Bed, c. 1810, with maker's brass plaque engraved, "Argles / late / Butler's / Patent / 13 & 14 / Catherine St. Strand." Courtesy Phillips of Hitchin (Antiques) Ltd.*

Opposite, left:
D.9. *The chair set up as a bed.*

Opposite, right:
D.10. *The chair disassembled, with back and sides removed.*

EDWARD ARGLES
(c. 1795–1813)

"Edward Argles traded as a cabinet-maker and upholsterer at Maidstone, Kent from 1795 until 1810 when he advertised the sale of his premises and stock 'having taken the business of Dr. Butler of Catherine-street in the Strand.' Butler had specialised in a range of patent furniture and Argles evidently continued these lines. . . . He succeeded in attracting Royal patronage. When, in 1813 he was declared bankrupt, his stock in trade was valued at £8,500."[3] A maker's brass plaque on a chair-bed quite similar to those produced by the firms of Thomas Butler and Morgan & Sanders is engraved, "Argles / late / Butlers / Patent / 13 & 14, / Catherine St. Strand." Argles advertised the firm as an "Upholsterer & Cabinet maker to the King & Queen, their Royal Highnesses Prince, Princess & Princess Charlotte of Wales, Duke of York & Princesses."[4]

D.11. *Detail of maker's engraved brass plaque.*

ARMY & NAVY CO-OPERATIVE SOCIETY
(1871–C.1935)

The Army & Navy Co-Operative Society, Limited, of 105 Victoria Street in Westminster, was the most popular military and civilian outfitter from its establishment in 1871 through World War II, by which time it had become the Army and Navy Stores Limited. Described by *The Field* in 1923 as a "National Institution," the firm was instrumental in assuming the majority of business from the Victorian manufacturers of campaign and invalid furniture after the death of Queen Victoria in 1901. Its lengthy, fully illustrated catalogues were distributed throughout the British Empire and offered a comprehensive selection of portable and folding furniture, as well as camp and cabin requisites, including traveling chests, portable and folding washstands, chairs, mirrors, stick racks, and wrought-iron and brass bedsteads. "In 1876—five years after the store was founded—the Army & Navy catalogue listed campaign furniture in two pages. (For many years the catalogue called it 'Barrack Furniture'). By July 1880, it occupied 20 pages with profuse illustration. And on the outbreak of war in 1914 it ran to 26 closely detailed pages."[5]

The firm offered a variety of folding camp equipment for maneuvers and expeditions, including marquees and tents of every description for sporting and camping purposes. The *1881 Price List*, for example, included illustrations for seven elegant campaign beds, each of which was designed to disassemble and fit within an iron-bound strong-chest. The designs included a "Folding Solid Iron Half Tester Bedstead;" a "Portable Folding Sofa Barrack Bedstead, with screw curtain rod and fly rails;" a "Portable Iron Couch Bedstead;" a "Portable Iron French Bedstead;" a "Portable Solid Iron Flat-roof Bedstead, 4 ft. 6 in. by 6 ft. 4 in.;" a "Portable Brass Sofa Bedstead;" and a "Portable Folding, solid Iron Tent Bedstead." For sheets, blankets, and pillows, the firm offered a three-foot-long, cylindrical, waterproof valise. For officers traveling with their families, the catalogue even included a "Patent Folding Crib, 2 feet by 4 feet" that could be packed flat "for removal or export."

The firm frequently marked leather items with a shield-shaped trade label impressed with the letters "A & NCSL" in gold. Alternately, the company's initials were sometimes impressed directly into the piece. Campaign furniture was also impressed with the initials "A & NCSL," though in some cases these initials were stamped on a brass plaque which was then affixed to the piece. Much of the campaign furniture manufactured by the Army & Navy Co-Operative Society, however, remained unmarked. The London commercial directory for 1875 lists the firm at 117 Victoria St., Westminster, with a warehouse at Johnson's Place, Lupus Street, in Pimlico. By 1902 it was trading at 105 Victoria Street in Westminster, where it was still located in 1935, at which time the firm had depots in Plymouth, England, Bombay, and Calcutta. In 1940 and 1950 the Society is listed in London only as Army & Navy Stores, Limited.

GEORGE AUSTIN
(c. 1840–1847)

In the 1840 *Dublin Almanac and General Register of Ireland*, George Austin is listed at 7 St. Andrew Street and 9 William Street, Dublin, as a "Cabinet maker, portable desk and work box manufacturer." In 1847 he is listed at the same address as a "Fancy cabinet, writing desk, dressing case, work-box, military canteen and plate chest manufacturer."

A mid-nineteenth-century brass-bound campaign spirits case (plates D.13–14), formerly the property of the Marquess of Normanby, of Whitley Wicklow, Ireland, and now in a private collection, bears the maker's paper label, "G<small>EO</small>. A<small>USTIN</small>. / Cabinet Maker / 7, St. Andrew St / One door from Wicklow St. Dublin / Manufac-turers of Portable Writing / Desks, Dressing Cases, Work Boxes, &c. / <small>MILITARY CANTEENS AND PLATE CHESTS</small>" (plate D.12).

D.12. Maker's paper label.

D.13 and D.14. Victorian Brass-Bound Mahogany Spirits Case, by George Austin, third quarter nineteenth century. H: 11½ in.; W: 14 in.; D: 9 in. Collection of Peter Bronson.

ALBERT BARKER, LTD.
(c. 1890–1939)

Albert Barker is first listed in the London commercial directories in 1890. The directories of 1897 and 1905 record the following: "Albert Barker Limited, by special warrants of appointment to Her Majesty the Queen and T.R.H. the Prince and Princess of Wales, manufacturers, inventors and patentees of the 'Royal Burlington' and other travelling dressing bags, gold and silver work, gem jewelry, writing cases, electro-plated goods, dressing cases, art stationery, fine cutlery, fancy goods of the finest English and foreign manufacture, 5 New Bond Street." The firm was still in business in 1939, but is not listed in the London commercial directory for 1940.

Above:
D.15. Table shown with legs folded into base, which becomes a packing case.

Right:
D.16. Late Victorian Brass-Bound Mahogany Campaign Table, with hinged legs, by Albert Barker, Ltd., c. 1900. H (open): 26 3/4 in.; H (closed): 3 1/2 in.; L (open): 31 in. Photo: Courtesy of Ross Hamilton Antiques, Ltd.

D.17. Late Victorian Oak Campaign Writing Desk, last quarter nineteenth century. The desk is engraved with the maker's ivory plaque of Albert Barker Ltd. of 5 New Bond Street, special warrant holder to Queen Victoria. H: 24 1/4 in.; W: 23 3/4 in.; D: 23 3/4 in. Private collection.
While folded for travel, the desk can be carried by means of a brass handle.

D.18. The desk unfolds to reveal a leather-lined interior with inkwells, ivory pens, and various compartments for paper and envelopes. Desks such as these were popular among British officers throughout the nineteenth century until the First World War. Shown with elephant-foot stool.

BAYLEY & BLEW
(1739–c. 1910)

William Bayley is listed in the 1779 London directory as a perfumer on Cockspur Street, Charing Cross. In 1784 the firm is listed as Bayley & Lowe, also on Cockspur Street. Bayley & Lowe is listed as a perfumer on Cockspur Street in 1795 and again the following year. Bayley, Son & Blew, perfumers, is recorded at 17 Cockspur Street from 1799 to 1885.

The entry for the firm Bayley & Co. in the 1885 London commercial directory states: "Bayley & Co. established in 1739, at the Old Civet Cat, 17 Cockspur Street, London, Perfumers to the Royal Family and Foreign Courts, whole distillers and sole manufacturers of Ess. Bouquet. From the perfume becoming the peculiar favourite of his late Majesty, George the Fourth, arose many imperfect imitations of the article and which continue to be sold under the name of Bouquet du Roi-Esprit de Bouquet of George the Fourth, &c.; but the Essence Bouquet, exclusively prepared by Bayley & Co. Cockspur Street, London is the only article entitled to those appellations, and which possess an unrivaled and distinct fragrance. This perfume has also become a peculiar favourite in every foreign Court and city. Bayley & Co., make the 'Ess.' But of one quality, of one manufacture, and of one price, without any alteration whatsoever. Highly perfumed soap tablets, spermaceti, Otto of rose and Ess. Bouquet."

In addition to manufacturing perfume, the company manufactured small cabinets and portable writing desks. From 1849 to 1875 the firm went by the name William Bayley & Co., perfumers and dressing case makers to the Royal Family, trading from 17 Cockspur Street, Charing Cross. From 1887 to 1895 Bayley & Co. is listed as "Wholesale Perfumers, 17 Cockspur Street." From 1897 to 1901 the firm is recorded as Bayley & Co. "Wholesale Perfumers & Fine Toilet Soap manufacturers, 94 St. Martin's Lane." From 1902 until the firm's final listing in 1910, the directory records: "Bayley & Co. . . . wholesale perfumers and fine toilet soap manufacturers, by special warrant to His Majesty the King, 94 St. Martin's Lane."

GEORGE, ROBERT, AND JOHN BENGOUGH
(c. 1843–1870)

In the 1841 London commercial directory there is a listing for Ann Bengough & Son, trunk maker and camp equipage manufacturer, at 4 Tichborne Street. From 1843 to 1851, her sons, George and Robert Bengough, are recorded as trunk makers working from the same address in Piccadilly. On August 8, 1855 George, Robert, and their brother, John Bengough, were granted a patent for their improved mule portmanteau (D.19). In 1860 George and Robert are recorded as trunk makers with premises at 4 Tichborne Street, 49 High Holborn, and 5 and 6 Cheapside.[6] From 1869 to 1870 George and Robert are recorded as working from 5 Cheapside. Their brother John is recorded in his own right from 1866 to 1868 as a "Trunk and Packing Case Maker" at 4 Tichborne Street, Piccadilly, the same address as George and Robert.[7]

D.19. The "Improved Mule Portmanteau," registered by the brothers George, Robert, and John Bengough, 4 Tichborne Street, Piccadilly, London. August 8, 1855. Watercolor and ink on paper. Public Record Office, London.

BLADES & PALMER
(c. 1802–1823)

"Thomas Blades of 177 Piccadilly formed a partnership with Palmer in about 1802."[8] In 1803 Blades & Palmer appears in Sheraton's list of master cabinet makers.[9] The firm is recorded in the post office directories for 1807 and 1813 as an upholsterer trading from 177 Piccadilly and 114 Jermyn Street. Blades & Palmer continues to appear in London directories through 1823.

JOHN BLAIR
(c. 1851)

John Blair, of Camphill Irvine, Ayrshire, Scotland was granted a patent on March 12, 1851 for his "military, tourist's, and emigrant's portable couch or bedstead."

BOWRING, ARUNDEL & CO.
(c. 1850–1930)

The outfitter Bowring, Arundel & Co. was granted a patent between 1881 and 1884 for its combination pack saddle boxes and bedstead. The firm is listed in the commercial directories from 1850 to 1930 as a shirt maker, hosier, and outfitter. In 1850 the company was located at 11 Fenchurch Street. By 1861 Bowring, Arundel & Co. had expanded to 11 and 50 Fenchurch Street and also 11 Old Bond Street, at least through 1875. In 1880 the company is listed at 11 and 50 Fenchurch Street and 39 Old Bond Street. Under "Outfitters" in the 1903 trade directory, Bowring, Arundel & Co. is listed at 11 and 12 Fenchurch Street. There is a second listing for the firm at 39 Old Bond Street. In 1920 the firm is recorded at 11 and 12 Fenchurch Street and 10 Grafton Street, New Bond Street, where it is still listed in 1925. In 1930 Bowring, Arundel & Co. maintained premises at 42 Mincing Lane and 10 Grafton Street, New Bond Street.[10]

WILLIAM BRADSHAW
(c. 1834–1855)

William Bradshaw, upholsterer, is listed in the Dublin directories from 1834 to 1847. In 1855 he received a patent for his design for a portable camp bedstead. According to the *Gentleman's Almanac*, he worked both at Queen's Square and 7 Camden Street in Dublin.

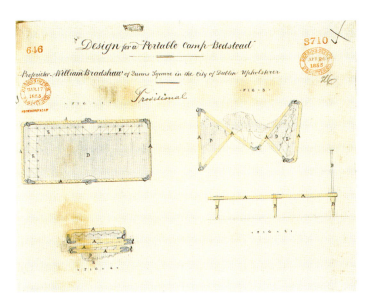

D.20. "Design for a Portable Camp Bedstead," registered by William Bradshaw of Queens Square in the city of Dublin, Upholsterer. April 26, 1855. Watercolor and ink on paper. Public Record Office, London.

BROWN BROTHERS
(c. 1851–1872)

Brown Brothers is recorded in the London commercial directories from 1851 to 1872 at 165 Piccadilly. In 1851 the firm is listed as "Patentees of the portable suspensory and invalid chairs, capable of instant conversion into camp or temporary beds," which Brown Brothers deemed "invaluable for emigration purposes and particularly adapted for warm climates." In the directory for 1860 the firm is recorded as "Patentees of the Royal Cambridge couch and bed, collapsing and very portable, also the patent canteen field bed; patentees and manufacturers of the suspensory chair, forming couch or bed, parallel folding tables, and camp, yacht, or garden chairs, bedsteads and other portable furniture, for home and export. . . . " In 1865 the firm appears as "army and navy outfitters and manufacturers of camp and barrack furniture, drawers, portmanteaus and overland trunks." Brown Brothers is also listed as a patentee and manufacturer of "the self-acting marvelous

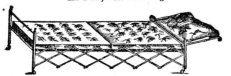

BROWN BROTHERS'
ROYAL PATENT
CAMBRIDGE COUCH AND BED,
For BARRACKS, HOME USE, or TRAVELLING;
NO NUTS OR SCREWS,
SIMPLE AND PORTABLE.

THE PATENT CANTEEN FIELD BED,
The Patent Livingstone Couch, Chair and Bed;
Also their PORTABLE SUSPENSORY CHAIRS, CAMP STOOLS, &c.
CATALOGUES FREE.
165, PICCADILLY, LONDON.

D. 21. *Advertisement for Brown Brothers of 165, Piccadilly, London, in* The Army List Advertiser, *1867. Ink on paper. Collection of Peter Bronson.*

perfect spring chair, suspensory chairs forming couch or bed, the folding camp bed, the Cambridge bed, garden and yachting chairs, and portable iron goods for the army and export, invalids and private use." The firm also acted as "special agents for patent India rubber and kamptulicon floor cloth, patent cork beds and mattress for field and home service." The directory for 1866 adds that Brown Brothers was a patentee of "the overland chair" and a manufacturer of "Capt. McGwire's patent field hammocks and special agents for cork beds and mattresses. . . ."

Brown Brothers placed an advertisement in *The Army List Advertiser* of 1867 for its "Royal Patent Cambridge Couch and Bed, For Barracks, Home Use, or Travelling; No nuts or screws, Simple and Portable. The Patent Canteen Field Bed, The Patent Livingstone Couch, Chair and Bed; Also their Portable Suspensory Chairs, Camp Stools, &c. . . ." The firm also offered an illustrated catalogue.

In 1869 the firm is listed in the commercial directory as "patentees of the new tent, fixed with 12 pegs and 2 ropes—no pole—for picnic parties, lawns, bathing, shooting, &c. &c.; patentees of Brown's patent field hammocks, 165 Piccadilly." The firm is last recorded in 1872.[11]

JOSEPH BROWN
(c. 1831–1864)

Joseph Brown is recorded in the London commercial directories for 1838 and 1842 as an upholsterer and chair maker with a workshop at 37 Minories, London. The 1849 directory refers to "Joseph Brown, upholsterer, cabinet maker and patent sea cot manufacturer, to prevent sea sickness, 37 Minories." A label on a piece of furniture that was brought to New Zealand in 1851 by Captain David Frazer, commander of the ship *City of Edinburgh* reads: "By Her Majesty's Letters Patent / Dated 2nd October 1852 / JOSEPH BROWN / 71 Leadenhall Street / CABINET MAKER & UPHOLSTERER / for improvements in / Swinging sofas, Chairs, Tables and Beds / for the Prevention of Seasickness / Supplied only at the Inventor's Manufactory / Also every article of Cabin Furniture, Beds / and bedding."[12]

Joseph Brown's business was located on Leadenhall Street, close to the India House, headquarters of the Honourable East India Company. The East India Company had evolved from a trading organization to a territorial power in India, with an immense income and powerful military and naval forces. The India House was situated on a narrow plot of land in the City of London, on the south side of Leadenhall Street and on the west side of Lime Street. Those in the employ of the East India Company must have found it convenient to have an outfitter such as Joseph Brown nearby. The firm is recorded in the London commercial directories from 1831 to 1864.

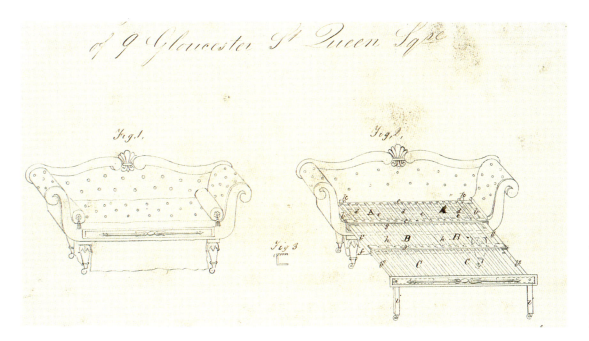

D. 22. "Design for an Expanding Sofa Bedstead," registered by Mr. Burdet of 9, Gloucester Street, Queen Square, 1847–1848. Ink on paper. Public Record Office, London.

BURDET
(c. 1847)

Mr. Burdet, of 9 Gloucester Street, Queen Square, was granted a patent in 1847 for his expanding sofa bedstead. He does not appear in the London commercial directories between 1841 and 1870.

THOMAS BUTLER
(c. 1787–1814)

Thomas Butler, once an attorney's clerk and part-time non-conformist minister in Hitchin, Hertfordshire, was in business prior to 1787 with Edward Johnson, an upholsterer and cabinet maker, at 14 Catherine Street, Strand, London (see Edward Johnson).[13] He was one of the first and most important of the Catherine Street manufacturers of patent campaign furniture, having employed both Thomas Morgan and Joseph Sanders as his foremen prior to their establishment of Morgan & Sanders in 1800 (see Morgan & Sanders). Butler also employed James Steains, his son-in-law, from 1793 to 1810. In 1810 Steains became a partner in the firm Pryer, Steains & Mackenzie (see Pryer, Steains & Mackenzie). Butler and Johnson dissolved their partnership in 1787, selling their stock at Christie's on March 28, 1787.[14] At the time, an announcement was made that in the future, Thomas Butler would be carrying on business from 14 Catherine Street. In 1801, much to the chagrin of Morgan & Sanders, Butler sold his business, including Butler's "sole Patent-right" for making his Patent Bedstead, together with all his "Stock in Trade, Engines, Tools, etc." to Thomas Oxenham, "Patent Mangle Maker to their Majesties and Royal Family," who had been employed by Butler to value his stock (see Thomas Oxenham).[15] According to Morgan & Sanders, Butler had repeatedly promised them his company, and in December 1800 had been "in treaty with him for it." On October 3, 1801, Morgan & Sanders placed the following announcement in *The Times*:

With the utmost reverence for Religion, and respect for real Preachers of the Gospel, we beg leave to observe, that T. Oxenham and T. Butler, are both Preachers; one has a Chapel at Wellyn, the other at Hitchin, in Hertfordshire; and we humbly submit the following text for their future meditation: 'Beware of false Prophets, which come to you in sheeps' clothing, but inwardly they are ravening wolves; ye shall know them by their fruits; do men gather grapes of thorns or figs of thistles?' Matthew, Chap. Vii, Verse 15.... If our enemies are disposed to continue such disgraceful conduct, Morgan and Sanders (though very much against their disposition), will take those steps that will shew to all the world the unjust treatment they have received.

Morgan & Sanders applied enough pressure to Butler and Oxenham that, by April 9, 1802 they were able to place an announcement in *The Times* which read, in part, "Morgan and Sanders are now called upon, as a duty they owe to those Ladies and Gentlemen who have so generously patronised them, and to inform the Public at large, that the said Mr. Oxenham has very wisely returned the Business back to T. Butler, who is now

D.23. *George III Mahogany and Beechwood Patented Camp Bedstead (lacking headboard), c. 1801, with maker's engraved brass label of Thomas Butler, "*Butler's */ Patent / N°. 14 / Catherine St. Strand / London." H: 6 ft.; L: 6 ft. 3 in.; W: 4 ft. 6 in. Courtesy of Sotheby's.*

D.24. *Detail of maker's engraved brass plaque.*

literally the Successor to T. Oxenham; any further remarks on what is so manifest and clear, would be an infringement on the good understanding and discernment of the Public at large."

From 1802 to 1810 Thomas Butler, now working from 13 and 14 Catherine Street, engaged in a bitter rivalry with his arch-rivals and neighbors, Morgan & Sanders of 16 and 17 Catherine Street, eventually selling the business for a second time in 1810 to Edward Argles (*see* Edward Argles). Argles carried the business for three years, but went bankrupt in 1813. Butler returned from retirement to trade from 1813 to 1814, but finally retired for the third and final time in 1814. In 1816 Morgan & Sanders acquired "a considerable part of Mr. Butler's late wareroom."

One of Butler's trade cards from 1806 contains the following information:

The Original Manufactory. For the Patent Bedsteads, Sofa Beds, Chair Beds & New Invented Dining Tables. 13 & 14 Catherine Street. T. Butler, Upholsterer and Cabinet Maker . . . To the King and Queen, Their Royal Highnesses Prince, Princess and Princess Charlotte of Wales, Duke of York and Princesses. SOFA BEDS, *upon the best and most approved principle, forming an elegant Sofa, and may be transformed with great ease into a complete Four Post Bed; with Bedding, Furniture &c., excellent seasonal Goose-feather Beds.* CHAIR BEDS, *upon the best and most approved principle, forming a handsome easy Chair, and is with great ease transformed into a Tent Bed, with furniture and Bedding complete.* PORTABLE CHAIRS; *Plain and with Arms, or Mahogany, or elegantly Japann'd, made to any pattern, a dozen of which, pack in the space of two common Chairs, with a variety of improv'd Camp and Navy articles.* IMPERIAL DINING TABLES, *forming an elegant Sett, any shape or size, to Dine, from four to seventy Persons, or any greater number. The whole Table shuts up into the space of a large Pembroke Table; the feet are so contrived as not to incommode the Company sitting, the whole will pack up in a box 16 inches deep . . .* PATENT BRASS-SCREW BEDSTEADS, *in Every Respect Superior to all Others. These elegant Four-post and Tent Bedsteads, with Lath or Sacking bottom, made upon the best and most approved principle, are fixed up or taken down in a few minutes, without the use of tools. The furniture is made upon a new plan; it can be put up, or taken down, without tools, tacks, nails, etc. A very convenient and highly approved of Sofa Bed, contrived on purpose for Captains' Cabins and Ladies or Gentlemen going to the East or West Indies; with every other Article, necessary for Voyages and use of Foreign Climates, Mosquito Nett-furniture, Bedding &c. No. 13 & 14, Catherine Street, Strand.*[16]

Another trade card dating from between 1803 and 1810 states:

D.25. Regency Mahogany Extending Dining Table, with the brass maker's plaque engraved, "BUTLER'S Patent Nº. 14 Catherine St. Strand London," c. 1805. Courtesy Phillips of Hitchin (Antiques) Ltd.
Whereas most tables of this general type have eight legs, this table has only four, which stay in the center, while the leaves are supported by sliding rails.

The Upholstery and Bedding Warehouse, Catherine Street, Strand. Butler's Patent Bedsteads, Admired for their Absolute Prevention of Vermin, their superior Elegance, and the facility with which they are fixt up and taken down. Also; The Improved Sofa & Chair Beds. This Bedstead may be made a Four-Post; a Tent; or in any other shape, with Sacking or Lath Bottom; it prevents the harbour of Vermin and may be fixt up in ten Minutes by any Person, without any Tool; are more Substantial and much more Elegant than those on the old Plan; they never become loose in the Joints, no Tacks or Nails are used in Bedstead or Furniture and is the most Portable of any Bedstead whatever. Butler's Improved: These Sofa Beds make a perfect and Elegant Sofa, Fashionable, Proportionate, very Portable and convert into a Bed with Furniture in five Minutes, is so simple in its transformation as to be done with ease by any Person. These Chair Beds with Cushions for Back, Seat & Sides, and Chints Cover, make a handsome Easy Chair, and when converted into a Bed, the Cushions make a Mattress, all very Portable, Shutting down into a square Box 7 Inches deep. / Dining tables that make different sizes to dine any number from 6 to 20 and occupy no more space than one large Card Table, without taking asunder. Ships cabins furnished, articles particularly adapted for travelling and exportation, manufacturers of: Patent tent beds and four poster beds which fold into settees, single canopied beds which fold into armchairs, 12 ft. tables which fit into a box 6 ft long and 4 inches deep, sets of 12 dining chairs which fit into a box 4 ft by 15 inches by 2 ft.[17]

D.26. The table shown as a drop-leaf table.

D.27. Detail of the maker's engraved brass plaque on drawer of table.

WILLIAM CALDWELL
(c. 1852–1870)

William Caldwell, cabinet maker and upholsterer, received a patent in 1852 for "the Berth Settee" for use aboard ship. He was located at this time at 136 and 146 West Nile Street, Glasgow. He is listed in the Glasgow postal directories from 1852 to 1870.

JOHN CAPPER & SON
(c. 1850–1940)

John Capper & Son, of Grace Church Street, London, received a patent on December 20, 1850 for a "Design for a Bassinette formed in parts to fold or collapse in order to render it portable." In the commercial directory for 1867, Capper, Son & Co. is listed at 169 and 170 Fenchurch Street and 69 and 70 Gracechurch Street. The listing for 1870 describes the firm as "linendrapers by appointment to the Queen & Prince of Wales, family linendrapers, silk mercers, shawl & lace workhousemen, hosiers, babies' & ladies' outfitters, mantle makers, dressmakers & milliners, 69 & 70 Gracechurch Street & 169 & 170 Fenchurch Street." By 1880 Capper, Son & Co. had expanded to 69 and 70 Gracechurch Street; 168, 169 and 170 Fenchurch Street; and 3 and 4 Ingram Court, Fenchurch Street. The firm is found at the same addresses in 1885.

In the 1905 directory Capper, Son & Co. is listed as "linen drapers by appointment to His Majesty the King and to the Prince of Wales, family linen drapers, silk mercers, ladies' & children's outfitters, tailors & habit makers, shirt makers & milliners" at 63 and 64 Gracechurch Street and 29 Regent Street, Piccadilly Circus, with American agents, Capper & Capper, at 45 and 47 East Jackson Boulevard, Chicago. In the 1935 directory Capper, Son & Co. is listed as a hosier at 14 Burlington Arcade. In the 1940 trade directory, under "Outfitters," Capper, Son & Co. is last listed at 225 Brompton Road.

JOHN CARMAN
(c. 1820–1863)

John Carman, trunk maker and manufacturer of canteen, military and camp equipage, traded from 20 Marylebone Street in Golden Square. He is first recorded there in 1820 and remained there until 1824. From 1826 to 1863 John Carman is listed at 2 Bruton Street.[18]

J. & A. CARTERS
(c. 1875–1972)

J. & A. Carters, invalid and surgical furniture manufacturer, was located at 6A New Cavendish Street, London. The firm appears in the commercial directories from 1875 to 1899. A caned oak chair with legs that unscrew, sliding forearms and rear carrying handles bears an engraved brass plaque for Carters of 6a New Cavendish Street, Portland Place, London (inventory no. 25719). An almost identical pattern of chair is illustrated in the 1907 Army & Navy Co-operative Society's *General Price List*, under the heading "Carrying Chair." It was constructed from French-polished beech, with a caned back and seat, and cost 47 shillings 3 pence. Unlike Carters's chair, whose legs could be unscrewed for transportation, the Army & Navy Co-Operative Society's *General Price List* advertised a "Portable Carrying Chair" the legs of which could be instantly folded by releasing a catch. According to the *Price List*, "[The Portable Carrying Chair] is a useful chair for travelling, as it can be placed under the seat of a railway carriage. Very light in weight, made of polished wood, with cane back and seat."

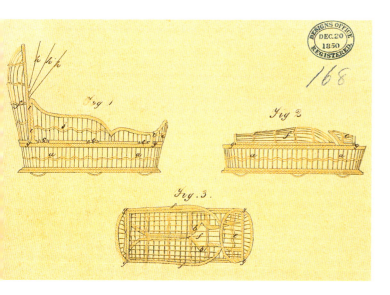

D.28. *"Design for a Portable Bassinette or Cradle," registered by John Capper & Son, Grace Church, December 1850. Watercolor and ink on paper. Public Record Office, London.*

In the 1903 commercial directory Carters is listed as "manufacturers of the 'Literary Machine,' bath chairs, invalid couches & appliances by Royal Warrant to H. M. The King & all the Courts of Europe &c. 6A New Cavendish street, Portland Place . . . Factories 15A, 17, 19, 21, 23, 25, 27, 29, 31, 33, 35 High St. Camden town." In 1940, J. & A. Carters is recorded in the trade directory under "Invalids' Carriage Makers" as well as "Invalids' Furniture and Appliances" as by appointment to the late King George V at 85, 87 and 89 New Cavendish Street and 125 to 129 Great Portland Street." In 1950 the firm is listed in the directory as "manufacturers of invalid furniture & invalid chairs of every type, invalid electric carriages & ambulance equipment. Contractors to H. M. Government, 125 to 129 Great Portland street W1; & 87 to 89 New Cavendish Street. . . . " Carters had the same listing in 1955, although by then the firm had moved to 65 Wigmore Street, where it continued to be listed through 1972 as providing "invalid furniture and appliances."[19]

THOMAS CHIPPENDALE
(C. 1747–1779)

Thomas Chippendale has been referred to as "the Shakespeare of English furniture makers."[20] Chippendale worked at Conduit Court, London Acre in 1749; Somerset Court, Strand in 1752; and at 60 to 62 St. Martin's Lane from 1754 to 1779. He apparently never printed a trade card, and does not appear in London directories for the period.[21]

Chippendale is best known for his influential publication, *The Gentleman and Cabinet Maker's Director* (first edition 1754; second edition 1763), which the firm described as "Being a large collection of the most Elegant and Useful Designs of Houshold [sic] Furniture in the Gothic, Chinese and Modern Taste. Including a great variety of Book-cases for Libraries or Private Rooms, Commodes, Library, and Writing-Tables, Buroes [sic], Breakfast-Tables, Dressing and China-Tables, China-cases, Hanging-shelves, Tea-chests, Trays, Fire Screens, Chairs, Settees, Sopha's [sic] Beds, Presses and Cloaths-chests [sic], Pier glass sconces, slab frames, Brackets, Candlesticks, clock-cases, Frets and other ornaments."[22]

For a history of Chippendale, *see* Beard and Gilbert, *Dictionary of English Furniture Makers 1660–1840*, pp. 164–66.

JAMES CLIFTON
(C. 1859–1873)

James Clifton, manufacturer of invalid carriages, Merlin wheelchairs and perambulators, is recorded in the London commercial directories from 1859 to 1873. From 1859 to 1860 he traded as an Infant Perambulator Manufacturer from 541 Oxford Street. From 1863 to 1873 Clifton is recorded as a "Manufacturer of Invalid & Recumbent Chairs, with all the latest improvements, of the best quality, 540 & 541 Oxford Street."[23]

An advertisement in the 1861 London commercial directory reads: "JAMES CLIFTON / MANUFACTURER OF / INVALID CARRIAGES / MERLIN WHEEL CHAIRS, AND PERAMBULATORS / OF THE BEST DESCRIPTION / 540 & 541 OXFORD STREET / AND 10, ROYAL ARCADE, LONDON / J. C. begs to call attention of Merchants and Shippers to his Establishment for / Invalid Chairs and Perambulators of the very best description, and at prices defying / competition."

EDWARD CORFIELD
(C. 1861–1918)

Edward Corfield is recorded in the London commercial directory for 1861 as a "Naval and military box manufacturer" trading from 6 Old Burlington Mews, Regent Street. From 1866 to 1870 he is listed as a "Military Box Manufacturer, tin plate worker and packing case maker, 6 Old Burlington Mews." From 1875 to 1910 Corfield is recorded as a tin plate worker trading from 4 Marlborough Mews, Great Marlborough Street. From 1915 to 1918 Corfield continues to be recorded as a tin plate worker, but has moved to 4 Ramillies Place, Great Marlborough Street.[24]

ALFRED COTTRELL
(C. 1854–1874)

Alfred Cottrell, a maker of portable metal beds, first appears in the London commercial directory in 1854 as "Alfred Pool Cottrell, Furniture Dealer, 20 Compton Street, Clerkenwell, London." An advertisement in the 1860 commercial directory reads, "Alfred Cottrell, Brass and Iron Bedstead and Bedding Manufactory, 232 Tottenham Court Road, London. All kinds of portable Bedsteads, suitable for the Export trade." Alfred Cottrell is listed in the 1862 directory as an "Iron & Brass bedstead manufacturer & furniture dealer" at 232 and 234 Tottenham Court Road West. From 1870 through 1874, Alfred Cottrell is listed in the directories as an upholsterer at the same address.

SAMUEL CREW
(c. 1709)

Samuel Crew of Falmouth, Cornwall, was an upholsterer who advertised in *The Post Boy*, December 21, 1709 that he made "all sorts of Field-Beds, Where all Gentlemen that go by the Packets for Portugal or Spain may be furnish't as in London."[25]

WILLIAM DAY
(1812–c. 1869)

William Day & Son, established in 1812, equipped British officers and travelers for journeys to all parts of the Empire. During the first quarter of the nineteenth century, the firm specialized in the manufacture of trunks and portable beds. A trade card describes the firm: "BY HIS MAJESTY'S ROYAL LETTERS PATENT . . . OF THE EXPANDING AND PRESS TRUNKS AND PORTMANTEAUS, Trunk Maker to HRH the DUKES OF YORK & SUSSEX. Sole Inventor of the Imperial Double Trunk & Trunk Canteen at his PORTABLE BEDSTEAD AND CAMP EQUIPAGE MANUFACTORIES."[26] A camp-bed dating from 1815 to 1826, once owned by Lieutenant-General F. C. C. Friboe and now in the collection of the Tøjhusmuseum in Copenhagen, is constructed from metal rods that screw together to form a frame and crossed legs. The frame bears two metal reliefs with the royal coat of arms surrounded by "W. Day, Patentee 353, Strand. London."[27]

William Day is recorded in the London commercial directory for 1838 as a trunk maker working from 353 Strand. In 1841 the firm is listed as a trunk and equipage maker at 353 and 378 Strand. The firm was awarded a Prize Medal in 1862 for "Excellence and Economy," and by 1865 was trading as William Day & Son, trunk and camp equipage makers, from the same addresses at 353 and 378 Strand. An advertisement in *The Army List Advertiser* of 1867 describes the firm as "Manufacturers of every variety of Portable Military Furniture for Barrack Room, Camp or Field, Patentees of the 'Eclipse' and Railway Compendium Portmanteaus." The firm also offered a fully illustrated catalogue, and its pieces were usually fitted with a Bramah lock and a black and white printed-paper label with the firm's name and address.[28] The firm is recorded in the London commercial directories from 1812 to 1869, when it is last listed as "Military outfitters and manufacturers of barrack room furniture; trunk, portmanteau and dressing case makers, 353 & 378 Strand."

ARTHUR WILLIAM DEAR
(c. 1880–1940)

Arthur William Dear & Co. first appears in London commercial directories in 1880. From 1897 to 1902 the firm is recorded in the directories as a portmanteau maker trading from 22 and 23 St. George's Place. Shortly after 1902 the company moved to 35 Knightsbridge, where it was still located in 1930, listed as a "Portmanteau maker, jeweler & silversmith." A mahogany camp table bearing the maker's engraved ivory plaque at this address is illustrated in plates D.29 and D.31. In the 1935 commercial directory A.W. Dear is listed as a "Vulcanite trunk maker" at 37 Knightsbridge. In the 1940 commercial directory the firm is listed at 37 and 39 Knightsbridge.[29]

JOHN DURHAM
(1820–c. 1835)

In 1820 John Durham, who had been employed as a foreman by Morgan & Co. of 16 Catherine Street, Strand, took over his former employer's business and established his own upholstery and cabinet manufactory (*see* Morgan & Sanders). On December 22, 1820 Durham published the following announcement in *The Times*:

UPHOLSTERY *and* CABINET MANUFACTORY, *16, Catherine-Street, Strand. - J.* DURHAM, *(late foreman to Messrs. Morgan and Co.,) most respectfully informs the Nobility, Gentry, and Public in general, that he has taken the above premises, and continues to manufacture, on the most improved principle, the Patent Four-post and Tent Bedsteads with furniture and bedding complete, the much-admired sofa and chair beds, patent dining tables and sideboards; portable chairs, and every other article in the above branches, of the best materials and workmanship, and on the most reasonable terms for prompt payment. N.B.: Articles for the East and West Indies, very portable.*

Durham used a brass plaque engraved, "(Patent) / JOHN DURHAM / Manufacturer / Successor to Morgan & Co / 16 Catherine St. Strand / London." Although Durham declared bankruptcy in 1826, the firm continued to trade at 16 Rupert Street, Haymarket from 1828 to 1835.[30]

D.29. Edwardian Mahogany Campaign Table, with green baize-lined top, c. 1900. The maker's ivory plaque is engraved, "A.W. DEAR / 35 KNIGHTSBRIDGE, LONDON." H: 27 in.; W: 30 in.; D: 26½ in. Private collection.

D.30. The campaign table folded to reveal the maker's engraved ivory plaque.

D.31. The table's original leather-trimmed canvas traveling case, with the monogram "A. L. G."

ANTHONY ECKHARDT
(c. 1771–1798)

Anthony Eckhardt, who in 1798 traded from Hans Place, Chelsea, was active in the last quarter of the eighteenth century.[31] He patented a portable table and chair in 1771, and a table built to this patent is currently housed in the Victoria and Albert Museum. Patent No. 995 dated 1771 reads: "A new portable table, with double or single folding flaps and folding feet, and also a new Portable Chair so contrived as to answer all the purposes of the common tables and chairs, and at the same time to lay in the compass of a small box, which would be of the greatest use to His said Majesty's navy and army, and to all seafaring people, as well as to His Majesty's subjects in general." Eckhardt designed his table to be used for serving tea, playing cards, or writing.

D.32. George III Mahogany Portable Table, 1771. Collection of the Victoria & Albert Museum, London. Photo: Victoria & Albert Museum; V & A Picture Library.

This portable table was originally conceived en-suite *with a portable chair. It was registered as Patent No. 995 by Anthony George Eckhardt of London on July 29, 1771.*

Eckhardt points out that "One advantage peculiar to this construction, added to the small space it is capable of being folded up in, is the facility of changing the sides of the flaps at pleasure, the one of which being of any beautifull [sic] wood, and the other covered with green cloth, it will then occasionally serve either as a tea table or as a card or writing table."

DAVID EDWARDS
(c. 1817–1871)

David Edwards, "Manufacturer of the Patent Military Mounted Writing and Dressing Cases," maintained a workshop at 21 King Street, Bloomsbury Square from about 1817 to 1837. By 1823 he is recorded in the London commercial directory as a "Manufacturer of Writing and Dressing Cases to His Majesty and the Royal Family." In the commercial directories from 1824 to 1831, Edwards is also listed as a manufacturer of writing and dressing cases by appointment to the Honourable East India Company. David Edwards is not recorded in 1839 and Edwards himself died in 1848.[32] Interestingly, in 1860 the firm enjoyed a brief revival, appearing in the London commercial directory as "David Edwards, dressing case, traveling bag and writing case maker, cutler &c. to the Queen, 166 New Bond Street (late of King Street, Bloomsbury Sq.)." From 1866 to 1871, the last year that the firm is listed in the commercial directory, David Edwards had expanded to include a location at 22 Albemarle Street.

D.33. *Regency Brass-Bound Mahogany Dressing-Table Box, by D. Edwards, London, c. 1825, with paper label* "D. EDWARDS, MANUFACTURER OF WRITING AND DRESSING CASES TO HIS MAJESTY THE DUKE OF YORK, NO. 21 KING STREET, BLOOMSBURY SQUARE." *W: 13 in. Courtesy Christie's Images.*

This dressing table box, fitted with ivory and silver-mounted glass boxes and trays, is of the type commonly designed for travel, as indicated by the recessed brass handles, brass banding, and lock.

THOMAS EDWARDS
(c. 1831–1850)

Thomas Edwards appears in the London commercial directories from 1831 to 1850. From 1831 to 1835 Thomas Edwards is listed as "Army-Contractor, 52 Upper Stamford Street." From 1838 to 1842, the listing reads, "Army-Contractor, 107 Upper Stamford Street, Blackfriars." The directory for 1847 records the firm at 104 Upper Blackfriar Street, Blackfriars. In 1849, the year he was granted a patent for both a "Military Folding Dressing Glass" and a "Camp and Cabin Shaving Glass," Thomas Edwards is listed as an "Army Clothier, 4 Charing Cross."

THOMAS EYLES
(c. 1851)

Thomas Eyles, of James Street in Bath, was granted a patent on February 26, 1851, for a folding table.

JAMES FINDON
(c. 1824–1851)

James Findon is first recorded in the London commercial directory in 1824. In the directory for 1838 he is listed as "patent water-closet manufacturer and coachsmith" trading from 190½ High Holborn. In the directory for 1842 Findon is recorded as a "Water closet & axletree manufacturer," trading from the same address. He was granted a patent for a water closet in 1848, on which he listed his name and address as "James Findon, Water Closet Manufacturer of Black Horse Yard, High Holborne, London." The London commercial directories for 1848 and 1851 record Findon as an "axletree & water closet manufacturer, 190½ High Holborn."[33]

GEORGE FLETCHER
(c. 1852)

George Fletcher & Co. was granted a patent on April 14, 1852 for an improved portable bedstead. At this time the firm was trading from Bilston Street, in Wolverhampton.

JOHN FRYER
(c. 1853–1859)

John Fryer, writing and dressing-case manufacturer, was granted a patent for a dispatch box in April 1853, when he was trading from 63 Charing Cross. He is recorded in the London commercial directories from 1855 to 1859 at this address.

WILLIAM GAIMES
(c. 1800–1823)

William Gaimes placed an advertisement in *The Times* on January 4, 1800, stating:

PORTABLE LETTER COPYING MACHINES, and DESKS,— WILLIAM GAIMES informs the Merchants and all Gentlemen concerned in Mercantile Affairs, that he has established a Manufactory, No. 23, Surry-road, for the sole purpose of improving and uniting the Machine to a complete Portable Secretary, adapted to hold all kinds of shaving, dressing and other instruments wanted in travelling. Portable Desks on much improved principles, and all sorts of Cases for travelling in any part of the world. The Machine is brought to that perfection that they [sic] must be a national advantage in facilitating with accuracy the great and weighty concern of the Counting-house of this country.... They have met with many opponents and difficulties in being introduced to Merchants, from their supplying the place of two copying Clerks. Much might be said to their recommendation, but I wish it to be known by their performance. Articles manufactured by him shall not be the lowest prices, but they shall be the best manufacture and materials of any in this Kingdom, and on equitable and respectable charges. Gentlemen curious in mechanics and conveniences may give their orders at the Manufactory, where they may see something quite new. Sold at his Shops, No. 54, St. Paul's-church-yard, and No. 56 Cornhill, and Wholesale, at No. 51, St. Paul's-church-yard.

The 1802 London commercial directory lists W. Gaimes as a "Cutler & Jeweller" at 56 Cornhill and 51, 53, and 54 St. Paul's Churchyard. In 1805 and 1808 the company is listed as "Cutler and Perfumer" at 53 & 54 St. Paul's Churchyard. The listing in 1813 describes Gaimes as a "Goldsmith and Portable Letter-copying-machine and Writing-desk Manuf. To their R. H. the Prince of Wales and Duke of Sussex & his Majesty's Public Offices, 53 St. Paul's Churchyard."[34]

GILLOW
(C. 1728–AFTER 1840)

Founded by Robert Gillow in about 1728, Gillow of Lancaster and London was among the most successful and prolific manufacturers of furniture during the late eighteenth and nineteenth centuries. Unlike almost all of the firm's contemporaries, Gillow's records survive and are currently housed in the Westminster County Archives in London.

*Their early work, in the 1750s, is now rare and poorly documented. . . . Much better known is the firm's later output, in the late eighteenth and early nineteenth centuries, in dark Cuban mahogany or exotic woods, veneers and inlays. . . . Gillows opened up a London branch in 1771 at '176 Oxford Road.' . . . The range of the furniture they produced was very wide, from Carlton House writing-tables to coffins and from highly finished and expensive inlaid pieces to the simplest oak and deal furniture. . . . Gillow furniture is often stamped with an incised mark in small capital letters 'GILLOWS LANCASTER' on a drawer edge or back of a seat frame. They were almost the only English maker to give a maker's mark consistently. . . . The firm was active throughout the nineteenth century.'*35

For a history of Gillow, see Beard and Gilbert, *Dictionary of English Furniture Makers 1660–1840*, pp. 341–43.

CHARLES GREEN
(C. 1846–1887)

Charles Green is recorded in the London commercial directories from 1846 to 1852 at 11 Church Row, Somers Town, as a "Cabinet Maker." In the 1855 to 1865 directories he is listed at 10 Church Row, St. Pancras Road. In 1870 he is listed at 1 Hungerford Road, Camden Road, and in 1875 at 155 Hungerford Road, Camden Town. On July 26, 1878, when Charles Green received a patent for a "Design for a Camp Stool," his address is listed as 80 Libra Road, North Bow, London. He is still listed at this address in 1887, the final year he appears in the commercial directory.

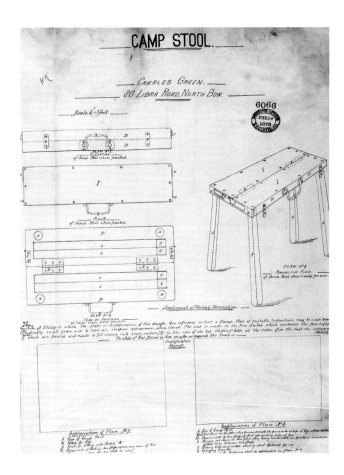

D.34. "Design for a Camp Stool," registered by Charles Green, 80 Libra Road, North Bow, London, July 26, 1878. Pen and ink on paper. Public Record Office, London.

Opposite, top:
D.35. Victorian Mahogany Folding Camp Stool, shown when ready for use, by Charles Green of 80 Libra Road, North Bow, London, stamped "Registered in London, 26th July 1878. No. 6066." H (folded): 2 in.; W (folded): 14 in.; D (folded): 3½ in.; H (open): 12 in.; W (open): 14 in.; D (open): 7 in. Collection of Peter Bronson.
   According to Charles Green, "The purpose of Utility to which the shape or Configuration of this design has reference is that a Camp Stool of suitable proportions may be made to occupy an exceedingly small space and to have an elegant appearance when closed. The seat is made in the form of a box, which contains the four legs, the ends of which are feruled and made to fit closely into brass sockets in the rim of the box. Sliding bolts at the sides give the seat the necessary stability. The whole of this design is new in so far as regards the shape or configuration thereof."[1]

1. Public Record Office, Kew. July 26, 1878, No. 6066.

Opposite, middle:
D.36. The interior of the camp stool when packed.

Opposite, bottom:
D.37. The camp stool shown packed.

GRESHAM & CRAVEN
(c. 1872–1902)

Gresham & Craven, engineers, manufacturers, and ironworkers, is recorded at 63 Sackville Street, Manchester, from 1872 to 1902. Among the pieces of campaign furniture manufactured by the firm was a wood-framed, officer's campaign bed decorated with cast-iron brackets.

JAMES HAKEWILL
(c. 1809)

In 1809 James Hakewill was granted a patent for tables, chairs and stools that would "pack together and fold easily" and could be used for "domestic, military and naval service."

HAMPTON & SONS
(c. 1868–1946)

Hampton & Sons first appears in the London commercial directories in 1868. The firm is recorded in the directory for 1875 as an upholsterer, carpet, cabinet and bedding manufacturer at 8 Pall Mall and 1 to 3 Dorset Place, Charing Cross. By 1908 the company had become Hampton & Sons Limited. A facsimile of Hampton & Sons's advertisement for a selection of officer's campaign furniture from about 1894 is reproduced in the *Regional Furniture Society Newsletter*:

A portable Douro Chair [named after the Douro River in Spain and Portugal, which became familiar to the British during the Peninsular War, 1808 to 1814] *in Birch, Stuffed Hair and covered in Leather; A case to contain the chair which also forms a table; An iron Folding Cambridge Bed Chair, with Horse Hair cushions, in Best Leather cloth; A Portable Iron Couch Bedstead, with Horsehair Mattress and Bolster, Feather Pillow, 3 Best White Blankets, a White Counterpane and Cretonne Cover and Valances Complete; A Strong Portable Brass Sofa Bed and Iron Bound Case to hold it; A Set of Portable Drawers, in Teak or Mahogany, with Case to Join Sideboard; Mahogany Folding Table; Mahogany or Teak set of Cavalry Drawers, with Table, Escritoire, Stationery Case, Cabinet Back Shelves, with Brass Pillars and Looking Glass in Center. A Strong Iron-bound case to hold it; Mahogany or Teak Book Shelves, with Brass Standards; A Set of Mahogany or Teak Book Shelves, with Glass Doors; Portable Toilet Glass in Teak or Mahogany; Mahogany or Teak Military Chest; Strong Iron-bound Cases,*

*forming wardrobe that also held chest; Mahogany or Teak Chest, with Secretary Drawer and Brass Corners and Handles; and a Mahogany or Teak Towel Airer.*36

In the London commercial directory for 1902, Hampton and Sons, Ltd. is described as "Builders, decorators, furnishers; electrical, gas, hot water, and sanitary engineers; designers and manufacturers of furniture, fitments, [and] panelling; parquetry, upholstery, bedsteads, bedding; British carpets; tapestries, silks, blinds, household linens, lace curtains; furnishing ironmongery, electrical fittings, cutlery, china and glass, etc. . . . Showrooms and chief offices, Pall Mall east, Trafalgar Square; cabinet, carpet and bedding factories and general works, Belvedere road." The firm continued to be listed in the directories until 1946.

HANDFORD & CO.
(C. 1800–1866)

In the 1802 London commercial directory, Handford & Son is listed as "Pocket-book-makers" at 98 Strand.37 In 1805, Thomas Handford is recorded as a "Pocket-book-maker" at 94 Strand. One of Handford's trade cards, dated 1808, states:

T. HANDFORD, / No. 94 Strand, / MANUFACTURER, / of Copying Machines, Writing Desks, and / all Kinds of Ladies & Gentlemen's / PORTABLE CASES / for every purpose Completed & adapted / for travelling in any part of the World. / MANUFACTURED / at No. 94, Strand, nearly opposite Southampton Street / LONDON. / where Old Desks are repaired or taken in Exchange. / Orders for the East or West Indies punctually executed and Country Dealers / supplied on the most reasonable terms.38

Thomas Handford, Jr., appears in the London commercial directories for 1835, 1838, and 1842 as "Patentee of the Waterproof travelling trunk, edged with brass, 6 Strand." In 1849 the firm is recorded as "Thomas Handford, trunk maker, 6 Strand." A trade label from a brass-bound leather trunk manufactured prior to 1852 reads: "T. Handford Patentee of the New Invented Light Water Proof Travelling Trunk particularly adapted for Officers of the Army & Navy. At his Manufactory No. 6 Strand near Charing Cross LONDON. Solid Leather Portmanteaus, Carpet, Coat & Enamell [sic] Bags HAT CASES &c."39 From 1852 to 1866, the last year the firm is listed in the commercial directory, the firm was located at 5 Strand under the name of Thomas Handford, Jr.

D.38. Trade Card of Handford, No. 94, Strand, London, c. 1808. Ink on paper. British Museum, Banks Trade Card Collection, Reference 28.73.

HARRODS
(1849–PRESENT)

Harrods was founded in 1849 by Charles Henry Harrod as a grocer's shop at 105 Brompton Road, and eventually grew to become a world-famous retailer. The firm became a Royal Warrant Holder and was famous the world over for its ability to procure "everything," including all variety of portable and campaign furniture. As the firm's export and shipping department advertised in *Harrods' Supplementary Export Price List* from about 1910, "Merchandise and Stores of every Description Packed and Shipped Abroad. Expeditions Completely Equipped to all parts of the World. Goods Packed for Head, Mule or Camel Loads." The firm also catered to "Explorers, Surveyors, Prospectors, Miners, Sportsmen, &c. . . . Exploring, Scientific and Shooting Expeditions

Completely Equipped and Provisioned for any Part of the World.... Full Equipment, Food Supplies, &c., packed and made up in suitable cases for CAMEL LOADS, MULE LOADS, PONY LOADS, NATIVE HEAD LOADS. Specialties in Portable Double Ridge Tents (made of Green Rot-Proof Canvas throughout) Portable Camp Beds, Mattresses, Mosquito Curtains, Water Carriers, Mule Panniers, Riding and Pack Saddles, Boots, Clothing, Guns, Rifles, Ammunition, Medical Stores, Provisions, &c., &c."

Much like the Army & Navy Co-Operative Society Ltd., Harrods supplied a large, fully illustrated catalogue from which one could place orders from the farthest corners of the Empire. To facilitate this process, during the Edwardian period (1901 to 1910), Harrods maintained agencies in Liverpool and Southampton in England, as well as in India, Gibraltar, the Federated Malay States, South Africa, and China.

CHARLES HAWKINS
(c. 1843–1860)

Charles Hawkins is recorded in the London directories from 1843 to 1851 as a "Camp equipage and trunk maker" trading from 86 Strand, the site of the firm of Lane & Billing in 1841 (see Lane & Billing). In 1860 Charles Hawkins is recorded for the last time as a portmanteau maker trading from 24 Arthur Street.

HEAL & SON
(C. 1810–PRESENT)

John Harris Heal founded Heal & Son as a feather-dressing business in 1810, the same year he married Fanny. The Heals had their first child, John Harris junior, in 1811.[40] When John Heal died in 1833, Fanny Heal took over the business with her son. In 1840 the firm moved to 196 Tottenham Court Road, where the flagship store remains today. In the London commercial directory for 1841, there is a listing for Fanny Heal & Son, "bed & mattress wa. [warehouse],196 Tottenham Ct. Rd." The listing for 1843 reads Fanny Heal & Son, "bed wa. & feath. dress" at the same address.

Heal & Son issued its first trade catalogue in 1848. Among the furniture the company sold were portable iron bedsteads intended for use by English officers posted abroad. "A whole bedroom—bedstead, horsehair mattress, bolster blankets, bed curtains, mahogany table and chair—fitted into two trunks, weighing no more than 98 lbs. for £ 16 9s 6d, and was illustrated for many years in the Officers' catalogues, strapped to a long suffering horse."[41]

Between 1866 and 1868 Heal & Son began to issue "catalogues of Bedsteads, Bedding and Bedroom furniture suitable for India, China and the Colonies."

In Heal & Son's 1870 *Illustrated Catalogue of Bedsteads & Bed-room Furniture with Price List of Bedding* "FOR INDIA, CHINA AND THE COLONIES," the firm offered

D.39. Heal & Son's Portable Furniture for an Officer's Tent, 1870. All of the pieces illustrated could be packed into the box shown in the foreground, which measured 2 feet 10 inches by 3 feet 7 inches by 1 foot 6 inches deep. When the furniture was knocked down and packed in the box for travel, it weighed 200 pounds. Courtesy Victoria & Albert Museum; V & A Picture Library.

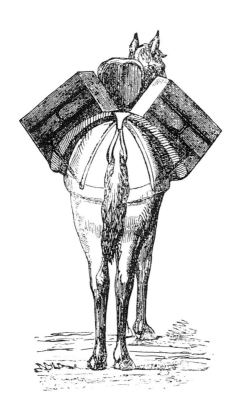

D.40. At the time of the Crimean War (1853–1856), Heal's illustrated in its officers' catalogues an entire bedroom suite, including a bedstead, horse-hair mattress, bolster, blankets, bed curtains, mahogany table, and chair, all designed to fit into two trunks, weighing no more than 98 pounds, that formed a balanced load when strapped on a horse's back. Courtesy Victoria & Albert Museum; V & A Picture Library.

PORTABLE FURNITURE NECESSARY FOR AN OFFICER'S TENT
. . . the whole of which will pack into a box, as shown . . . measuring 2 ft. 10 in. by 3 ft. 7 in. and 1 ft. 6 in. deep. Weight 200 lbs. A degree of comfort is attained with these articles which cannot otherwise be had with so little weight, and so small a compass; thus forming the very best and most convenient equipage for an Encampment. The Bedstead, by a single movement, forms a comfortable Arm Chair. The Box forms a Wardrobe, with mahogany doors and shelves inside. The outside of the Box forms the table. The Bath, Washstand, Glass, and Legs of Table, together with the Bedstead and Bedding all pack into the Box.

Among the articles listed with prices are a

Patent Portable Chair Bedstead, with Horsehair Cushions, in Cotton . . . £3.0.0., Horsehair Pillows 3/4 . . . £0.5.6., 1 pair 7/10 Blankets . . . £0.18.0., half do. 8/4 do. 10/6 . . . £0.5.3., 1 9/4 White Counterpane . . . £0.10.0., a large Japanned Bath . . . £1.8.0., Japanned Iron Washstand . . . £0.1.0., Zinc Basin . . . £0.4.0., Looking Glass, 8 in. by 10 in . . . £0.6.0., The Box with doors and shelves, to form a Wardrobe and an Outer Cover with Legs to form a Table . . . £4.0.0.; Ditto with Mahogany Doors . . . extra £0.15.0. Total £12.2.9. The Cushions in Worsted Damask, 15s extra.

Also available was a selection of bedroom chairs in cherry, mahogany, and imitation mahogany that came apart for packing, folding cane-seated "Darby" chairs in birch at 13s and walnut at 16s, and portable iron camp bedsteads and iron couches. The "Officers' Portable Iron Bedstead with cloth sacking, japanned black, brass vases and castors" fit into a box 2 feet 9 inches by 6 feet 6 inches and cost £2.15.0. For an additional 15s the box could be painted with the officer's name. The "Officers' Portable French Bedstead [with both headboard and footboard], with cloth sacking, japanned black, brass vases and castors," 6 feet 8 inches high, fit into a slightly larger box 3 feet by 6 feet 6 inches at £2.17.0. This box could also be painted with the officer's name for an additional 17s. Heal & Son also offered the "Officers' Superior Portable Tent Bedsteads of iron Tubing $1\frac{1}{4}$ inches in diameter, with cloth sacking, japanned black, brass mountings, vases and castors, 6 feet 8 inches high." This bedstead fit into a box 3 feet by 6 feet 6 inches and cost £4.0.0. For £6.0.0 an officer could have the same bed a foot wider. This larger bed could fit into a box 4 feet long, 11 inches wide, and 8 inches deep. It cost 17s to paint the officer's name on the smaller box, and £1.0.0 to paint the name on the box for the larger bed.

The firm continued to expand under the leadership of John Harris Heal's grandson, Sir Ambrose Heal. By 1940 the listing in the commercial directory reads, "makers of beds & bedding. By Appointment to the late King George V, cabinet makers, upholsterers, house furnishers, china & glass dealers, carpet warehousemen, bedding restorers & interior decorators, 195 to 199 Tottenham court road; factories, Torrington place WC1; Alfred mews W1." The same listing appears in 1950. In the 1965 commercial directory Heal & Son is listed "By appointment to Her Majesty the Queen / upholsterers & suppliers of bedding. / Cabinet makers, upholsterers, house furnishers. / China & glass dealers, carpet warehousemen / bedding restorers, interior decorators & church furnishers," at 191 to 199 Tottenham Court Road, with factories at Torrington Place.

The Heal family sold the business in 1983 to Habitat/Mothercare, which became Storehouse PLC. In 1990 there was a management buyout, and in 1997 the business became a public company. Today Heal & Son has two stores in London and two in the southeast of England.[42]

GEORGE HEPPLEWHITE
(C. BEFORE 1786)

The cabinet maker George Hepplewhite worked from Redcross Street, St. Giles's, Cripplegate.⁴³ Very little is known about him, and his name does not appear in the London directories of the period. In fact, no pieces of furniture marked by Hepplewhite have ever been found.⁴⁴ Two years following Hepplewhite's death, I. & J. Taylor published a book of furniture designs entitled *The Cabinet-maker and Upholsterer's Guide*, from drawings by 'A. Hepplewhite & Co., Cabinet-Makers.' It has been suggested that Hepplewhite's widow, Alice, took over his business.⁴⁵ Hepplewhite's "fame rests entirely on the pattern book issued by his widow; none of the plates are signed so even his authorship of the designs is open to doubt. However, the *Guide* provides a valuable record of respectable household furniture dating from the mid 1780s which, in the words of the preface seeks 'to unite elegance and utility, and blend the useful with the agreeable. . . .'"⁴⁶

PETER HEWLIN
(C. 1802–1820)

Peter Hewlin, cabinetmaker, upholsterer, and Tunbridge-ware manufacturer, worked at 2 Strand from 1802 to 1803, and at 164 Strand from 1807 to 1814.⁴⁷ He was on Thomas Sheraton's list of Master Cabinet Makers in 1803. A brass-bound portable writing box has been recorded that contains a maker's paper label printed: "HEWLIN'S, / (from No. 2 Strand) / CABINET, UPHOLSTERY, AND / TUNBRIDGE WARE MANUFAC-TURER. / No. 164 / near Somerset House, / An elegant assortment of Copying / Machines, Portable Desks, LADIES & GENTLEMEN'S DRESSING CASES, / Knife Cases &c. / FUNERALS FURNISHED."⁴⁸ A maker's paper label affixed to a small brass-bound leather trunk reads, "HEWLIN'S CABINET, UPHOLSTERY, AND TUNBRIDGE WARE MANUFACTURER opposite the NEW CHURCH Strand, an elegant assortment of Copying Machines, Portable Desks, LADY'S & GENTLEMAN'S DRESSING CASES, FUNERALS FURNISHED."⁴⁹ The firm is recorded in the London trade directories until 1820.

JOHN HILL
(C. 1841–1872)

The London commercial directories for 1841 and 1842 list John Edward Hill as a trunk maker and camp equipage manufacturer at 3 York Place, Upper Street, Islington. In 1843 he moved to 5 York Place, Upper Street, Islington. In 1846 "John Hill, trunk & military equipage manufacturer," is listed at 97 Quadrant, Regent Street." By 1849 he is also listed at 2 Jermyn Street. From 1852 until 1872 he is recorded at 97 Quadrant, Regent Street and 212 Piccadilly. Although he joined forces with Richard Millard to form the celebrated military outfitter Hill & Millard about 1853, it appears that Hill continued to trade under his own name until at least 1873. In 1854, for example, while trading from 212 Piccadilly, he was granted a patent for "Hill's New Camp Bedstead." Similarly, the commercial directory for 1865 refers to Hill as a "travelling equipage manufacturer, case maker, and perambulator manufacturer, 212 Piccadilly and 97 Quadrant, Regent St." He is no longer listed under his own name in 1874; the directory listing is for Hill & Millard (*see* Hill & Millard).

HILL & MILLARD
(C. 1854–1935)

Hill & Millard, a high-end military outfitter and trunk maker formed by John Hill and Richard Millard, was granted a patent in 1854 for its "Design for an adjusting arm for reclining chairs, registered for a Henry Hill and Richard Millard of No. 7 Duncannon Street, London." In the London commercial directories from 1855 to 1865, the firm is recorded as "military outfitters and trunk makers, 7 Duncannon St., Strand." From 1870 to 1875 Hill & Millard is also listed with its warehouse at 21 Villiers Street, Strand. There is no listing for the firm in 1880 or 1885, although Richard Millard is listed at the firm's address (*see* Richard Millard). From 1890 to 1930 there is a listing for Hill, Millard Limited, "Military outfitters," at 7 Duncannon Street, Strand. In 1935 the firm is listed as trunk makers at 103 Jermyn Street.⁵⁰

In 1867 the firm placed the following advertisement in *The Army List Advertiser*: "Hill & Millard, Military Outfitters, By Appointment to the 1st Life Guards, Grenadier, Coldstream & Scots Fusilier Guards. Manufacturers of Barrack and Camp Furniture. Patentees of the Army Chair. 7, Duncannon Street, Trafalgar Square, Opposite St. Martin's Church. A Complete Outfit for £28:10s. Illustrated Catalogue post free. Estimates for 'Mess' Furniture. Hill & Millard, 7 Duncannon Street, Trafalgar Square, W.C. (Opposite St. Martin's Church)."

While most manufacturers of military campaign furniture used locks provided by Bramah, Lever, or Hobbs & Co., makers of patent protectors and lever locks to Queen Victoria, Hill & Millard stamped all of the firm's important brass fittings "Hill & Millard."

HILL & PERKINS
(c. 1823–1839)

Hill & Perkins was an auctioneer, cabinetmaker, and upholsterer trading from 2 Common Land or 2 Commercial Hard, Portsea, in Portsmouth from about 1823 to 1839.[51] A maker's paper label affixed to an oval campaign dining table (*see* D. 42–43) states in part:

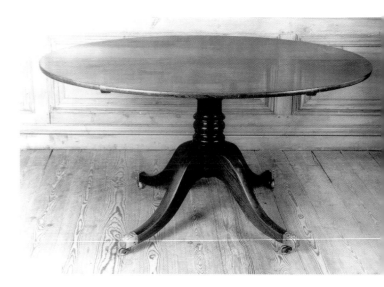

D.42. Regency Mahogany Campaign Breakfast Table, with ring-turned baluster standard on four down-swept legs ending in brass caps and casters, second quarter nineteenth century, with the maker's paper label of Hill & Perkins, Portsmouth. Courtesy Neil Wibroe.

D.41. Advertisement for Hill & Millard of 7 Duncannon Street, Trafalgar Square, London, in The Army List Advertiser, *1867. Ink on paper. Collection of Peter Bronson.*

D.43. Breakfast table showing the legs removed and the top separated ready for travel.

"Upholsterers By Appointment to His Majesty: Sea Cots, Mattresses, Blankets, Counterpanes, Sheets, and Pillow-Cases, Sea Chests, Portmanteaus, Trunks, Valises, and Carpet Bags in Great Variety, at Hill and Perkins's Portable Furniture and Canteen Manufactory & General Outfitting Warehouse . . . Portable Bedsteads in Iron, Wood and Brass. . . ."

INCE & MAYHEW
(c. 1758–1811)

The renowned London cabinetmakers William Ince and John Mayhew were in partnership from about 1758 until Ince's death in 1804.[52] The firm, which traded from Broad Street, Golden Square in 1762, and at 20 and 47 Marshall Street, Carnaby Market until 1811,[53] has been described as "one of the most significant, probably the longest lived but, as far as identified furniture is concerned, the least well-documented of any of the major London cabinet makers of the 18th century."[54] Largely in response to the publication of Thomas Chippendale's *The Gentleman and Cabinet Maker's Director* in 1754, Ince and Mayhew published their *Universal System of Houshold* [sic] *Furniture* in parts between 1759 and 1762. It consisted of three hundred designs in what the partners characterized as "the most elegant taste, Both useful and Ornamental, finely engraved, in which the nature of ornament and perspective is accurately exemplified." As Ralph Edwards has observed, "Sheraton, towards the end of the century, pronounces the *Universal System* 'to have been a book of merit in its day, though much inferior to Chippen-dale's which was a real original, as well as more extensive and masterly in design.'"[55]

For a history of Ince & Mayhew, see Beard and Gilbert, the *Dictionary of English Furniture Makers 1660–1840*, pp. 589–93.

Right:
D.44. *"Design for a Portable Backgammon, Chess and Draught Board,"* registered by John Jacques, 102 Hatton Garden, London, June 10, 1858. Watercolor and ink on paper. Public Record Office, London.

ISAAC & CAMPBELL
(c. 1850–1870)

In 1850 Isaac & Campbell, of 21 St. James's Street and 71 High Street, Chatham, received a patent for the firm's "Design for barrack, college and cabin furniture." In 1852 Isaac & Campbell is listed for the first time in the London commercial directory as "army contractors" at 21 St. James's Street. In 1855 the firm is recorded at 21 and 27 St. James's Street, and in 1861 at 71 Jermyn Street. In 1865 the firm is listed as "Isaac, Campbell & Co., merchants," at the same address. In 1870 the firm is recorded "Isaac, Campbell & Co (in liquidation), Merchants, 1 East India Avenue, Leadenhall Street," near the old headquarters of the Honourable East India Company.

JOHN JACQUES
(c. 1858)

John Jacques, of 102 Hatton Garden, London, was granted a patent for his design for a portable backgammon, chess, and draughts board on June 10, 1858.

JOHN JAMES
(c. 1847)

John James of Middlesex was granted a patent for a "traveler's boudoir or combined dressing case, escritoire, and drawers" in 1847.

JOHN, WILLIAM, & MATTHEW JARVIS
(c. 1875–1880)

J. W. & M. Jarvis, "wholesale & export cabinet makers & upholsters [sic], CLUB, OFFICE, DRAWING, HALL, DINING, AND LIBRARY, BED ROOM FURNITURE OF EVERY DESCRIPTION, 60, CITY ROAD" is listed in the London commercial directories from 1875 to 1880. The firm placed an advertisement in the directory for 1879 featuring three pieces of campaign furniture: "A PATENT FOLDING SPRING LATH BEDSTEAD OR COUCH," which was adaptable for any climate, and came in two sizes, from 6 feet x 2 feet to 6 feet x 3 feet 6 inches; "THE ADJUSTABLE, FOLDING EASY CHAIR. / Very strong, with cast brass Mounts, reclining back, altering to 3 positions, specially recommended as an Easy Chair. / 12 Best Gents' pack in a case 4 feet 6 inches x 3 feet 8 inches x 1 foot 10 inches"; and "THE COLONIAL DINING TABLE." With pine top and frame and hardwood legs, this table came in sizes from 3 feet 6 inches x 5 feet, with one flap, at a cost of £40, to 4 feet x 8 feet, with two flaps, at £62. Remarkably, six of these dining tables, each measuring 3 feet 6 inches x 5 feet, could be packed in a space 3 feet 6 inches x 3 feet 8 inches x 3 feet.

In the 1880 commercial directory, the firm of John, William & Matthew Jarvis is listed as "wholesale & export manufacturing upholsterers & cabinet makers, club & hotel furnishers & office fitters, bagatelle & miniature billiard table makers, specialité for solid mahogany, ash walnut &c. furniture (without veneer), recommended for hard wear & hot climates, exporters to India, China, Australia & the Cape, 60 City road (nr. Finsbury)."

An advertisement in the directory that year offers "SOLID Furniture for hard wear and tropical climates" and also features a "PATENT / FOLDING SPRING LATH BEDSTEAD / OR COUCH." Below a line drawing of the bed both open and closed, the advertisement explains, "As represented above it forms a most luxurious Bedstead, / or Couch, is cleanly, and adapted for any climate."

D.45. "Traveler's Boudoir or Dressing Case, Escritoire, Drawers Combined," registered by John James of Middlesex, 1847. Watercolor and ink on paper. Public Record Office, London.

EDWARD JOHNSON
(c. 1838–1851)

In 1838 Edward Johnson is listed in the London commercial directory as a "Trunk maker, 155 Leadenhall Street. The following year the company placed an advertisement in Pigot & Co.'s *Royal, National, and Commercial Directory*, which read:

BY ROYAL LETTERS PATENT. / *Newly Invented Metallic Folding Bedstead, &c. &c.* / E. JOHNSON, / *(late Merriman)* / CAMP, TRAVELLING EQUIPAGE AND CABIN FURNITURE / MANUFACTURER, / *By Appointment,* / TO THE HONOURABLE EAST INDIA COMPANY, / *No. 155,* / LEADENHALL-STREET, LONDON, / *sole proprietor,* / Solicits the attention of the Nobility, Gentry and the Public in general, to his newly invented / Metallic Folding Bedsteads, Couches, Chairs, &c.

The advantages of durability and freedom from insects, possessed by Metallic Bedsteads, would, it is believed, have secured their general adoption long ago, had any plan been discovered for obviating the objections so justly brought against them, of weight, expensiveness and inelegance. So completely, however, have these objections been overcome in the New Patent Bedsteads, that their simplicity and elegance of construction, combined with their economy, render them worthy of the attention of all classes of society: they are equally suited to those Gentlemen who may require the accommodation of a bed in their Chamber or Offices, or to the Cottage, particularly those of Sporting Gentlemen, who frequently, during the season, find difficulty in accommodating their numerous guests with beds. In the day they form an elegant piece of drawing-room furniture, and at night can be converted into a bed in a few minutes.

To officers of the Army and the Honourable East India Company's Service, these Bedsteads are particularly suited; as, in addition to their other advantages, for warm climates, they possess the invaluable quality of requiring neither mattress nor bolster, and can be used during a voyage as ship-sofas and swing cots. For the Barrack room they will be found superior to all other inventions of the kind.

To Emigrants to the Canadas, Van Dieman's Land [Tasmania], Sydney and South Australia, they are invaluable.

They are strongly recommended to all who may have occasion for a number of beds on a sudden emergency; as, from their folding perfectly flat, they can be put aside when out of use in less than one-twelfth part of the room occupied by the common French bedstead....

An inspection of the Specimens at the Proprietor's is earnestly requested, where may also be had every description of Camp or Cabin Furniture, viz., Ship sofas, double and single. Swing cots. Bedsteads, brass and iron, and couches of every description. Elastic spring mattresses, horse hair, wool and others. Solid mahogany and other portable Drawers, Wardrobes, Bookcases, &c. Wash-Hand Stands, to form Tables: Portable Tables. Swinging Trays, Trunks, Sea Chests, &c. Looking Glasses . . . Camp and Cabin Recumbent & Easy Chairs. Cabin Lamps and Candle Sticks. . . .[56]

The 1840 and 1841 commercial directories list Edward Johnson at 155 Leadenhall Street as a "Travelling equipage and cabin furniture manufacturer and patentee of the folding hinged bedsteads, etc." In 1842 Edward Johnson is listed as a "Travelling equipage &c. maker" at the same address. In 1847 the firm is recorded as a "Camp equipment Manufacturer & Patentee of the metallic folding hinged bedsteads &c., 160 Piccadilly (late of Leadenhall Street) & Jermyn Street (*see* Merriman)."

From 1849 to 1851 the firm is recorded as a "Camp equipage, portmanteau, and iron and brass bedstead manufacturer and patentee of the metallic folding hinged bedsteads, etc, 160 Piccadilly Lane, Late of Leadenhall Street."[57]

JOHNSTONE & JEANES
(C. 1842–1885)

Johnstone & Jeanes was "one of the most illustrious furniture manufacturers of the nineteenth century, being the successor to Johnstone Jupe & Co., whose fame centers on Mr. Jupe's patented dining tables."[58] The London commercial directory for 1842 records the firm as "Johnstone & Jeanes, cabinet maker and upholsterer, 67 New Bond Street," and the 1849 and 1852 directories place them at 67 New Bond Street, as well as at 15 Clipstone Street, which in the earlier directory is identified as Portland Place and in the later, as Fitzroy Square. Johnstone & Jeanes exhibited at the 1862 London Exhibition, where *The Art Journal's Illustrated Catalogue of the Exhibition* described the firm as "one of the oldest in London, having been established in New Bond Street for upwards of a century; its renown has been obtained not only by a good and substantial manufacture, but by continual study to introduce Art into all their works."[59]

By 1865 Johnstone & Jeanes had expanded to 15½ Clipstone Street, in addition to maintaining its premises at 67 New Bond Street. The firm is recorded in 1875 as "Johnstone Jeanes & Co., (Johnstone Wetherell and Norman), cabinet makers, upholsterers and house agents, 67 New Bond Street W and 20½ Clipstone street, Fitzroy square W." In the early 1880s it began manufacturing Regency revival pieces, and in 1885 the firm changed its name to Johnstone, Norman & Co. In 1887 the firm of Johnstone, Norman & Co. is listed in the commercial directory as "Cabinet makers, 67 New Bond Street & 15 Clipstone Street, Fitzroy Square & Estate Agents." The year 1889 finds the firm listed as "Cabinet makers, Upholsterers, House Decorators, Builders & Estate Agents" at the same locations and also in New York, where the firm continued to be listed until 1898, although the London address changed to 91 New Bond Street in 1895.

In 1899 the firm was apparently sold to Morant & Co., as the 1899 and 1900 directories cross-reference Johnstone, Norman & Co. with Morant & Co., "Interior Decorators, Painters, Upholsterers, Undertakers, Estate & House agents, Appraisers & Surveyors, Carvers, Guilders, Cabinet makers, Carpet Manufacturers, &c., by appointment to Her Magesty, 91 New Bond Street & 4, 5, 6, & 7 Woodstock Street."

GREGORY KANE
(c. 1829–1865)

In 1829 Gregory Kane was a trunk maker working from 8½ Fishamble Street, Dublin.[60] From 1830 to 1835 he was at 1 Fishamble Street and also at Essex Quay. In 1838 he was the "only manufacturer of solid leather portmanteau in Dublin."[61] In the 1840 *Dublin Almanac and General Register of Ireland*, Gregory Kane is listed as a trunk maker trading from 81 Dame Street, Dublin. The 1847 *Almanac* lists him as a "Trunk and portmanteau maker" trading at 69 Dame Street. In 1857 and 1858 the firm manufactured at Sycamore Alley.[62] In 1865 Gregory Kane is listed at "68 & 70 Dame Street, Residence at Shamrock Lodge, Glenageary, Kingstown," as "Portmanteau maker to the Lord Lieutenant." That year the firm also manufactured at 7 Crampton Court. From 1868 to 1888 Gregory Kane is listed solely at 68 to 70 Dame Street.[63]

On his trade card Kane billed himself as "Portmanteau and Dressing Case Manufacturer to His Excellency the Lord Lieutenant and the officers of the Garrison. Camp Furniture, Military and Naval Chests, Canteens, Imperials, Carriage Trunks, Tarpaulins, Hair-Mattresses, Bed Valises, Carpet Bags, &c, &c. Inventor of the Lady's Portmanteau and Gentleman's Improved Triple Portmanteau." Kane won prizes in the Exhibition of Manufacturers in 1841, 1844, and 1847.

The firm's trade card is reproduced in *Furniture History: Journal of the Furniture History Society*.[64]

KEY, MITCHELL & GRIEG
(c. 1850)

The firm of Key, Mitchell & Grieg of 103 Newgate Street, London, was granted a patent in 1850 for its "convertible bedstead."

LANE & BILLING
(c. 1813–1841)

In 1813 T. Lane "Trunk Chest &c. Maker" is listed in the London commercial directory at 74 St. Paul's Church-yard. By 1821 the firm is recorded as "Lane & Billing, Trunk makers, 22 Coventry Street & 60 St. Paul's Church-yard," where it is still listed in 1825. In the 1826 and 1827 directories, Lane & Billing is recorded as "Trunk manufacturers, 86 Strand, & 60 & 74 St. Paul's Church-yard." The directory listing for 1831 records Lane & Billing as "Trunk and Portable Desk Manufacturers, 60 & 74 St. Paul's Church-yard, & 22 Coventry Street, Haymarket." In 1835 the firm is listed at 74 St. Paul's Church-yard and 86 Strand; and in 1838 solely at 86 Strand. From 1839 to 1841 Lane & Billing is recorded as "Camp Equipage and Trunk Makers" with premises at 86 Strand.[65]

LEVESON & SONS
(c. 1870–1915)

Leveson & Sons, a manufacturer of "bath chairs, invalid furniture, perambulators," is recorded in the London commercial directories from 1870 to 1915. In the 1870 directory Leveson, Lewis & Co. is listed as "Merchants, commission agents & ship & insurance brokers" at 6 Lime Street. In 1875 E. J. Leveson & Co. "East-India merchants" is listed at the same address. In 1880 Edward John Leveson, "East-India merchants," is recorded at 32 Great St. Helen's, and in 1885 at 8 Crosby Square. In 1890 Leveson & Sons is listed as "manufacturers of bath chairs, invalid furniture, perambulators, &c." at 90 and 92 New Oxford Street, and 21 Parkside, Knightsbridge. From 1895 to 1900 the firm is listed with additional premises at 30 Kensington High Street, and manufactories in Manchester, Liverpool, and Leeds.

From 1902 to 1915 the firm is listed as having premises at 90 and 92 New Oxford Street, 7 Park Side, Knightsbridge, and 85 Victoria Street, with manufactories located at 1, 2, 3, 4, 6, 7, and 9 Lawrence Street, and in Manchester, Liverpool, and Leeds. In 1916 Leveson & Sons incorporated with John Ward, Ltd. (*see* John Ward). The directory listing for 1920 reads, "LEVESON & SONS (incorporated with John Ward Ltd.), makers of bath chairs, invalid furniture, baby cars, perambulators &c . . . control office & works, Leveson house, Lawrence St. Bloomsbury . . . baby car showrooms, 26 Knightsbridge . . . also at 35 Piccadilly, Manchester & 89 Bold street, Liverpool." The 1930 commercial directory listing for Leveson & Sons, "makers of invalid furniture & baby cars; incorporated with John Ward Ltd.," gives the address of 246 Tottenham Court Road.

ABRAHAM LEVY
(c. 1852–1855)

"Trunk and camp equipage manufacturer," Abraham Levy, is listed in the 1852 London trade directory at 49 Pall Mall. The following year he is recorded at 44 Pall Mall. In 1854 he is listed once again at 49 Pall Mall. The final listing for Abraham Levy in 1855 is at 44 Pall Mall.

SAMUEL LEVY
(c. 1835–1865)

In the London commercial directory for 1835 Samuel Levy is recorded as an "Outfitter" at 2 Hemmings Row, St. Martin's Lane. From 1839 to 1865, Samuel Levy is listed as a "Naval and military outfitter, portable bedstead, and camp furniture manufacturer" with premises at 28 King William Street, Strand. There is no listing for the firm in 1866.

RICHARD LOADER
(c. 1824–1866)

Richard Loader, "Cabinet, Chair and Looking-Glass manufacturer," appears in the London commercial directories from 1824 to 1866. The firm is recorded at 35 Finsbury Pavement in the London commercial directory for 1838. In 1842 Richard Loader is described as a cabinet, chair, looking glass, and floor cloth manufacturer trading from 23 and 24 Finsbury Pavement. The commercial directory for 1849 refers to "Richard A. C. Loader, wholesale and retail upholsterer, cabinet maker and plate glass factory" at 24 Finsbury Pavement. By 1852 the firm had expanded to 6 Little Moorfields. The directory for 1865 records Richard Loader as a wood turner at 45 Finsbury Market.

J & W LOWNDES
(c. 1790–1850)

The trunk maker James & William Lowndes is listed in the London commercial directories from 1790 to 1847 at 18 Haymarket, London. A trade card of J & W Lowndes from about 1803 records the following details: "Military & Camp Equipage Warehouse / J & W Lowndes / No. 18, Hay Market. / Marquees Tents & all Sorts of Camp Furniture. / Camp Bedsteads / Bed & Bedding / Camp & Sea Cots / Military Canteens / Liquor Cases / Mahogany Writing Cases / Dressing Cases / Saddle Bags / Leather Portmanteaus / Trunks of Every Description / and various other Articles for the equipment of / Military & Naval Officers."66 In 1849 and 1850 the firm is recorded as "William & James Lowndes, Scotch Muslin manufacturers & Manchester Warehousemen, 7 Watling Street."67

D.46. *Trade Card of J & W Lowndes, No. 18 Hay Market, London, c. 1803. Ink on paper. British Museum, Banks Trade Card Collection, Reference 132.74.*

HENRY MANNING
(c. 1838–1872)

Henry Manning supplied Government House in Auckland, New Zealand with its furnishings. The London commercial directories of 1838 through 1852 record Henry Manning as a carpenter and builder at 251 High Holborn, London. From 1855 to 1870 the listing reads, "251 High Holborn & Portable House Manufacturer, Richardson's yard near the canal bridge, Commercial Road East, Limehouse, builder and iron fence maker." Henry Manning last appears in the commercial directories in 1871 and 1872 as a "Builder & Iron Fence Maker" at 251 High Holborn.[68]

JOHN MAPLE
(1841–c. 1997)

The firm John Maple & Co. was founded in 1841. According to the London commercial directory for 1875, John Maple & Co., upholsterers, was trading from 142, 143, and 145 to 149 Tottenham Court Road, and maintained a carpet warehouse at 1 to 15, 27, and 31 Tottenham Place, and 2 to 6, 12, 13, 14 and 15a Grafton Street East. The firm's manufactories were located at Beaumont Place and Midford Place. By 1897 the firm had been renamed Maple and Co., Limited and is described in the commercial directories as "Cabinet makers, upholsterers, carpet factors and importers of Indian, Turkey and Persian carpets, bedding manufacturers, linen factors, parquet flooring, and wood paneling manufacturers, carvers and gilders, furnishings ironmongers, interior decorators and general furnishing warehousemen, timber merchants, china, glass and earthenware dealers, clocks, bronzes and ornamental china, plumbers, gasfitters and hot water engineers." The firm was located at 141 to 145, and 150 Tottenham Court Road, and at Euston Road, Grafton Street, and Gower Street. Near the turn of the twentieth century, Maple and Co. provided furnishings for such illustrious residences as the Viceregal Lodge in Simla, the throne room of the king of Siam's Royal Palace in Bangkok, the Jockey Club in Buenos Aires, and Czar Nicholas II's Winter Palace in St. Petersburg. In 1997 the trade name "Maples" was purchased by Allders, one of Britain's largest depart-ment store groups.

JOHN MEAD
(c. 1864)

John Mead, of Abridge, Essex, was granted a patent on February 20, 1864 for his design for a portable folding "whatnot" dinner wagon or sideboard.

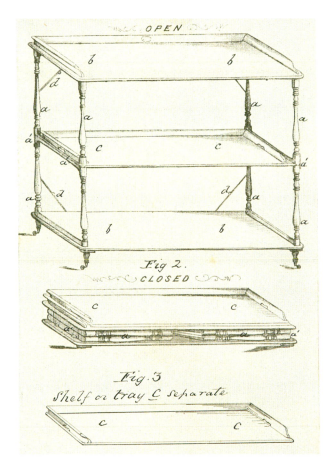

D.47. "A New Design for the Shape or Configuration of a Portable Folding Whatnot, Dinner Wagon or Sideboard," registered by John Mead, Abridge, Essex, February 20, 1864. Ink on paper. Public Record Office, London.

MERRIMAN & SONS
(c. 1795–1835)

According to the London commercial directories from 1795 until 1813, the firm of Merriman & Sons was listed as trunk makers at 155 Leadenhall Street. In the 1821 commercial directory there is a listing for G. Merriman "Trunk-makers" at 155 Leadenhall Street and 102 Cheapside. There is no listing in 1823. In 1825 G. F. Merriman is listed as a trunk maker at 155 Leadenhall Street. The firm is recorded in 1826 and 1827 at both 154 and 155 Leadenhall Street. The listings for 1831 and the final year, 1835, are for G. F.

Merriman, trunk maker, at 155 Leadenhall Street.[69] By 1838 the firm appeared under the name of Edward Johnson at the same address (*see* Edward Johnson).

MILES & KINGTON
(c. 1817–1889)

Miles & Kington, West India and general merchants, is recorded in *Mathew's Bristol Trade Directories* at 61 Queen Square, Bristol, from 1817 to 1851. On August 31, 1854 Articles of Partnership were drawn up between Philip William Skynner Miles, Edward Peach William Miles, Henry Cruger William Miles, all from King's Weston, Gloucestershire, and Thomas Kington of Charlton House, Somerset. They agreed to act as co-partners in a business of "West India and General Merchants & Ship Owners" from September 1, 1853 to April 30, 1864. The firm was to be known as Mileses [*sic*] & Kington and to be carried on at 60 and 61 Queen Square, Bristol. Shares in the partnership were to number sixteen and to represent £5,000, the whole capital being £80,000. At the time this would have made Mileses & Kington one of the largest companies in Bristol. The Articles of Partnership also addressed the imbalance between the three members of the Miles family and Thomas Kington by stating that Kington could, with the consent of his partners, introduce his son Philip Oliphant Kington as a partner in the business anytime after May 1, 1856.

The firm of Mileses & Kington continued to trade from 61 Queen Square in 1855 and 1858. According to the "notes on shipping history" made by a Mr. Lowless and now at the Bristol Record Office, Thomas Kington died at the age of 62 on February 20, 1857 at Charlton House, Somerset. He was buried at Wraxall on February 27th. In 1863 the firm was renamed again, to Mileses, Brothers & Co., merchants. They continued to trade at 61 Queen Square from 1864 to 1876, moving to 71 Queen Square from 1877 to 1889, the last year that the firm is recorded in the directories.

A chair stamped "MILES KINGTON & CO, / SOLE AGENTS FOR THE /AUSTRALIAN / COLONIES" was imported by the Government of New Zealand for their House of Representatives.[70] Philip Oliphant Kington and Fulbert Archer, both working in Melbourne, Australia, acted as merchants to Philip William Skynner Miles, Edward Peach William Miles, and Henry Cruger William Miles.[71] The 611-ton *Bosworth*, owned by Mileses & Kington, sailed from Bristol to Melbourne on November 9, 1858 with a cargo consisting primarily of Mileses & Kington exports, though six other merchants also supplied goods. Mileses & Kington's cargo included 330 firkins of butter; 2,450 sacks of oats; 1 wooden house; 87 cases of slate chimney pieces; 2 carts; 2 cwt metal nails; 1 thrashing machine; 127 packages of passengers' baggage; 1 cwt of printed books; 3,000 pieces of common earthenware; 1 cwt of confectionary; 62 tons of coal; 18 iron quartz crushers; 20 loads of timber; 4,000 bushels of white salt; 110 tons of freestone; 1 bull and 3 cows.[72]

On Wednesday, January 26, 1859, *The Lyttelton Times* of New Zealand reported under shipping news, "In the *Canterbury*, T. B. Craig, agent . . . 2 sofas, Miles, Kington & Co." The *Canterbury* was a schooner of thirty-eight tons built at Pigeons Bay, Banks Peninsula, New Zealand.

RICHARD MILLARD
(c. 1845–1885)

Richard Millard, trunk maker of 12 Craven Street, Strand, London, was granted a patent for a portable recumbent and easy chair in 1845. By 1854 he had joined forces with John Hill to form the celebrated military outfitters Hill & Millard, although he continued to be listed under his own name in London commercial directories in 1880 and 1885 at 7 Duncannon Street, Strand, the same address as the firm Hill & Millard (*see* Hill & Millard).

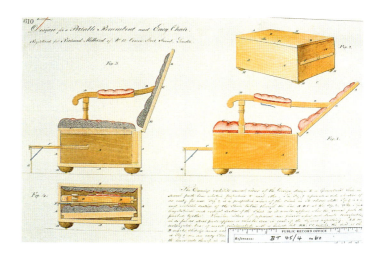

D.48. *"Design for a Portable Recumbent and Easy Chair," registered by Richard Millard of No. 12 Craven Street, Strand, London, 1845–1846. Watercolor and ink on paper. Public Record Office, London.*

WILLIAM MILLARD
(c. 1812–1855)

William Millard's trade card from 1812 states: "William Millard, / Military, Naval, Travelling and Commercial / Trunk Manufacturer / No. 392 Oxford Street, / London / Regulation Trunks for the Royal Military Establishments & Every Description of Camp Equipage / Trunks & Imperials Fitted to Carriages-Ladies Fancy Work Trunks & Cases for Musical Instruments &c. &c. &c."[73]

A trunk maker named William Millard is recorded in the London commercial directories for 1838 and 1842 at 9 Skinner Street, Snowhill, and again from 1849 to 1855 at 19 Greville St., Hatton Garden.[74]

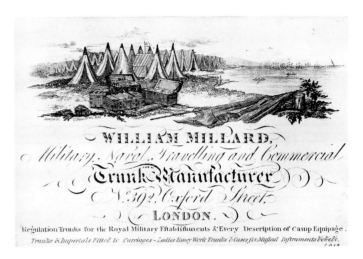

D.49. Trade Card of William Millard, No. 392 Oxford Street, London, c. 1812. Ink on paper. British Museum, Banks Trade Card Collection, Reference 120.12.

THOMAS MILLS
(c. 1847–1848)

Thomas Mills of Birmingham was granted a patent for his design for an expanding and contracting table between 1847 and 1848.

MORGAN & SANDERS
(1801–1820)

Thomas Morgan worked as a linen-draper in Newgate Street, and after that in Newport Street, before being employed in Thomas Butler's counting-house as an under clerk in about 1790. Together with Joseph Sanders, who had also been employed as a clerk by Thomas Butler, they established the celebrated firm of Morgan & Sanders in 1801.[75] They situated their business at 16 and 17 Catherine Street, two doors from that of their archrival Thomas Butler (*see* Thomas Butler). On September 29, 1801 the firm ran an advertisement in *The Times* that read in part:

New Invented IMPERIAL DINING TABLES *and* PORTABLE CHAIRS, *by the real Inventors,* MORGAN *and* SANDERS, *at their Manufactory for Improved Sofa Beds, Chair Beds, and the much-admired Four-Post and Tent Bedsteads, which entirely prevent the harbour of vermin; are fixt up and taken down by hand, requiring no tools, with Furniture and Bedding complete, Couch Beds; patent Boethemas or rising Mattresses, Children's Crib Beds, and Swing Cots, Army and Navy Equipage, Musquito Net Furniture, and every other article suitable for Ladies and Gentlemen going to the East and West Indies, and all foreign climates; also Sofa Beds upon an improved principle, and much admired for their conveniency on ship-board. The above highly useful invention and improvements . . . are most respectfully recommended to the Nobility and Public, as being the most portable, fashionable, and convenient of any that have hitherto been invented. . . . The bed furniture are all made upon a new plan of having no nails or tacks, are fixt up and taken down in a few minutes without tools. Canopy and dome beds, with window curtains, &c. in suit, executed in the first style of fashion and taste by Morgan and Sanders, Upholsterers, and Cabinet Makers, No. 16 & 17, Catherine-Street, 3 doors from the Strand, nearly facing Somerset House, London.*

Their rivalry with fellow-manufacturers of patent, metamorphic furniture, such as Thomas Butler, Thomas Oxenham, and Edward Argles is well documented in *The Times* between 1800 and 1820. Morgan & Sanders renamed their premises Trafalgar House about 1807, in honor of Admiral Nelson's great victory. Several years earlier, Morgan & Sanders had designed an "imperial" dining table and matching sideboard for Merton Place, Nelson's country house in Surrey. Morgan & Sanders outlasted all of their competitors along Catherine Street. The year 1816 must have been a particularly memorable year for the firm, for it was then that Morgan & Sanders purchased "a considerable part of Mr. Butler's late Ware-rooms

adjoining their own"[76] and expanded to 15, 16, and 17 Catherine Street.

Joseph Sanders died in 1818, and the firm was renamed Morgan & Co. The company's premises were scaled back to 16 Catherine Street. In 1820 Morgan & Co. was acquired by John Durham, who had been a foreman at the late firm (*see* John Durham). Despite declaring bankruptcy in 1826, Durham continued to trade from 16 Rupert Street, Haymarket, until 1835.

One of Morgan & Sanders's broadsheets, c. 1803, contains the following information:

Morgan & Sanders's Manufactory for their New Invented Dining Tables and Portable Chairs, The best & most approved Sofa Beds, Chair Beds, handsome Four Post and Tent Bedsteads, with Furniture and Bedding complete at their Upholstery & Cabinet Ware-Rooms, No. 16 & 17 Catherine Street. Three doors from the Strand, London. Morgan & Sanders's New Invented, Imperial Dining Table forming an elegant Sett, to Dine from Four to Twenty Persons, or any greater Number; the whole Table shuts up into the space of a Large Pembroke Table, the Feet are completely out of the way & the whole may be packed in a Box only 10 Inches deep. Portable Chairs, a Dozen of which packs in the space of 2 Common Chairs. The best and most approved Sofa Beds,

Top:
D.50. Regency Mahogany "Imperial" Dining Table by Morgan & Sanders, c. 1810, with the brass handle engraved, "Patent / Morgan & Sanders / Inventors & Manufacturers / 16 & 17 Catherine Street / Strand London." *Courtesy Michael Sim, Fine English Furniture, Kent.*

The table is shown fully extended. When fully extended, by means of a pull-out mechanism, the table measures 9 feet by 3 feet 8 inches and can seat ten diners. Morgan & Sanders also produced similar tables that had legs that unscrewed, allowing the table to be folded into a box ten inches deep.

Above, right:
D.51. "Imperial" Dining Table with additional leaves removed.

Above, left:
D.52. Detail of engraved brass handle.

DIRECTORY /193

D.53. Detail of maker's engraved brass plaque.

forming an elegant Sofa, and may be transformed with great ease into a compleat Four Post Bed, with Furniture, Bedding, &c. The best & most approved Chair Beds, forming a handsome easy Chair, and is with great ease transformed into a Tent Bed, with Furniture and Bedding compleat. This elegant Four Post and Tent Bedstead, with Lath or Sacking bottom, made upon the best & most approved principle, are fixed up or taken down in a few minutes, without the use of tools, &c. The Furniture are made upon a new Plan, of taking off or on, without Tools, Tacks &c. A very convenient & highly approved of Sofa Bed, contrived on purpose for Captains Cabins & ladies or Gentlemen going to the East or West Indies with every other Article necessary for Voyages & use of Foreign Climates, Musquito Nett Furniture, Bedding & also Army & Navy Equipage, compleat. The above Inventions and Improvements with every other Article in the Upholstery and Cabinet Branches, executed in the most Fashionable and best manner.[77]

Another one of the firm's broadsheets from the turn of the nineteenth century states:

Patronized by their Majesties and the Royal Family. Morgan and Sanders's Manufactory for their New Invented Imperial Dining Tables and Portable Chairs, The best & most approved Sofa Beds, Chair Beds, Patent Brass Screw Four Post & Tent Bedsteads, with Furniture and Bedding complete at their Upholstery and Cabinet Ware-Rooms 16 & 17 Catherine Street, Strand London. Patent Camp Beds. Army & Navy Equipage. Morgan and Sanders's, New Invented, Imperial Dining Tables, forming and elegant Sett, to Dine from 4 to 20 Persons or any greater Number, the whole Table shuts up into the space of a Large Pembroke Table, the Feet are completely out of the way, & the whole may be packed in a box, only 10 inches deep . . . Portable chairs, plain and with arms, of Mahogany, or elegantly Japan'd, made to any pattern, a dozen of which pack in the space of two common Chairs. The best and most approved Sofa Beds, forming an elegant Sofa, & may be transformed with great ease into a complete Four Post Bed, with Bedding Furniture &c. The best and most approved Chair Beds, forming a handsome easy Chair and is with great ease transformed into a Tent Bed, with Furniture & Bedding complete. Patent Brass Screw Bedsteads, in every respect superior to all others. These elegant Four Post and Tent Bedsteads, with Lath or Sacking bottom, made upon the best and most approved principle, are fixed up or taken down, in a few minutes, without the use of tools. The furnitures are made upon a New Plan of taking off or on, without Tools, Tacks, &c. A very convenient & highly approved of Sofa Bed, contrived on purpose for Captains Cabins & Ladies or Gentlemen going to the East or West Indies; with every other Article necessary for voyages and use of Foreign Climates: Mosquito Nett furniture, Bedding &c. The above Inventions & Improvements, with every other Article, in the Upholstery & Cabinet Branches, executed in the first stile of elegance & fashion.[78]

WILLIAM OVERLEY
(C. 1710–1732)

William Overley, joiner and cabinetmaker, is perhaps the oldest maker of sea chests for whom any records survive. He was actively trading on Leadenhall Street from about 1710 to 1732.[79] One of his trade cards states: "Will'm Overley Joyner at the Sign of / the East India House in Leaden-hall Street LONDON / Makes all sorts of Sea Chests in Deal or Wainscot / Ruff or Smooth Packing Chests or Cases, and Cases / of Bottles, & Boxes of all Sizes, Presses in Deal or / Wainscot, & Bedsteds, Tables, Desks, Book Cases, Bu-/'rows [sic], & Writing Desks, Letterholes . . . for Shops. / Allso Counters and all sorts of Joyners worke done / at Reasonable Rates."[80] Of note, Overley worked before the age of regular mahogany imports to Great Britain, which began in quantity from the West Indies only after 1724. He therefore advertised his furniture as being made from deal or wainscot.

On his trade card Overley depicts himself installed in a small shop close to the entrance of the East India Company's first headquarters. William Foster, historian of the East India Company, notes that it was Overley's representation of the East India House on his trade card that enabled Thomas Babington Macaulay to describe the building (demolished about 1726) as "an edifice of timber and plaster, rich with the quaint carving and lattice work of the Elizabethan Age. Above the windows was a painting, which represented a fleet of merchantmen tossing on the waves. The whole was surmounted by a colossal wooden seaman, who from between two dolphins looked down on the crowds of Leadenhall Street."[81]

After further examination of Overley's trade card, Foster writes:

... we note that the ships ... appear to be carrying the Union flag, first introduced in the reign of Queen Anne; further, that the royal arms are ... in reality those of George I (1714–27). The latter is a very perplexing discovery, for how can we reconcile it with the fact that the Old Company's arms are shown as still in position, and that some other features distinctly indicate that the print is considerably earlier than [another view published in 1711]? The only explanation that commends itself is that Overley did at one time occupy the little shop near the entrance; ... that while there he had a shop-bill prepared to advertise his wares; that after a while, as the Company's needs in the matter of accommodation increased, he was dispossessed and moved to other premises in Leadenhall Street, retaining the East India House as his sign; and that, at some date during the reign of the first Hanoverian, he had a fresh bill prepared, in which the artist, while copying the old one in the main, inserted the new royal arms. This view is supported by the fact that in a scarce little book entitled New Remarks of London ... collected by the Company of Parish Clerks (London, 1732) it is stated that the last house on the south side of Leadenhall Street within the bounds of the parish of St. Andrew Undershaft was that of 'Mr. Ovely, a box-maker,' who is no doubt our worthy joiner. This would place him a little on the east side of Leadenhall, and four or five doors from his old premises at the India House. This has ... been confirmed by an examination of the deeds relating to a house in the position indicated which was acquired and pulled down by the Company in 1826. William Overley is named as one of the tenants previous to 1747.[82]

THOMAS & SAMUEL OXENHAM
(c. 1795–1832)

"When late in 1800 [Thomas] Butler took a decision to dispose of [his] business and Joseph Sanders and Thomas Morgan, two of his employees stated an interest in taking over, Thomas Oxenham was called in to value the stock. To the outrage of Morgan and Sanders, Butler sold the business to Oxenham"[83] (see Morgan & Sanders and Thomas Butler). On October 1, 1801 Thomas Oxenham placed an advertisement in *The Morning Herald* that announced, "THOMAS OXENHAM, Patent Mangle Maker to their Majesties and Royal Family, respectfully informs the Nobility, Gentry, and Public at large, that he has purchased of Mr. Thomas Butler, of No.14 Catherine-street, Strand, Patent Bedstead Maker to their Majesties, his sole Patent-right for making the said much-admired Bedsteads, for the prevention of vermin; together with all his Stock in Trade, Engines, Tools, &c. and that he carries on the same in all its branches." Among the items offered at this time were "Curious new invented Folding Chair Beds on various constructions; Sofa Beds for Merchant's ships and travelling in general...."[84]

By April 1802 Oxenham had sold the business back to Butler, though he continued to make inexpensive reproductions of Butler's patterns. On October 8, 1803, for example, he placed the following announcement in *The Times*:

CHEAP MANUFACTORY. - SOFA & CHAIR BEDS, *Brass screw Bedsteads, and Dining Tables, from 10 to 20 per Cent cheaper than the boasted Manufactories in Catherine-street. Messrs.* OXENHAMS, *No. 354, Oxford-street, near the Pantheon, beg leave to inform the Public, that they manufacture the above*

D.54. Trade Card of Samuel Oxenham & Co., 354 Oxford Street, London, c. 1803. Ink on paper. British Museum, Banks Trade Card Collection, Reference 28.108.

articles, (for ready money only) from 10 to 20 per Cent under what is commonly charged. As a proof of the above assertion, single sofas and furnitures, usually sold at 18 and 19 guineas, they sell at 16 guineas; double sofa beds, usually sold at 21 and 22 guineas, they sell at 18 guineas; chair beds, usually sold at 11 guineas, they sell at 9 guineas; royal dining tables, usually sold at 30 guineas, they sell at 25 guineas;—camp bedsteads and furniture, &c. complete, usually sold at 17 guineas they sell for 14 guineas; also every other article in the Upholstery and Cabinet Branches equally cheap. Gentlemen going abroad, or Merchants, will find, on inspection, the truth of the above assertion.

Samuel Oxenham, who subscribed to Thomas Sheraton's *Cabinet Directory* in 1803, listing the 354 Oxford Street address, was Thomas Oxenham's partner.[85] The firm's trade card from that year provides the following information: "Sam'l. Oxenham & Co. Manufactory for the new Invented Dining Tables and Portable Chairs. The best and most approved Sofa-Beds, Chair-Beds, handsome Four-Post and Tent Bedsteads, with Furniture and Bedding complete at their Upholstery and Cabinet Ware-Rooms, No. 354, Oxford Street, near the Pantheon, London."[86]

Thomas Oxenham retired from his business in 1832. The firm eventually went into the auction and appraisal business, appearing in trade directories from 1838 through 1852 as "Sam'l Oxenham & Son, Auction & Appraisers, 353 Oxford Street." The London commercial directory for 1865 makes reference to "Hugh & Henry Oxenham, auctioneers and valuers, 353 & 354 Oxford St."

LAWRANCE PHILLIPS
(c. 1843–1880)

In the 1843 London commercial directory Lawrance Phillips is recorded as a "Tailor and habit maker, 28 Strand." In 1849 the firm is listed as "Army and Navy clothier, sword cutler, gold lacemen, embroiderer and accoutrement maker, military hat and cap maker, hosier, shirtmaker, outfitter and portable camp and cabin furniture manufacturer, 28 Strand." Lawrance Phillips was still operating at the same address in 1860. In 1866 and again in 1869, the listing is for Lawrance Phillips & Son, "army contractor, naval, military, and court tailors and general outfitters, sword cutlers, gold lacemen and embroiderers and manufacturers of portable barrack furniture, trunks and portmanteaus, 13 George Street, Hanover Square (from 28 Strand)." From 1870 the firm is listed in the directories as "tailors," "military outfitters," or "court and military tailors." Lawrance Phillips & Son remained at the same address through the last directory listing in 1880.

WILLIAM POCOCK
(c. 1802–1824)

William Pocock, a cabinet maker, upholsterer, and undertaker, is recorded at 26 Southampton Street, Covent Garden, in the London commercial directories from 1802 to 1824. Pocock was joined by his son about 1809, when the firm began trading as Pocock & Son, or Pocock & Co.[87] The firm invented and manufactured "patent" furniture, much like the more well-known Thomas Butler and Morgan & Sanders of Catherine Street.

By 1814 Pocock's was printing the line "By His Majesty's Royal Letters Patent" on the firm's trade cards. One of these cards, from 1814, advertised "Patent Camp or Barrack Sofa Beds" which it claimed made "a comfortable and convenient Sofa and Bed, suitable either for Camp or Barracks, or on Board a Ship, or even for an elegant Drawing Room; and yet are very portable by folding into a very small Compass for the Convenience of Carriage. They have been highly approved by distinguished Officers of the Army and Navy."

During the Peninsular Wars (1808 to 1814), Pocock's also specialized in invalid furniture. An advertisement from this period illustrates the firm's "Patent Boethema or Rising Mattress."[88] This was "for the Use of Invalids to raise them up in their Beds; or for any Person accustomed to sit up while in Bed; can be laid upon any Bedstead, and is so constructed as to be applicable to a Sofa."

MRS. ELIZABETH POWELL
(c. 1843–1852)

Mrs. Elizabeth Powell is recorded in the London directory for 1843 as a whip maker trading from 33 Bryanstone Street in Bryanstone Square. She is not listed in 1848, but in 1849 appears in the London directory as a trunk maker with premises at 100 New Bond Street and 59 Paddington Street, Marylebone, where John Powell is also listed. In 1851 and 1852 she is listed as a "Trunk and Portmanteau Maker, & Inventor of military portable equipage," at 100 New Bond Street.[89] (*see* John Powell.)

JOHN POWELL
(c. 1839–1860)

John Powell is first listed in the London directory in 1839. From 1839 to 1842 he is recorded as a trunk maker trading from 59 Paddington Street, Marylebone. In 1843 he is listed at 50 Paddington Street, and in 1848 he is recorded as a "trunk maker" with premises at 59 Paddington Street and as a "traveling equipage manufacturer" with premises at 100 New Bond Street. In 1849 he appears as a "Travelling equipage manufacturer" at 100 New Bond Street. In 1851 John Powell is listed as a "Trunk maker" back at 59 Paddington Street, where he is also recorded in 1852. (*see* Mrs. Elizabeth Powell.) He is listed for the last time in the 1860 directory as a "Trunk and packing case maker" and "camp equipage manufacturer" at 59 Paddington Street.

EDWARD PRATT
(c. 1857–1871)

From 1857 to 1860 Edward Pratt is listed in the London commercial directory as a "Patent Compendium Portmanteau & Camp equipage manufacturer" at 19 Cockspur Street, Charing Cross, the same address where Samuel and Henry Pratt were listed in 1841 (*see* Samuel & Henry Pratt). By 1861 Edward Pratt had moved to 36 New Bond Street. The directories for 1866 to 1870 record Edward Pratt as "Late Richardson, hatter, trunk maker, and patent compendium portmanteau manufacturer," trading from 37 Old Bond Street.[90]

SAMUEL & HENRY PRATT
(c. 1813–1867)

Samuel Pratt first appears in the London directory in 1813. His trade card from 1825 reads: "Patentee of Real Solid Leather Wardrobe Travelling Trunks / Imperials, / Carriage Trunks / & Plate Case Maker, / By Appointment to His Majesty, / At his Camp Equipage & Portable Brass Bedstead Manufactorys / 47 New Bond Street, & 190, Regent Street, & 19, Cockspur Street." In 1826 Samuel Pratt was granted a patent for a bed to prevent seasickness. In the commercial directory for 1838 he is listed with a partner as "Samuel and Henry Pratt, Upholsterers &c., 47 New Bond Street." They are both listed in 1841 at 19 Cockspur Street. The directories for 1842 and 1849 refer to "Samuel Pratt, senior, camp equipage manufactory and patentee of the new patent compendium for travelling, 19 Cockspur Street, Charing Cross." In 1852 Henry Pratt is listed as "patent travelling wardrobe, portmanteau, and camp equipage manufacturer, 19 Cockspur Street, Charing Cross, and 123 New Bond Street." That same year,

D.55. *Receipt from Samuel Pratt, 47, New Bond Street, & 190 Regent Street, & 19 Cockspur Street, London, dated May 21, 1825. Ink on paper. British Museum, Banks Trade Card Collection, Reference 120.14.*

1852, Samuel appears as "Samuel Pratt, Cabinet Maker, importer of ancient furniture, etc., 47 New Bond Street." The directory for 1865 records a "Samuel Luke Pratt, cabinetmaker" at the 47 New Bond Street address. He is last recorded in the directory in 1880. From 1859 to 1868 Henry Pratt, Jr. is listed as a trunk maker at 13A Chester Terrace, Eaton Square.[91]

PRYER, STEAINS & MACKENZIE
(c. 1810–1837)

George Pryer, James Steains, and John Mackenzie were all foremen to Thomas Butler of Catherine Street. Upon Thomas Butler's second retirement in 1810, Pryer, Steains, and Mackenzie established themselves in business as a "fashionable upholstery and Cabinet Manufactory" at 30 Brydges Street, Catherine Street, Strand (see Thomas Butler). On July 10, 1810 the firm published the following announcement in *The Times*:

FASHIONABLE UPHOLSTERY and CABINET MANUFACTORY, 30, Brydges-street, Catherine- street, Strand.—PRYER, STEAINS, and MACKENZIE, (late Foremen to Mr. T. Butler, of Catherine-street) respectfully take this method of informing the Nobility and Gentry, they have opened the above premises, where they manufacture every description of useful and fashionable furniture, which, from their long experience and having for many years severally conducted the different departments of Mr. Butler's late Manufactory (he having retired, and sold the same) and being resolved to get up all their work of the best materials, under their own immediate inspection, and on the most moderate terms, they flatter themselves they can fully recommend; and hope, by a steady attention to the interest of those who may honour them with orders, to merit their favours and recommendation. Manufacturers of the much admired Patent Dining-Tables of various descriptions, with considerable improvements; also the Sideboards with a new improved Dining-Table enclosed, the Patent Brass-screw Bedsteads, Sofa-Beds, and Chair-Beds—many of the above so improved as to be particularly portable for travelling and foreign climates; Camp Beds, Portable Chairs, Ship Sideboards, and Sofa Beds.

"By 1817 Steains had withdrawn from the partnership; thereafter the firm traded as Pryer & Mackenzie until the latter ceased his involvement in 1837."[92]

CHARLES ROBINSON
(c. 1849–1852)

Charles Robinson is recorded in the London commercial directory for 1849 as an iron bedstead manufacturer with workshops at 11 Bath Place, New Road, and 6 and 7 Greenland Place, Judd Street, Brunswick Square. He was granted a patent for a telescopic military bedstead in 1851. In 1852 he is listed as a brass and iron bedstead manufacturer working at 14 Elm Street and 6 and 7 Greenland Place, Cromer Street, Gray's Inn Road.

ROBINSON & SONS
(c. 1865–1875)

The firm of Robinson & Sons is listed in the 1865 directory for Yorkshire. Robinson & Sons stamped a portable caned mahogany campaign day bed from about 1875 "Robinson & Sons / Original Inventors and Makers / Ilkley." A similar campaign bed fashioned from walnut and dated 1873 bears the label, "Robinson & Sons, Manufacturers, Steam Cabinet Works, Ilkley, Yorkshire." Both beds, one in a private collection, the other sold at auction in 1999, are almost identical in appearance to the campaign day beds being manufactured by Leveson & Son and the Army and Navy Co-Operative Society about 1875.

D.56. *Victorian Caned Mahogany Adjustable Campaign Daybed, third quarter nineteenth century, stamped Robinson & Sons. H: 13 in.; L: 75 in.; W: 22 in. Private collection.*
 This campaign bed with a caned seat and ratcheted ends has removable feet, which are stamped with the mark of Robinson & Sons, manufacturers whose "Steam Cabinet Works" were located in Ilkley, Yorkshire.

E. ROSS
(C. 1821–1907)

Together with Hill & Millard, Ross & Co. is one of the most respected names in campaign furniture, and the Victorian Army's manufacturer of choice. The British Army's Kabul Committee on Equipment wrote in 1882, for example, ". . . the committee now considers the question of camp furniture for officers. . . . The majority of the committee consider it to be necessary for the comfort of an officer, that he should have a bed, and they find that the pattern made by Ross of Dublin is the most suitable. It weighs under 20 lbs."

The firm of E. Ross was founded by James Ross Murphy and Patrick Murphy. Their business was located throughout its existence at Ellis's Quay in Dublin, although there are inconsistencies in the directory listings. E. Ross was located at 6 Ellis's Quay, Dublin, from 1821 to 1825; at 6 and 7 Ellis's Quay from 1834 to 1836; and at 5 and 6 Ellis's Quay from 1842 to 1844.[93]

While trading under the name of "E. Ross, Camp Furniture Manufacturers," James Ross Murphy and Patrick Murphy were granted a patent for their design for a portable combined chair and couch on July 1, 1853. On August 11th they were granted a patent for their design for a portable reclining chair (*see* D.58).

In 1855, E. Ross is listed in the Dublin Street Directory as "army cabinet furniture, portmanteau, and camp equipage manufactory" at 9, 10, and 11 Ellis's

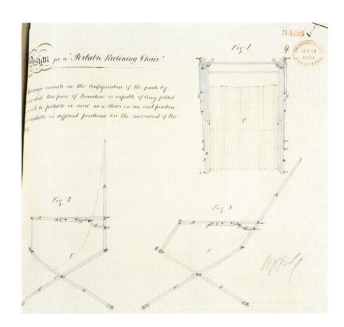

D.58. *"Design for a Portable Reclining Chair," registered by James Ross Murphy and Patrick Murphy, trading under the name or style of E. Ross, Camp Furniture Manufacturers, Dublin, August 11, 1853. Watercolor and ink on paper. Public Record Office, London.*

Quay. Under "nobility, gentry, merchants and traders" in the same directory, the firm is listed as E. Ross, "army furniture warehouse and portmanteau manufactory, 9 and 10 Ellis's Quay." E. Ross is listed solely at 9, 10 and 11 Ellis's Quay in 1856.

E. Ross changed its name to "Ross & Co." in 1860. Brass plaques affixed to various pieces of furniture made in 1863 as a wedding present for Captain Benjamin Simner of the 76th Regiment are embossed, "Ross & Co. / Manufacturers / 9, 10 & 11, Ellis's Quay / Dublin." The 1864 street directory lists the company at 8, 9, and 10 Ellis's Quay as "Ross & Co. camp furniture manufacturers and upholsterers to H.R.H., the Prince of Wales—factory, 35 Tighe Street." In the same directory under Tighe Street, there is a listing at number 35 for "Ross, E. furniture stores." In 1865 Ross & Co. exhibited at the Dublin International Exhibition, where the firm was recorded as a camp furniture and portmanteau manufacturer trading from 8 Ellis's Quay, Dublin. The firm is recorded at 8, 9, and 10 Ellis's Quay with its factory at 35 Tighe Street in the Dublin street directories from 1867 to 1880. The street directory for 1883 notes that Ross & Co. is at 8, 9 and 10 Ellis's Quay, and that number 11 is vacant. Under 35 Tighe Street the firm is listed as "Ross & Co. furniture stores."

D.57. *Adjustable campaign bed folded for travel. The legs also unscrew.*

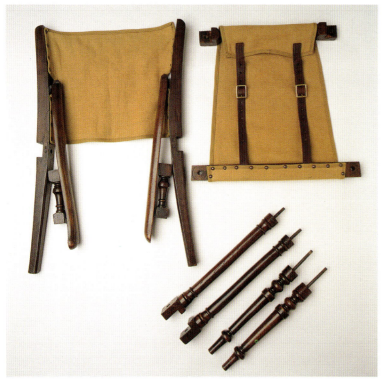

Left:
D.59. Irish Victorian Mahogany Campaign Chair, with slung canvas back secured by brass tacks, third quarter nineteenth century. The right rear leg is affixed with the maker's ivory plaque engraved, "Ross & Co. / Manufacturers / 9-10 & 11 Ellis's Quay / Dublin." H: 30¼ in.; W: 22 in.; D: 20 in. Private collection.

Below, left:
D.60. The chair knocked down for travel.

Below:
D.61. Detail of stamped numbers on turned legs for assembly of frame.

D.62. Detail of maker's engraved ivory plaque.

200 / DIRECTORY

In 1896 the firm is recorded at 8, 9, and 10 Ellis's Quay as "Ross & Co. camp furniture manufacturers and upholsterers to H.R.H. the Prince of Wales, invalid furniture manufacturers." There is an additional listing for James Ross Murphy, Esq., but no listing at all in the directory for Tighe Street. In the 1909 directory, 8, 9, and 10 Ellis's Quay are listed as vacant, surrounded on either side by tenements.

The firm marked the overwhelming majority of their pieces with a brass or ivory plaque giving its name and current address.

Left:
D.63. Victorian Mahogany Side Chair, with legs that unscrew and a seat that detaches from the back, c. 1846–1859, with the maker's brass plaque embossed, "E. Ross / cabinet maker upholsterer / camp equipage / and / portmantua [sic] manufacturer / 9 & 10 Ellis's Quay / Dublin." H: 33 ½ in.; H (to seat): 17 in.; W: 19 in.; D: 18 ¾ in. Private Collection.

Below, left:
D.64. Chair shown disassembled. Legs that unscrewed were commonly used on campaign chairs from about 1800. In the late eighteenth century, by contrast, it was common for campaign chairs to fold inward, by means of concertinalike action.

D.65. Detail of maker's embossed brass plaque.

D.66. Victorian Mahogany Traveling Mirror, in box frame, third quarter nineteenth century. The maker's ivory plaque is engraved, "ROSS & CO. / MANUFACTURERS / 8, 9, 10 ELLIS'S QUAY / DUBLIN." H (closed): 2 ¼ in.; H (open): 1 ft. 4 in.; W: 1 ft. 2 ¼ in.; D: 1 ft. 6 ½ in. Courtesy Phillips of Hitchin (Antiques) Ltd.

D.67. When in use, the mirror is lifted out, and its ratcheted back is supported by one of the ends of the case, allowing for the mirror to be adjusted at different angles.

D.68. Victorian Mahogany Pot Cupboard, by Ross & Co., Dublin, third quarter nineteenth century. This piece bears the brass plaque embossed, "ROSS & CO. / MANUFACTURERS, 9, 10 AND 11 ELLIS'S QUAY, DUBLIN." H: 2 ft. 7 in.; W: 1 ft. 2¼ in.; D: 1 ft. ½ in. Courtesy Phillips of Hitchin (Antiques) Ltd.

Although pot cupboards are rather simple in design, this would appear to be the only one so far recorded specifically made for traveling.

D.69. Pot cupboard shown with its legs unscrewed.

Below:
D.70. *Set of Six Victorian Oak Campaign Dining Chairs, with the maker's ivory plaque engraved,* "Ross & Co. / camp furniture makers / 8, 9 & 10 Ellis's Quay, / Dublin," *second half of the nineteenth century. H: 2 ft. 10 in.; H (to seat): 1 ft. 7 in.; W: 1 ft. 6 in.; D: 1 ft. 5 in. Courtesy Phillips of Hitchin (Antiques) Ltd.*

Right:
D.71. *Detail of maker's engraved ivory plaque, on three of the six chairs.*

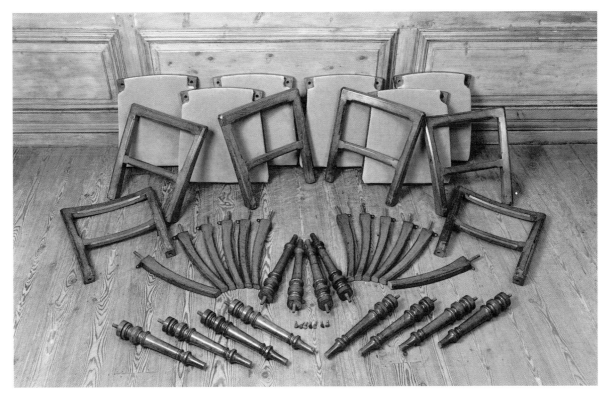

D.72. *The chairs with the seat frames and backs separated, and all the legs unscrewed.*

DIRECTORY /203

D.73. Victorian Military Chest of Drawers, in two sections, with feet that unscrew (replacements of correct design), second half nineteenth century. The maker's brass plaque is embossed, "Ross & Co. / Manufacturers / 9, 10 & 11, Ellis's Quay / Dublin." H: 3 ft. 9 in.; W: 3 ft. 3 in.; D: 1 ft. 7 1/4 in. Courtesy Phillips of Hitchin (Antiques) Ltd.

This chest of drawers has a relatively unusual arrangement. The lower section has the more typical arrangement of two long drawers, whereas the upper section contains four short drawers and one long drawer.

WILLIAM WHITE ROUCH
(c. 1858–1959)

William White Rouch, photographic apparatus manufacturer of 180 Strand, was granted patents in 1858 and 1861 for his designs for a portable photographic dark operating chamber. The firm is listed in the London commercial directories for an entire century, from 1859 to 1959. The directory for 1865 lists the firm as "William White Rouch & Co., chemists and druggists, chemical glass and photographic apparatus manufacturers, general scientific and chemical agents and opticians, 180 Strand." By 1875 the firm advertised that it had been awarded medals at the principal international exhibitions and is listed as "operative chemists, chemical glass and photographic apparatus manufacturers, general scientific and chemical agents and opticians, 180 Strand WC and 43 Norfolk Street, Strand." By 1902 the firm is recorded in the London commercial directory simply as "photographic specialists" trading from 161 Strand.

RUDALL, ROSE, CARTE
(c. 1855–1925)

The firm Rudall, Rose, Carte & Co. is listed in the 1855 London commercial directory at 100 New Bond Street as, "Council and prize medal musical instruments manufacturers, sole agents in Gt. Britain for Sax's military instruments, music sellers & publishers." The firm was granted a patent on November 6, 1856 for its design for a portable iron military music stand. According to the patent, "The object of this Design is so to construct and combine the several parts of a Music Stand that they may be folded up so that the entire stand legs and all may be brought into a small space, and made more conveniently portable than the stands in ordinary use."

From 1861 to 1870 Rudall, Rose, Carte & Co. is listed at 20 Charing Cross, as "Instrument makers to Her Majesty, the Army & Navy." In 1875 Rudall, Carte & Co. is listed at the same address. By 1880 the firm had moved to 23 Berners Street, Oxford Street, where it remained until 1925.

SAVORY & MOORE
(c. 1838–1908)

Savory & Moore, chemists by appointment to Queen Victoria, is listed in the London commercial directories from 1838 to 1908. The firm supplied a small brass and mahogany medicine chest for the Honourable Henry Herbert to take with him to the Crimean War upon his graduation from Eton in 1854, at a cost of 54 shillings. It contains a mortar and pestle, beaker, set of scales, and twelve glass bottles, and bears a maker's ivory label incised "Savory & Moore / Chemists to the Queen / 143, New Bond Street / and 220, Regent St., London." The medicine chest is now housed in Powis Castle, North Wales.

WILLIAM SCHNELL
(c. 1855–1860)

On January 25, 1855 the upholsterer and cabinetmaker William Schnell, of 12 Denmark Street, Soho received a patent for what he termed "The People's Sofa Bed." Although he is not listed in the commercial directory the year that he received the patent, he is recorded in 1857, 1859, and 1860 as "Upholsterer & Cabinet maker, 63 Charlotte Street, Fitzrovia Square."[94]

SEDDON
(c. 1753–1868)

Seddon was one of the largest manufacturers of furniture in eighteenth century London, employing about four hundred workers in 1786. Like Morgan & Sanders and Thomas Butler, the firm made a large number of patent metamorphic pieces for travel, including tables, beds and chairs that packed flat. George Seddon I established the firm about 1753 on Aldersgate Street, where it was to remain until 1837. George Seddon I was joined by his sons Thomas I and George II in 1785, and by his son-in-law, Thomas Shackleton, between 1788 and 1798.[95] For a short time the firm went by the name "Seddon, Sons & Shackleton." In 1815 the business passed to the late George Seddon II's nephew, Thomas Seddon II. He, in turn, was joined by his brother, George Seddon III in about 1817.

The brothers continued to trade from Aldersgate Street, but expanded in 1826 to 16 Lower Grosvenor Street.[96] The firm was awarded a Royal Warrant in 1832 and left its Aldersgate address in 1837. From about 1817 to 1840 the firm affixed a maker's paper label to many of its pieces that read: "T & G Seddon, / LONDON HOUSE, / Aldersgate Street."[97]

The firm is recorded in the London commercial directory for 1838 as "Thomas and George Seddon, Cabinet manufacturers, &c., to Her Majesty, Calthorpe place, Gray's-inn-road." The firm eventually established premises between 1853 and 1854 at 67 New Bond Street.

The London commercial directory for 1865 records "Charles Seddon & Co., cabinet-makers &c., Avery Row, Grosvenor Street, & 58 South Molton Street." The firm is listed in 1867 and again for the last time in 1868 as Seddon & Co. "Cabinet manufacturers, upholsterers, decorators, undertakers, house & estate agents to Her Majesty, 70 Grosvenor Street."

ANGELO SEDLEY
(c. 1861–1868)

Angelo Sedley, of 210 Regent Street, London, was granted a patent for his "Compendium Dressing Tables" in the mid-nineteenth century. The London commercial directory for 1861 lists Angelo Sedley & Co. "(late John Wells & Co.) cabinet makers & upholsterers, 210 Regent street; manufactory, 6½ Tyler street, Golden square." An advertisement in the same directory states: "CABINET-MAKERS & UPHOLSTERERS / DRAWING & DINING ROOM FURNITURE / OF SUPERIOR DESIGN AND MANUFACTURE / RICH CARPETS, DAMASKS AND CHINTZES / at Moderate Prices." The London commercial directory for 1865 records the firm as "Angelo Sedley & Co., Burlington Furniture Galleries, cabinet-makers & upholsterers, patentees & manufacturers of equilibrium chairs, couches, etc. 38 Conduit St., London." Sedley's advertisement for 1865 states: "THE BURLINGTON FURNITURE GALLERIES / 38 CONDUIT STREET, W. / SEDLEY'S / PATENT EQUILIBRIUM CHAIR / Prices as shown / Chair, with Arms Stuffed in canvas £2.12 / Leg Rest, Extra £0.3 / Castors, Extra £0.4. / ALSO THE VICTORIA EQUILIBRIUM CHAIR, COUCH & BED, COMBINED. / The above combine ease, economy, and comfortable utility. / UPHOLSTERY & CABINET WORKS / Illustrated Catalogue Gratis / Removed from 210, Regent Street, W. to larger premises." The firm last appears in the commercial directory in 1868.

THOMAS SHEARER
(C. 1788)

Shortly after the publication of A. Hepplewhite & Co.'s *The Cabinet-maker's and Upholsterer's Guide*, the London Society of Cabinet-Makers published *The Cabinet-Maker's London Book of Prices* in 1788. Seventeen of its twenty plates were signed by Thomas Shearer, who may have been a "journeyman cabinet maker rather than a professional designer."[98] "The plates, which illustrate objects described in the text, are in a fluent style that bridges the short interval between Hepplewhite's *Guide* and Sheraton's *Drawing Book*."[99] Among the designs for portable furniture illustrated or discussed in the second edition (1793) are a "Travelling Bidet" designed to rise out of a chest, four variations on a "Portable Writing Desk," a "Strong Travelling Box" with optional lacquered brass corners and straps, and a "Gentleman's Portable Desk," also with optional lacquered brass corners and straps.[100]

JOHN SHEPHERD
(C. 1808–1898)

From 1808 until 1839 J. Shepherd is listed in the London commercial directories as a "Trunk-maker, 90 Bishopsgate within [the City of London]. In the 1841 directory John Shepherd is listed as a "Trunk and bag maker" at 90 Bishopsgate. From 1842 to 1849 the firm is listed as "Trunk maker and undertaker" at the same address. The 1851 listing reads, "Trunk and iron bedstead maker, undertaker, camp and cabin manufacturer, 90 Bishopsgate." In 1860 and 1861 John Shepherd is recorded as "Trunk and iron bedstead maker, undertaker, camp and cabin furniture maker and outfitter," at 90 Bishopsgate and Summit Place, Upper Clapton. In 1867 the firm is also listed as a shipping agent, and the address has changed from 90 to 55 Bishopsgate and Summit Place, Upper Clapton. The listing for 1870 records the firm simply as "Trunk maker," at 55 Bishopsgate. From 1875 to 1885 John Shepherd is once again recorded as "Trunk and iron bedstead maker, undertaker, camp and cabin furniture maker and outfitter, and shipping agent" at both 55 Bishopsgate and Tottenham Green, Middlesex. In 1890 and 1891 there is no mention of the firm as a shipping agent, but rather as "Trunk and iron bedstead maker, undertaker, camp and cabin furniture maker and outfitter and funeral carriage master" at the same addresses. From 1893 to 1898 the last year the firm is listed in the commercial directory, John Shepherd is recorded as "Trunk maker, Undertaker & Outfitter & Funeral Carriage Master" at 26 Leadenhall Street and Tottenham Green, Middlesex.

THOMAS SHERATON
(C. 1791–1805)

Thomas Sheraton was a designer of furniture, and it is doubtful whether he ever set up a workshop of his own. Sheraton was located at 41 Davies Street, Grosvenor Square in 1793; 106 Wardour Street in 1795; and later at 8 Broad Street, Golden Square.[101] He devoted himself mainly to the production of designs, which he published between 1791 and 1805. His principal work is *The Cabinet Makers' and Upholsterers' Drawing Book*, originally issued in four parts between 1791 and 1794. In 1803 he published his celebrated and influential *Cabinet Dictionary*, which features a number of campaign pieces. With regard to his design for a camp or field bedstead, Sheraton writes that it is "made to fold close together, so that a case of about 15 inches square, and 3 feet 8 inches long, will hold both the frame and tester lath." His design for a camp table consists of "two flaps, about 14 inches wide each, and 2 feet 8 inches in length, of Honduras, hinged at the under side. . . . The triangular legs which support it, are fixed in the centre, the same as a fishing stool, by means of an iron triangle, with three screw pins and nuts. . . . These tables are both simple, and will bear any degree of hardship. . . ." Lastly, his camp chair "folds up, and the back, foot, and stump of the elbow, are hinged to the side rail, and the back, feet, and seat, are stayed with girth webbing, so that the whole will draw together, and lie flat. Some cover the seats with leather, but it is not soon dry as webbing, which, therefore, is most approved of."

For a history of Thomas Sheraton, see Beard and Gilbert, *Dictionary of English Furniture Makers 1660–1840*, pp. 808–9.

JAMES SHOOLBRED
(C. 1820–1930)

James Shoolbred & Co. is first listed in the 1820 London commercial directory as "Schoolbred [*sic*] & Co., Linen-drapers & Hosiers, &c. 155 Tottenham-court-road." In the directory for 1824 Shoolbred & Co. is listed as "Linen-drapers & Hosiers" at the same address. In 1838 the firm is recorded as "Shoolbred, Cook & Co., Linen & Woollen Drapers, Mercers,

Hosiers, Haberdashers & Carpet Warehousemen, 154, 155 & 156 Tottenham Court road." By 1842 Shoolbred had expanded to 43 & 44 Grafton Street. In 1849 the firm is listed as "James Shoolbred & Co., linen and woollen drapers, silk mercers, hosiers, haberdashers, and carpet warehousemen, 154, 155 & 156 Tottenham Court Road; and 37 to 39 and 41 to 44 Grafton Street." The firm is recorded in the London commercial directory for 1865 as "Linen and Woollen Drapers, Silk Mercers, Hosiers, Haberdashers & Carpet Warehousemen, 151–156 Tottenham Court Road, 37–45 Grafton St. east; 23–27 Sussex St. & 33 University St."

James Shoolbred & Co. eventually grew to become one of London's most important department stores, specializing from the 1870s in furniture and decorations. In 1876 the firm advertised "Every description of camp and folding bedsteads." James Shoolbred & Co. exhibited a very extensive selection of items in the 1878 Paris Universal Exhibition and was granted a Royal Warrant by the mid-1880s. The firm continued to be listed in the commercial pages until 1930.

SILBER & FLEMING
(c. 1864–1902)

Silber & Fleming is recorded in the London commercial directory for 1865 as "warehousemen" with premises at 56 and 56½ Wood St., City, and 24 Rue Vendôme, Paris. In 1875 the firm is described as "manufacturers, importers of and dealers in British and foreign fancy & leather goods, jewelry, watches, clocks, bronzes, perfumery, stationery, cutlery, cabinet goods, pictures, glass, china, musical boxes and instruments, toys, pipes, beads, lamps etc., 56, 56A, 56½, 61 and 62 Wood street, Cheapside; 2 London Wall; 3 and 4 Bird Court, Philip Lane; 32 Summer row, Birmingham, and 40 Rue de Paradis Poissonnière, Paris." Silber & Fleming's illustrated catalogue from this period offers a selection of portable barrack, camp, ship, and garden furniture. In the 1897 London commercial directory the firm is recorded as "Manufacturers, importers, warehousemen and agents, wholesale and export" with departments that sold fancy leather goods, trunks, and ladies & gentlemen's traveling bags, trading from 56½, 57–62, and 71 Wood street, Cheapside; 2 London Wall. By 1902 the firm had been absorbed by Faudel, Phillips & Son.

S. W. SILVER
(c. 1838–1959)

Stephen Winckworth Silver & Co. is recorded in the London commercial directories from 1838 to 1959. In the 1838 directory the firm is listed as "Clothiers" with a "Ready-made Linen and Outfitting Warehouse" at 10, 66, and 67 Cornhill, and 4 St. George's Crescent South, in Liverpool. In 1842 S. W. Silver & Co. is recorded at 10, 66, and 67 Cornhill; 4½ Bishopsgate, London; and 4 and 5 St. George's Crescent South, Liverpool. The firm is also recorded as having workshops at 33 Nassau place, Commercial Road East, London. The 1849 and 1852 directories record S.W. Silver & Co. as "clothiers, outfitters and contractors," trading at 10, 66, and 67 Cornhill, with an "emigrants' fitting out warehouse" at 4½ Bishopsgate, and 10 and 11 St. George's Crescent, Liverpool. The firm's workshops were situated at 33 and 34 Nassau Place, Commercial Road East. In 1861 the firm placed an advertisement in the London commercial directory which read, in part, "Furniture for Camp, Barrack, Cabin, and Colonial Use, embracing every variety of Cabinet Work, Canteens, Trunks, Portmanteaus, etc., Portable, and Suitable for all Climates. Outfitting Requirements of every description, for Naval and Military Officers, Cadets, Civilians, [and] Midshipmen."

The firm was awarded a prize medal in 1862, and in 1865 it exhibited in the New Zealand Exhibition. The *Reports and Awards of Jurors* from 1866 states: "The only British exhibitor in the furniture section was the firm of S.W. Silver & Co., London, Exhibit No. 2978. Their entry covered a variety of furniture for dining and drawing rooms, library, hall and bedrooms, but the judges took special note of their folding chairs. The suitability of some of the exhibits of furniture, where lightness, portability, and convenience are required, is particularly noticeable in some chairs, which, although fit for luxuriantly furnished apartments in point of appearance, can yet be folded and removed with all the readiness of a camp stool."[102]

In 1865 S. W. Silver & Co. is recorded as a contractor and manufacturer of camp, cabin, and portable furniture, as well as "Rhodes" tents and portmanteaus. By 1875 the firm had set up an "Explorer's Room" at 60 and 67 Cornhill, which it claimed contained "every article of equipment for voyage, camp, travel &c. for ladies and gentlemen." S. W. Silver & Co.'s "office of the Colonies" was at 4 Sun Court, Cornhill, and its retail outlets for "clothing, shirts, accoutrements, household, cabin and portable furniture, mattresses, camp equipage, tents &c" were at 5 Bishopsgate and at

100 Market Street in Manchester. Its factory was at Canal Cut, Limehouse and the counting house was at Sun Court, Cornhill. The firm also acted as "army, navy and colonial agents," with offices at 66 and 67 Cornhill, as well as inventors, having been granted a patent on March 10, 1876 for its design for a "reconvertible chair and bedstead for camp use."

In 1897 S. W. Silver & Co. offered "Every article of equipment for voyage, camp, travel, and for colonists, explorers and settlers, colonial agents and manufacturers of clothing, trunks, firearms, portable furniture, tents &c. Sun Court, 67 Cornhill." By 1902 the firm is listed as "S. W. Silver & Co. & Benjamin Edgington Limited, every article of equipment for voyage, camp and travel, etc. for colonists and explorers & firearms, portable furniture, tents, etc. Sun Court, 67 Cornhill." In the London trade directory for the following year, S.W. Silver & Co. & Benjamin Edgington Limited offered an "Illustrated Catalogue containing particulars of complete equipments [sic] for every part of the world. Colonial handbooks &c." The firm was trading as late as 1959. A caned settee manufactured by S.W. Silver & Co. is in the Dominion Museum in New Zealand.[103]

WILLIAM SMEE & SONS
(c. 1806–1885)

William Smee was active as a cabinetmaker and upholsterer from 1806 to 1840. He worked at 5 Pavement, Moorfields from 1806 to 1838, at which time the firm became William Smee & Sons, and the address was renumbered to 6 Finsbury Pavement. From 1835 the firm occupied additional space at 34 Little Moorfields.[104] In 1861 William Smee & Sons is listed in the commercial directory at 6 Finsbury Pavement, 34 Little Moorfields, and 7 Finsbury Circus as "Wholesale cabinet makers, upholsterers, bedding warehousemen, timber merchants, appraisers." In 1865 the firm appears as wholesale cabinetmakers, upholsterers, bedding warehousemen, and appraisers trading from 6 Finsbury Pavement and 34 Little Moorfields. From 1870 to 1885 the firm is recorded as William A. & Sylvanus Smee, "wholesale cabinetmakers, upholsterers and bedding warehousemen and appraisers, 6 Finsbury Pavement; 34 Little Moorfields and Finsbury Cabinet works, King Henry's Walk, Ball's Pond." The 1880 listing for the firm also states, "Prize Medal Paris Exhibition." In 1890 the name of the firm is listed as Smith & Cobay at the same addresses, where it is also recorded in 1895. In 1900 and 1905 Smith & Cobay is listed at 139 New Bond Street, with factories at King Henry's Walk & Bloomsbury Place.[105]

JOHN SOUTHGATE & CO.
(c. 1848–1907)

The London commercial directory for 1848 lists "Southgate and Alcock, trunk and packing case manufacturers, 76 Watling Street and 3 George Yard, Bow Lane." The following year the firm is recorded at 76 Watling Street and 5 George Yard, Bow Lane. The firm is listed at the same addresses in 1852 as "Trunk and packing case, canteen, portmanteau and camp and military equipage manufacturers, and saddlers' ironmongers." The 1860 and 1861 directories list John Southgate & Co. as also manufacturing an "enameled travel bag." The 1866 directory records that the firm has expanded to 75 and 76 Watling Street and 5 George Yard, Bow Lane and is manufacturing "Solid leather portmanteau, carpet and enameled leather bag and military equipage, canteen and trunk and packing case[s]. . . ."

From 1867 to 1880 John Southgate & Co. continued to manufacture the same items at the same addresses. From 1900 to 1905 the firm is recorded as John Southgate & Sons, "leather trunk makers, 76 Watling Street; 13 Well Court, Queen Street, 93 Gray's Inn Road; 4, 5 & 6 Brownlow Mews." In 1906 the firm is listed in the London commercial pages as John Southgate & Co. (Wolfsky & Co., Ltd.) "leather goods manufacturers; works, 17, 18, & 19 Bridgewater Square (late of Watling Street). The same is recorded in 1907. The 1910 directory lists "Wolfsky & Co., leather goods manufacturers: 17, 18, & 19 Bridgewater Street."

CHARLES STEWART
(c. 1810–1827)

In 1810 Charles Stewart, cabinetmaker and upholsterer, was granted patent No. 3339 for "improvements in the construction of dining and other tables." His extending table was constructed with a sliding frame and hinged flaps, which reduced to a pier table when the leaves were removed. He was located at 115 St. Martin's Lane until 1820 and at 24 Regent Street from 1821 to 1827.[106] The following three inscriptions on brass plaques affixed to extending dining room tables have been recorded:

"Stewart, / INVENTOR, / AND Patentee / 115 St. Martin's Lane / Charing Cross, / LONDON"

"Stewart, / INVENTOR, / AND Patentee / 24 Regent St. Piccadilly, / from St Martins Lane, / LONDON."

"Stewart, Inventor, and Patentee, 315 Oxford Street & 115 St. Martins Lane, London."

The last of these maker's brass plaques was affixed to a campaign dining table that has been described as a "particularly ingenious example of campaign furniture, suitable for an officer's mess or governor's residence. Usable as a side table . . . it extends, with four leaves inserted, to a dining table about 11 ft long . . . supported with the aid of a system of sliding bearers on only four legs which unscrew, so that the whole thing could be packed into a remarkably small space."[107]

CHARLES SYMONS
(c. 1853–1855)

Charles Symons, a plate chest maker and joiner at 1 Princes Street, Fitzroy Square, London was granted a patent on November 18, 1853 for a table bedstead, which he intended to be used as a table, bedstead, or writing desk. Symons is recorded in the London commercial directories in 1854 and 1855.[108]

MARGARET TAIT
(c. 1813–1831)

Margaret Tait, perfumer and writing-desk manufacturer, traded from 41 Cornhill, London. Her firm appears in the London commercial directories from 1813 to 1831. According to a paper trade label affixed to the interior of a portable mahogany desk from about 1825, Tait "supplies merchants, captains and country traders on the most reasonable terms. NB. An elegant assortment of pocketbooks, ladies' and gentlemen's dressing cases, etc., writing desks and copying machines. Manufactured and sold wholesale and retail."

D.74–75. *George IV Brass-Mounted Mahogany Traveling Desk, with green baize-lined writing slope and fitted interior. This piece bears the maker's paper label, "Margaret Tait / 41 Cornhill," c. 1825. H: 5½ in.; W: 1 ft. 7¾ in.; D (closed): 10 in.; D (open): 20 in. Courtesy Phillips of Hitchin (Antiques) Ltd.*

D.76. *Detail of the maker's paper label.*

BENJAMIN TAYLOR & SONS
(c. 1805–1876)

Benjamin Taylor & Sons, designers, manufacturers, and upholsterers, traded first from Kent Street, Southwark, from 1805 to 1821, and subsequently from Great Dover Street, Southwark, until 1873. The firm is recorded in the London commercial directory for 1838 as "Benjamin Taylor & Sons, upholsterers and auctioneers, Dover Road." Benjamin Taylor & Sons was trading from 167 Great Dover Street, Southwark in 1851, the year that the firm received honorable mention for a line of "furniture in cork" for a yacht or steam ship cabin which it exhibited at the Great Exhibition of Works of Industry of All Nations at the Crystal Palace."[109] In 1855 the firm is listed as "Cabinet makers, upholsterers, patent cork floating bed, steam packet furnishers"; in 1861, as "patentees of the sliding tables for ships' use." In 1865 and 1870 the firm is again recorded as "Cabinet makers, upholsterers, bedding manufacturers, steam packet furnishers, patentees of the sliding table for ships' use, inventors and manufacturers of the patent cork floating bedding, 167 Great Dover Street, S.E." In 1875 and 1877 the firm is listed at 97 New Bond Street.[110]

HENRY EDWARD THOMPSON
(c. 1846–1858)

Henry Edward Thompson is recorded on patents from 1847 and 1849 as a "Camp Equipage Manufacturer" trading from Long Acre, London. He is listed in the London commercial directories from 1846 to 1850 as "Henry E. Thompson, travelling equipage manufacturer to the Queen, and patentee for the metallic military bedstead, 116 Longacre." On July 30, 1852 a patent was granted to "Henry Edward Thompson, Iron Bedstead and Travelling Equipage manufacturers, 351 Oxford Street, London." That same year he is listed in the directory at 116 Long Acre, but no longer supplying to the Queen. He is not listed in the directories from 1855 to 1860, although on a patent granted in 1858, Henry E. Thompson is recorded as trading from 302 Strand, London. (*see* John Thomas Thompson.)

JOHN THOMAS THOMPSON
(c. 1816–1852)

John Thomas Thompson & Co. advertised its business as "cabinet maker, army upholsterer, auctioneer, appraiser, military bed and camp equipage maker to their Majesties, patentee of the light military traveling bed"[111] On January 1, 1816 the firm placed an advertisement in *The Times* for its "PATENT EAST and WEST INDIA WELLINGTON BED":

This elegant and portable BEDSTEAD *is made of Wrought Iron Tubes, plated with brass, thereby rendering it extremely light, not liable to rust, or harbour vermin, by its ingenious and simple construction being only one piece, it forms in two*

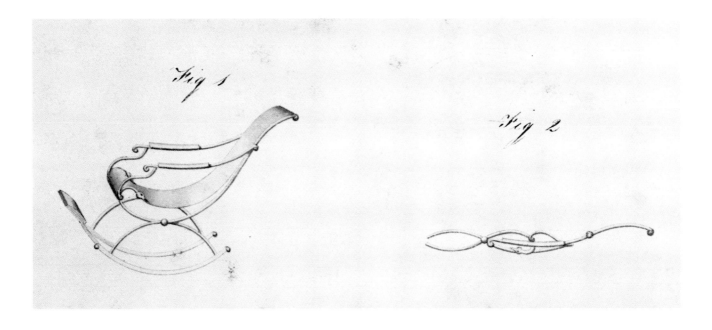

D.77. "Design For a Portable Folding Rocking Chair," registered by Henry Edward Thompson of Long Acre, London, September 11, 1847. Ink on paper. Public Record Office, London.

minutes into a most complete bed, weighing only 56 lbs, with the bedding complete; and by its portability and very small size into which it folds, will fix to any part of a carriage; to the invalid in particular traveling for health it has been invaluable, as by the elasticity of the sacking, turning in bed is rendered less painful and when in a warm climate its use will enable them to enjoy the blessing of sleep, often denied to them in the beds of the country which cannot be kept from vermin. As a spare bed in a house it has been found to be extremely useful, it being soon put up, and also forming an elegant couch; a very extensive assortment of different sizes, fitted up with an entire new pattern of Mosquito-Nets are now on show at the warerooms of the patentee J.T. Thompson 116 Longacre.

This is believed to be the first of three patents Thompson received for iron bedsteads and testers.[112]

The firm is recorded in commercial directories from 1817 to 1842 at 116 Long Acre, London as "Travelling equipage maker." The directories of 1841 and 1842 record John Thomas Thompson at the Longacre address as "Travelling Equipage-maker to the Queen & Patentee for the Metallic Military-bedstead." The firm does not appear in the directory of 1846, at which time Henry E. Thompson is listed at the 116 Longacre address. (*see* Henry Edward Thompson.)

JOHN TROTTER
(c. 1790–1808)

John Trotter & Sons is recorded in the London commercial directory for 1790 as "John Trotter & Coutts/Army and Navy Warehouse, 43, Frith Street, Soho." On July 5, 1793 Messrs. Trotter & Co. supplied Lieutenant Robert Ballard Long of the 1st Dragoon Guards with forty-nine articles of camp equipment prior to his embarking on the Flanders campaign. A copy of his "Invoice of Camp Equipage" is reproduced in plates 37 and 38.

By 1793 the firm was trading under the name John Trotter, Jr. & Co. By 1802 the firm had moved its Army & Navy Warehouse to 7 Soho Square. From 1806 to 1808, the last year the firm is listed in the commercial directory, John Trotter, Jr. & Co. is recorded as merchants trading from 6 Soho Square.

WILLIAM HENRY VAUGHAN
(ACTIVE C. 1866–1918)

W. H. Vaughan & Co. was a firm of upholsterers that specialized in the manufacture of folding chairs. The firm is recorded in the London commercial directories from 1866 to 1918. In 1875 the firm is listed as trading from 332 and 334 Old Street, Shoreditch. By 1897 it was also trading from 41 Rivington Street, East London. Between 1903 and 1910 the firm is listed as upholsterers at 332 and 334 Old Street. From 1911 to 1918 the firm is listed as cabinetmakers at the same address.

JOHN VERRINDER
(c. 1850)

John Verrinder, of Lincoln, was granted a patent in 1850 for his design for a portable box-table and sofa-bedstead that could be folded into a box.

JOHN COLLARD VICKERY
(c. 1895–1937)

John Collard Vickery is listed in the 1895 and 1897 commercial directories as a "Dressing case, travelling bag maker, jeweler, silversmith, stationer, importer" at 183 Regent Street, London. In 1900 the firm is listed at 181 and 183 Regent Street "by Royal Warrant of appointment to Her Majesty the Queen & H.R.H. the Princess of Wales." In 1903 the firm placed an advertisement in *The Connoisseur*, in which it described itself as "Jeweller, Gold & Silversmith, High-Class Leather Goods and Fitted Travelling Bag Manufacturer. To Their Majesties The King and Queen and Their Royal Highnesses The Prince and Princess of Wales. Novelties in all departments."[113]

By 1905 John Collard Vickery had expanded to 179, 181, and 183 Regent Street, and 1 New Burlington Place, Regent Street. From 1910 to 1925 the firm is listed at the above addresses and also at 177 Regent Street. From 1930 through 1932 John Collard Vickery is listed as "goldsmith, silversmith, jeweller, dressing case & high-class leather goods manufacturer &c. to His Magesty the King & Her Magesty the Queen, at 145 and 147 Regent Street. In 1933 and 1934 the firm is also listed at 143 Regent Street. From 1935–1937 the firm is recorded only at 145 and 147 Regent Street.[114]

JOHN WARD
(c. 1762–1958)

According to an advertisement in the 1861 London commercial directory for 1861, John Ward Ltd. had been in business for 99 years. The advertisement describes the firm as follows: "By appointment to the Queen and Royal Family, the Empresses of France, Russia &c., &c. / 5 & 6, & 12 LEICESTER PLACE ... PATENTEE AND MANUFACTURER of / Bath and Brighton Wheel Chairs, Children's Perambulators / PATENT SELF-PROPELLING AND SELF-ACTING CHAIRS / AND BEDS OF EVERY DESCRIPTION FOR THE USE AND COMFORT OF INVALIDS FOR SALE OR HIRE." Beneath a line drawing of their "PATENT ALBERT CHAIR," is the following description:

This elegant and simple invention, for which LETTERS PATENT *have been obtained, is made in* IRON, *and is very superior / to anything of the kind yet made for camp use.*

It forms a chair in every position, or a Bed, at pleasure, and folds into a small compass / for shipment; they are also made in Wood, and form a luxurious Chair or Lounge for the Drawing Room or Library. They are known as WARD'S PATENT ALBERT LOUNGING CHAIR.

An advertisement from 1875 records the following:

"*John Ward, 5 & 6, Leicester Square, London W.C. Patentee and Manufacturer of Bath and Brighton Wheel Chairs, Children's Perambulators, Patent self-propelling and self-acting chairs, and beds of every description for the use and comfort of invalids for sale or hire. By Special Appointment to the Queen and Royal Family, the Empresses of France, Austria and Russia, and the King of the Belgians, etc., etc. Prize Medals Awarded: London, 1851; International Exhibition, London, 1862, Dublin, 1865; International Exhibition in Paris, 1867; Vienna, 1873, Medal for Merit and one for Progress; also Honourable Mention, Paris, 1855; London, 1862; Paris, 1867; and Vienna, 1873.*"

In 1897 the firm is recorded as:

Invalid chair manufacturer to the Queen and Royal Family, the Empresses of France, Austria and Russia and the King of the Belgians, inventor and patentee of every description of easy chair, carriage or bed, every appliance for the use and

D.78. Advertisement for *John Ward of Leicester Square, Furniture Makers by Appointment to Her Majesty The Queen*, from Kelly's Post Office Directory for London, *1879, Vol. II, p. 127. Courtesy Victoria & Albert Museum; V & A Picture Library.*
This photograph depicts a lady being carried in a chair similar to that designed by John Alderman of Soho Square.

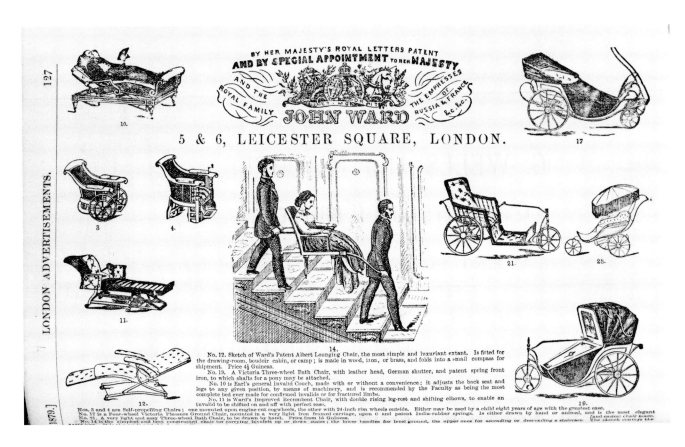

comfort of invalids; perambulators, children's carriages &c. (the only prize medal holder at the Exhibition of 1851 and at the French Exhibition of 1855; and the only prize medal holder at the International Exhibition of 1862, and the only silver medal and honourable mention awarded at the French Exhibition of 1867 and Vienna 1873; also two silver medals Paris 1878), 246 & 247 Tottenham court road. Late of 5 & 6 Leicester Square.

The listing for John Ward, Ltd. in the London commercial directory for 1919 reads, "Invalid chair makers by appointment to their Majesties the King and Queen, 246 & 247 Tottenham Court Road (late of Leicester Square-established nearly 200 years)." By this time John Ward had incorporated Leveson & Sons, a firm that continued to manufacture invalid furniture and baby cars (*see* Leveson & Sons). John Ward, Ltd. is listed in the commercial directory for 1930 as "Invalid chair makers by appointment to their Majesties the King and Queen; builders of the 'Leveson' baby cars; established nearly 200 years; incorporating Leveson & Sons & Alderman, Johnson & Co. . . . invalid furniture head-quarters, 246 & 247 Tottenham court road . . . baby car showrooms, 26 Knightsbridge, SW1. . . . " (*see* John Alderman).

In 1940 John Ward, Ltd. is listed at 247 Tottenham Court Road as "invalids' chair makers" and also at 26 Knightsbridge. In 1950 John Ward, Ltd. is recorded as perambulator dealers at 21 Lamb's Conduit Street. In the 1955 directory the firm is described as "nursery outfitters & perambulator dealers" at the same address. The last year that John Ward, Ltd. appears in the London trade directory is 1958 as perambulator dealers at 21 Lamb's Conduit Street.

WELLS & LAMBE
(c. 1802–1890)

Wells & Lambe, portable writing desk and dressing case manufacturers, was founded in about 1802 by J. Wells.[115] According to the London commercial directories, Wells's partner, John Lambe, ran a Mineral Water Warehouse from 153 New Bond Street and 2 Leadenhall Street from 1790 to 1817. The directory for 1813 records the firm of J. Wells & Co., Portable Desk Manufactory, as trading from 34 Cockspur Street. The directory for 1823 lists Wells & Lambe, dressing case makers, at 44 New Bond Street. By 1825, the firm had moved to 29 Cockspur Street, where they are recorded through 1890.

GEORGE LANGFORD WILLIAMS
(c. 1854–1880)

George Langford Williams, trunk and camp equipage maker, was located at 41 New Bond Street in 1854, when he patented his design for a traveling bag. He is recorded in the London commercial directory for 1865 as a "trunk & portmanteau manufacturer, 41 New Bond Street." Williams last appears in the commercial directories in 1880.

THOMAS WILMOT
(c. 1800–1840)

Thomas Wilmot [*sic*], is listed in the London commercial directory for 1802 as a "Cabinet-maker" at "16 John-street, Oxford-street," London. Thomas Wilmott [*sic*] was mentioned in Sheraton's list of Master Cabinet Makers in 1803.[116] In 1805, T. Wilmot "Cabinet-maker" is recorded at 16 Great Portland Street, Oxford Street. From 1808 until 1824, T. Wilmot, "Cabinet-maker" is listed at the 16 John Street, Oxford Street address.

A maker's paper label affixed to a mirror at Phillips of Hitchin (Antiques) Ltd. reads: "T. Wilmott, / Upholder / Cabinet maker and Undertaker / No. 16, / John Street, Oxford Street / Imperial Dining Tables. / Sofa & Chair Beds on an Improved Principle."

There is no listing for this maker in the 1831 directory. In 1835 and 1838, Thomas Wilmot is listed as "Auctioneer & Appraiser" at 19 Grosvenor Street, W. Pimlico. In 1840, the listing reads: "Thomas Wilmot, Auctioneer & Appraiser, Estate & House agent and surveyor, 18 Grosvenor Street west, Eaton Square."

WILLIAM WILSON
(c. 1825–1850)

During the second quarter of the nineteenth century, the Scottish cabinet maker William Wilson used a paper label printed, "William Wilson, Edinburgh, 21 George St., Travelling and Dressing Cases, Portable Writing-Desks, Every Article in the Fancy Wood and Leather Line."

WINFIELD & SIMMS
(c. 1840–1853)

The firm of Winfield & Simms is recorded as a "Camp equipage manufacturer" at 26 New Bond Street in the London commercial directories from 1841 to 1852. In 1853 the firm is recorded as a camp equipage manufacturer at 141 Fleet Street.[117] (see Robert W. Winfield.)

ROBERT W. WINFIELD
(c. 1835–1890)

Robert Walter Winfield, who had an office at 141 Fleet Street, London, and a factory at Cambridge Street Works, Birmingham, was a patentee and manufacturer of plain and ornamental cased and patent tubes. Although his firm manufactured such everyday Victorian items as cornice-pole and curtain rings, picture hooks, rods and brackets, stair and carpet rods, brass name, door, and stall-board plates, it also manufactured portable brass arm chairs complete with Morocco leather arms and seats, as well as portable brass campaign beds. Winfield claimed he was "proprietor of the original patent" for his "metallic military bedsteads,"[118] one of which was illustrated in the official catalogue of the Great Exhibition in 1851.

In 1835, R.W. Winfield is listed in the commercial directory as "Brass-founder, Belle Sauvage Yard, Ludgate Hill."[119] In 1838 Robert W. Winfield is at 1 Belle Sauvage Yard, Ludgate Hill, and in 1839 and 1840 at 11 Belle Sauvage Yard, Ludgate Hill. In the 1842 and 1843 London commercial directories, Robert W. Winfield is listed as "Brassfounder, 141 Fleet Street." The firm maintained this London address at least until 1880, with works at Cambridge Street, Birmingham. In the 1852 and 1860 London commercial directories, the firm is recorded as "Brass bedstead maker and brass founder." An addendum to an advertisement in the 1861 commercial directory includes the following:

R W Winfield & Son's new and extensive show rooms contain specimens of their Patent Metallic Military / Travelling, and House Bedsteads, so much in use at home and abroad; with many other Articles of Furniture in Brass, Bronze Or-molu [sic] / and imitation of Silver; together with Gas Fittings of every description, and a variety of other Articles of Manufacture. The Portable / Bedsteads are admirably adapted for use in the Camp, or for travelling; also well-suited for Officers in the Army and Navy.

The Patent Ship Cot and Sofa is recommended to Invalids and Officers refitting; it will be found to prevent Sea-Sickness / and afford all of the comforts of a Bed upon Shore.

Robert W. Winfield & Co. placed the following advertisement in the London commercial directory for 1865:

R.W. Winfield & Co., Cambridge Street Works, Metal Rolling and Wire Mills, Birmingham, and 141, Fleet Street, London. Proprietor of the original patent for BRASS & IRON BEDSTEADS; and manufacturers of Sofas, Couches and Chairs; Gas chandeliers, Pillars, Brackets and Fittings, Patent Shades and Burners, of all kinds, and in various styles; Plain and Ornamental Tubing of every description, Rough and Finished; Patent Tubes, by the New Patent Process, whether Taper or Double; Brass Desk, Pew, Organ, and other Railing; Window Cornices, Patent Curtain Bands and Ends; Glass Cornice Rings; Locomotive Railings and Mouldings; Brass and Zinc name-plates; Shop Fronts; Sash Bars, etc.

Awards: The Council or First Class Medal was awarded in London at the Great Exhibition, 1851, to R.W. Winfield, for General Brass Foundry, Metallic Bedsteads, and Chandeliers. A Medal for Excellence of Workmanship in Bedsteads and Ornamental Tubing, was awarded to R.W. Winfield & Son, at the International Exhibition, 1862.

In the 1867 trade directory, the firm of Robert W. Winfield & Co., tube drawers, is still listed at 141 Fleet Street EC, with works at Cambridge Street, Birmingham. According to an advertisement placed in the 1880 London directory, the firm was awarded one bronze and three gold medals at the Paris Exhibition of 1878.

In the London commercial directories from 1884 to 1887 there is a listing for Robert W. Winfield at "47 Holborn Viaduct and 49 Farringdon Street; works, Cambridge Street, Birmingham." There are no listings for Robert W. Winfield after 1887, but the 1890 directory records "Winfield's Limited, brass and iron bedstead manufacturers, Cambridge Street works, Birmingham and 49 Farringdon St. [London]."(see Winfield & Simms.)

WREN BROTHERS
(c. 1852–1868)

In 1854 the firm of Wren Brothers was granted a patent for its design for a portable bed. In 1855 Wren Brothers is listed in the commercial directory at 232 Tottenham Court Road and 9 Sloane Street, Knightsbridge, as "Iron bedstead makers." From 1861 to the firm's last directory listing in 1868, John Wren is recorded at 231 Tottenham Court Road, as "Upholsterer."

Following is a list of the directories consulted:

FOR BRISTOL:

Mathew's Annual Bristol Directory (Bristol, published by Joseph Mathews): 1815, 1817, 1822, 1826, 1832, 1836, 1841, 1842, 1845, 1851, 1854, 1855, 1858, 1863, 1864, 1866, 1868, 1871, 1876, 1877, 1880, 1885, 1889, 1890, 1891.

FOR DUBLIN:

The Dublin Almanac and General Register of Ireland (Dublin: Pettigrew and Oulton): 1834, 1840, 1847.

Alexander Thom, *Thom's Irish Almanac and Official Directory* (Dublin): 1834, 1840, 1847, 1855, 1856, 1864, 1865, 1867, 1870, 1873, 1876, 1879, 1880, 1883, 1896, 1909.

FOR GLASGOW:

The Post Office Annual Directory for Glasgow, (Glasgow): 1852, 1869, 1870.

FOR LINCOLNSHIRE:

Kelly's Post Office Directory for Lincolnshire (London: Kelly & Co.): 1868.

FOR LIVERPOOL:

John Gore, *Gore's Liverpool Directory* (Liverpool: Young): 1805, 1810, 1825, 1864.

FOR LONDON:

Kelly's Post Office London Directories (London: W. Kelly & Co.): 1790, 1795, 1799, 1802, 1805, 1806, 1807, 1809, 1812, 1813, 1816, 1817, 1820, 1821, 1823, 1824, 1830, 1832, 1835, 1838, 1839, 1840, 1841, 1842, 1843, 1846, 1847, 1848, 1849, 1850, 1851, 1852, 1853, 1854, 1855, 1856, 1857, 1859, 1860, 1861, 1862, 1863, 1864, 1865, 1866, 1867, 1868, 1869, 1870, 1871, 1872, 1873, 1874, 1875, 1876, 1877, 1879, 1880, 1882, 1884, 1885, 1887, 1888, 1889, 1890, 1891, 1892, 1893, 1895, 1897, 1898, 1899, 1900, 1901, 1902, 1903, 1905, 1906, 1907, 1908, 1909, 1910, 1911, 1913, 1914, 1915, 1916, 1917, 1918, 1919, 1920, 1925, 1930, 1931, 1932, 1933, 1934, 1935, 1937, 1938, 1939, 1940, 1941, 1946, 1950, 1955, 1956, 1957, 1958, 1959, 1961, 1965, 1970, 1972, 1973, 1974, 1980.

Kent's Directory for London (London: Richard and Henry Causton): 1779, 1795, 1805, 1808, 1821, 1823, 1825.

The Post-Office London Directory (London: Richard G. Gunnell and William Shearman): 1831.

Lowndes' London Directory (London: T & W Lowndes): 1784, 1790, 1796, 1799.

Critchett & Woods Directory for London, The Post Office London Directory (London: Chapman & Roe): 1802, 1805, 1806, 1807, 1808, 1809, 1811, 1812, 1813, 1815, 1817, 1820, 1824, 1830, 1831, 1832, 1835.

Robson's London Commercial Directory (London: Robson, Blades & Co.): 1826, 1827.

FOR MANCHESTER:

Directory of the English Counties, Lancashire General Directory (Manchester): 1818, 1819, 1820, 1855, 1872, 1885, 1893, 1902.

FOR YORKSHIRE:

Kelly's Directory of Yorkshire (London: W. Kelly): 1854, 1865.

Notes

1. Issue 9, May/June, 1995, 10–11.
2. J. W. Allen is not recorded in the London commercial directory for 1914.
3. Christopher Gilbert, *Pictorial Dictionary of Marked London Furniture 1700–1840* (London: Furniture History Society and W. S. Maney and Son, 1996), 15.
4. Geoffrey Beard and Christopher Gilbert, eds. *Dictionary of English Furniture Makers 1660–1840* (London: The Furniture History Society and W. S. Maney and Son, 1986), 17.
5. Peter Johnson, "Camp Comforts," *Art & Antiques* (Feb 8, 1975), 18.
6. George and Robert Bengough do not appear in the London commercial directory for 1872.
7. John Bengough does not appear in the London commercial directory for 1869.
8. Gilbert, 18.
9. Beard and Gilbert, 78.
10. Bowring, Arundel & Co. does not appear in the London commercial directory for 1935.
11. Brown Brothers is not listed in the London commercial directory for 1873. The only listing in 1874 is for "Brown Brothers & Co., engineers, patentees and manufacturers of direct acting hoisting machinery, steam cranes, over-head steam travelers, hydraulic machinery, etc., at 80 Cannon Street."
12. Stanley Northcote-Bade, *Colonial Furniture in New Zealand* (Auckland, New Zealand: A. H. & A.W. Reed), 47.
13. Gilbert, 20.
14. Gilbert, 20.
15. *The Morning Herald*, Oct. 1, 1801.
16. British Museum, Banks Trade Card Collection, Reference 28.26.
17. British Museum, Banks Trade Card Collection, Reference 28.27.
18. John Carman is not listed in the London commercial directory for 1864.
19. J. & A. Carters is not listed in the London Commercial directory for 1973.
20. Beard and Gilbert, 164.
21. Sir Ambrose Heal, *London Furniture Makers 1660–1840* (London: B. T. Batsford, 1953), 36.
22. Title page reprinted in Oliver Brackett, *Thomas Chippendale: A Study of His Life, Work and Influence*, (London: Hodder & Stoughton, 1924), 39.
23. There is no listing for James Clifton in the 1874 London commercial directory.
24. Edward Corfield is not listed in the London commercial directory for 1919.
25. Beard and Gilbert, 209.
26. Beard and Gilbert, 236.
27. J. B. Saunders, "Camp Furniture for the Victorian Officer," *Army Museum '81:* 59.
28. See Helenka Gulshan, *Vintage Luggage*, 99.
29. A.W. Dear & Co. is not recorded in the London commercial directory for 1941.
30. Gilbert, 26.
31. Gilbert, 26. Anthony Eckardt does not appear in the London commercial directories for 1799 or 1802.
32. Gilbert, 27.
33. James Findon is not recorded in the London commercial directory for 1852.
34. There is no listing for William Gaimes in the London commercial directory for 1820.
35. Geoffrey Beard, *The National Trust Book of English Furniture* (London: Viking, 1985), 164.
36. Summer, 1996 (no. 24), 338B.
37. Handford & Son does not appear in the London commercial directories between 1790 and 1799.
38. British Museum, Banks Trade Card Collection, Reference 28.73.
39. Helenka Gulshan, *Vintage Luggage*, 108.
40. I would like to thank Jane Taylor, Publicity Manager at Heal & Son Limited, for providing information on the company's history.
41. Information kindly provided by Heal & Son Limited.
42. Information kindly provided by Heal & Son Limited.
43. Sir Ambrose Heal, 81.
44. Heal, 81.
45. Beard and Gilbert, 422.
46. Beard and Gilbert, 422.
47. Gilbert, 34.
48. Gilbert, 34.
49. Sotheby's London, June 4 1999, lot 224.
50. Hill & Millard is not recorded in the London commercial directory for 1937.
51. Beard and Gilbert, 432.
52. Beard and Gilbert, 589.

53. Sir Ambrose Heal, 95.
54. Beard and Gilbert, 589.
55. Ralph Edwards, introduction, *The Universal System of Household Furniture* by Ince and Mayhew (1762; London: Alec Tiranti, 1960), j.
56. James Pigot & Co., *Royal, National, and Commercial Directory*, 97.
57. Edward Johnson is not recorded in the London commercial directory for 1852.
58. W. R. Harvey, *Mrs. Plante's Dressing Table*, (London: W. R. Harvey & Co.), 40.
59. Art Journal, *Illustrated Catalogue of the London Exhibition* (1862), 207.
60. *See* Desmond FitzGerald, the Knight of Glin, "Dublin Directories & Trade Labels," *Furniture History* (1985), 268.
61. "Dublin Directories and Trade Labels," in *Furniture History* (1985), 268.
62. "Dublin Directories and Trade Labels," 268.
63. "Dublin Directories and Trade Labels," 268.
64. XXI, Leeds, 1985, 279.
65. Lane & Billing is not recorded in the London commercial directory for 1842.
66. British Museum, Banks Trade Card Collection, Reference 132.74.
67. There is no listing for J & W Lowndes in the London commercial directory for 1851.
68. There is no listing for Henry Manning in the London commercial directory for 1873.
69. Directories for the years 1836 and 1837 were not available in either the National Arts Library, London, or the New York Public Library.
70. The chair is illustrated in Northcote-Bade's *Colonial Furniture in New Zealand*, 105, fig. 72.
71. Bristol Record Office, Document no. 12151 (15).
72. Ambrose Foote, ed., *The Bristol Presentment: or, BILL OF ENTRY*, vol. XL, no. 4136, November 11, 1858.
73. British Museum, Banks Trade Card Collection, Reference 120.12.
74. There is no listing for William Millard in the London commercial directory for 1856.
75. *The Repository of Arts*, London: R. Ackermann, July 1809, 122.
76. *The Times*, April 3, 1816.
77. British Museum, Banks Trade Card Collection, Reference 28.99.
78. British Museum, Banks Trade Card Collection, Reference 28.100.
79. William Foster, *The East India House* (London: John Lane, The Bodley Head, 1924), 128.
80. The trade card is reproduced in the December 1784 issue of the *Gentleman's Magazine*, as well as in *The East India House* by William Foster, p. 129, and *The London Furniture Makers 1660–1840* by Sir Ambrose Heal, 133.
81. William Foster, 128–29.
82. William Foster, 127–28.
83. Beard and Gilbert, 668–69.
84. Beard and Gilbert, 669.
85. Beard and Gilbert, 669.
86. British Museum, Banks Trade Card Collection, Reference 28.108.
87. Gilbert, 45.
88. London, Public Record Office, F.O. 185/50, Spain 1814.
89. Mrs. Elizabeth Powell is not recorded in the London commercial directory for 1853.
90. Edward Pratt is not recorded in the London commercial directory for 1872.
91. There is no listing for Henry Pratt, Jr. in the London commercial directory for 1869.
92. Gilbert, 46.
93. Desmond FitzGerald, the Knight of Glin, "Dublin Directories and Trade Labels," *Furniture History* (1985), 271.
94. William Schnell is not listed in the London commercial directory for 1861.
95. *See* Gilbert, 48.
96. Gilbert, 48.
97. Gilbert, 48.
98. Beard and Gilbert, 806.
99. Beard and Gilbert, 806.
100. *See* London Society of Cabinet-Makers, *The Cabinet-Maker's London Book of Prices*, 1788, 219, 222, 225; plate 25, and fig. 3.
101. Sir Ambrose Heal, 166.
102. *Reports and Awards of Jurors*, New Zealand, 1866, 290.
103. It is illustrated in Northcote-Bade, *Colonial Furniture in New Zealand*, 36, fig. 14.
104. Beard and Gilbert, 823.
105. There is no listing for Smith & Cobay in the London commercial directory for 1906.
106. Gilbert, 51.
107. Peter Philp, "Campaigning In Style," *Antique Dealer and Collector's Guide*, Aug. 1990: 36–40.
108. Charles Symons is not listed in the 1856 London commercial directory.
109. *Great Exhibition of the Works of Industry of all Nations, 1851: Official Descriptive and Illustrated Catalogue*, vol. 2 (London: Spicer Brothers, 1851), 730.
110. Benjamin Taylor & Sons is not recorded in the London commercial directory for 1877.
111. Gilbert, 52.
112. Gilbert, 52.
113. Vol. 6, May–August, nos. 21–24.
114. The firm is not recorded in the London commercial directory for 1938.
115. Gilbert, 55.
116. Gilbert, 56.
117. Winfield & Simms is not recorded in the London commercial directory for 1855.
118. Beard and Gilbert, 991.
119. R. W. Winfield is not recorded in the London commercial directory for 1831.

Bibliography

Ackermann, Rudolph. *The Repository of Arts, Literature, Commerce, Manufactures, Fashions, and Politics.* London: R. Ackermann, 1809–1814.

Allen, Charles. *A Glimpse of the Burning Plain: Leaves from the Indian Journals of Charlotte Canning.* London: Michael Joseph, 1986.

Allen, Charles, ed. *Plain Tales From the Raj: Images of British India in the Twentieth Century.* London: Andre Deutsch, 1975.

Annesley, George. (Lord Valentia). *Voyages and Travels to India, Ceylon, the Red Sea, Abyssinia and Egypt in 1802–1806*, 3 vols. London: F. C. & J. Rivington, 1809.

Anonymous. *The Navy "At Home,"* 3 vols. London: William Marsh, 1831.

Anonymous. *Tom Raw, The Griffin: A Burlesque Poem, In Twelve Cantos.* London: R. Ackermann, 1828.

Archer, Mildred. *India and British Portraiture 1770–1825.* London: Sotheby Parke Bernet, 1979.

Art Journal. *Illustrated Catalogue of the London Exhibition.* London: 1862.

Austen, Brian. "Morgan & Sanders and the Patent Furniture Makers of Catherine Street," *The Connoisseur* (Nov. 1974), 180–191.

Austen, Jane. *Persuasion.* (1818; Oxford, Oxford University Press, 1988).

Barty-King, Hugh. *Maples: Fine Furnishers.* London: Quiller Press, 1992.

Beard, Geoffrey. *The National Trust Book of English Furniture.* London: Viking, 1985.

Beard, Geoffrey, and Christopher Gilbert, eds. *Dictionary of English Furniture Makers 1660–1840.* London: Furniture History Society and W. S. Maney & Son, 1986.

Boyd, Hugh. "Fashion in Men's Clothes," *The Indian Observer*, XIX, Dec. 10, 1793.

Brackett, Oliver. *Thomas Chippendale: A Study of His Life, Work and Influence*, London: Hodder & Stoughton, 1924.

Burton, Richard. *Tigers of the Raj: The Shikar Diaries of Colonel Burton 1894 to 1949.* Gloucester, England: Alan Sutton, 1987.

Carew, Tim. *How The Regiments Got Their Nicknames.* London: Leo Cooper, 1974.

Chippendale, Thomas. *The Gentleman and Cabinet-Maker's Director.* Third ed. London: Privately printed, 1762.

Conner, Patrick. *100° in the Shade: Military and Domestic Life in India, 1800–1860.* Exhibition

Catalogue. Martyn Gregory Gallery, London, 1999.

Curzon, George Nathaniel. *Tales of Travel.* London: Century, 1988.

Deitz, Paula. "Providing the Comforts of Home in War," *New York Times*, July 1, 1982, C10.

De Plas, S. *Les Meubles à Transformation et à Secret.* Paris: G. Le Prat, 1975.

Dickinson, Lt. Col. R. J. *Officer's Mess: Life and Customs in the Regiments.* Tunbridge Wells: Midas, 1973.

Eden, Emily. *Up the Country: Letters Written to Her Sister from the Upper Provinces of India.* Oxford: Oxford University Press, 1930.

Edwardes, Michael. *The Nabobs at Home.* London: Constable, 1991.

Edwards, Clive. "Folding Chairs," *Antique Collecting* (August 24, 1990), 5–8.

"Equipping an Officer and a Gentleman," *The Armourer* (May/June 1995), 10–11.

Farwell, Byron. *Mr. Kipling's Army*. New York: W. W. Norton, 1981.

Fastnedge, Ralph. *Sheraton Furniture*. London: Faber and Faber, 1962.

FitzGerald, Desmond, the Knight of Glin, "Dublin Directories & Trade Labels," *Furniture History Society Journal*, 1985.

Foster, William. *The East India House: Its History and Associations*. London: John Lane, The Bodley Head Ltd., 1924.

Galton, Francis. *The Art of Travel; or, Shifts and Contrivances Available in Wild Countries*. Eighth ed. London: John Murray, 1893.

"Georgian Knock-Down Furniture," *The Times* (Sept. 5, 1964), 11.

Gilbert, Christopher. *English Vernacular Furniture 1750–1900*. New Haven and London: Yale University Press, 1991.

———. *Pictorial Dictionary of Marked London Furniture 1700–1840*. London: Furniture History Society and W. S. Maney and Son, 1996.

Goradia, Nayana. *Lord Curzon: The Last of the British Moghuls*. Delhi: Oxford University Press, 1993.

Graham, Col. Henry. *History of the Sixteenth, The Queen's, Light Dragoons (Lancers), 1912–1925*. Devizes, Wiltshire: George Simpson & Co., 1926.

Great Exhibition of the Works of Industry of all Nations, 1851: Official Descriptive and Illustrated Catalogue. 3 vols., vol. 2. London: Spicer Brothers, 1851.

Gronow, Captain Rees Howell. *Gronow's Last Recollections; Being the Fourth and Final Series of his Reminiscences and Anecdotes*. London: Smith, Elder & Co., 1866.

Grose, Francis. *Advice to the Officers of the British Army* (1783; New York: Agathynian Club, 1867).

Gulshan, Helenka. *Vintage Luggage*. London: Philip Wilson, 1998.

Harris, R. G. *Bengal Cavalry Regiments 1857–1914*. London: Osprey, 1979.

Hay, Kate. "Just Sit Back and Enjoy Yourself," *Country Life* (May 21, 1998), 68–69.

Heal, Sir Ambrose. *London Furniture Makers: From the Restoration to the Victorian Era 1660–1840*. London: Portman Books, 1988.

Hepplewhite, A. & Co. *The Cabinet-Maker and Upholsterer's Guide*. (1787; New York, Towse Publishing Company, 1942).

Hibbert, Christopher. ed. *Captain Gronow: His Reminiscences of Regency and Victorian Life 1810–60*. London: Kyle Cathie, 1991.

———. *The English: A Social History 1066–1945*. New York: W. W. Norton, 1987.

Hughes, G. Bernard. "Furniture for the Regency Traveller," *Country Life* (March 2, 1967), 452–453.

———."Regency Patent Furniture," *Country Life* (January 2, 1958), 10–12.

Ince, William, and John Mayhew. *The Universal System of Household Furniture*. London: 1759–62.

James, Charles. *The Regimental Companion, Containing the Pay, Allowances, and Relative Duties of Every Officer in the British Service*. 4 vols., seventh ed., London, 1813.

Johnson, Peter. "Camp Comforts: A Roll-Call of Campaign Furniture," *Art & Antiques* (Feb. 8, 1975), 18–23.

———. "Camp Following," *Country Homes and Interiors* (January 1991), 26–27.

Joy, Edward T. "Early Nineteenth-Century Invalid Etc. Furniture," *Furniture History* (1974), 74–77.

———. "Pocock's—The Ingenious Inventors," *The Connoisseur* (February 1970), 88–92.

———. *English Furniture 1800–1851*. London: Sotheby Parke Bernet, 1977.

Kaye, M. M., ed. *The Golden Calm: An English Lady's Life in Moghul Delhi*. New York: Viking, 1980.

Kemp, Peter K., ed. "Boscawen's Letters to His Wife," *The Naval Miscellany*, 4. London: Navy Records Society, 1952, 163–256.

Lejeune, Anthony. *The Gentlemen's Clubs of London*. London: Studio Editions, 1984.

Lloyd, Christopher, and R. C. Anderson, eds. *A Memoir of James Trevenen*. London: Navy Records Society, 1959.

Loudon, J. C. *An Encyclopaedia of Cottage, Farm, and Villa Architecture and Furniture*. (1833; London: Longman, Brown, Green, and Longmans, 1853).

Lunt, James. *Charge to Glory! A Garland of Cavalry Exploits*. London: Heinemann, 1960.

Luxton, Brian. "Campaign Comfort," *Phillips Review* (June 1990).

Macaulay, Thomas Babington. Critical and Historical Essays, 3 vols. vol. 2. New York and Boston: Houghton Mifflin & Co., 1901.

MacMillan, Margaret. *Women of the Raj*. New York: Thames and Hudson, 1988.

MacQuoid, Percy, and Ralph Edwards. *The Dictionary of English Furniture: From the Middle Ages to the Late Georgian Period*. Second ed., 3 vols. London: Country Life, 1954.

Maiden, Sydney J. "A Wedding Present of 1863: An Officer's Travelling Furniture," *The Connoisseur* (May 1957), 168–171.

Martin, Thomas. *The New Circle of the Mechanical Arts.* London: J. Bumpus, 1819.

Meadmore, Clement. *The Modern Chair: Classics in Production.* New York: Van Nostrand Reinhold & Co., 1975.

Mercer, General Cavalié. *Journal of the Waterloo Campaign.* Edinburgh; London: William Blackwood and Sons, 1870.

Morris, James. *Heaven's Command: An Imperial Progress.* San Diego, New York, and London: Harvest, 1973.

———. *Farewell the Trumpets: An Imperial Retreat.* New York: Harcourt Brace Jovanovich, 1978.

Munday, John. "Captains and Cabins," *The Connoisseur* (Feb. 1979), 90–97.

Myerly, Scott Hughes. *British Military Spectacle.* Cambridge, Massachusetts: Harvard University Press, 1996.

Newark, George and Christopher. *Kipling's Soldiers.* Essex: The Pompadour Gallery, 1993.

Northcote-Bade, Stanley. *Colonial Furniture in New Zealand.* Auckland: A. H. & A. W. Reed, 1971.

Nutting, Wallace. "Double-Purpose Furniture," *The Magazine Antiques* (October 1940), 160–62.

O'Malley, L. S. S. *The Indian Civil Service 1601–1930.* London: John Murray, 1931.Penzer, Norman Mosley. "Thoughts on Coasters," *Apollo* (June 1954), 197–98.

Phillips, Jerome. "Exhibition of Furniture for Travel 1760–1860." (June 6–30, 1987), Phillips of Hitchin (Antiques) Ltd., Hitchin, Hertfordshire.

———. "Exhibition of Travelling and Campaigning Furniture 1790–1850." (June 3–30, 1984), Phillips of Hitchin (Antiques) Ltd., Hitchin, Hertfordshire.

Philp, Peter. "Campaigning in Style," *Antique Dealer and Collector's Guide* (August 1990), 36–40.

Reports and Awards of the Jurors, New Zealand Exhibition, 1865. Dunedin, New Zealand: Mills, Dick & Co., 1866.

Rieder, William. "Campaign Furniture: Ingenious Designs that Combine Style and Portability," *Architectural Digest* (July 1995), 102–107, 140.

Rosoman, Treve. "Field Furniture," *Traditional Homes* (February 1985), 38–43.

———. "Military Furniture," *Antique Collectors' Club* (April 1985), 44–46.

———. "Some Aspects of Eighteenth-Century Naval Furniture," *Furniture History*, 33, 1997, 120–27.

Roth, Rodris. "Seating for Anyplace: The Folding Chair," in *Victorian Furniture: Essays from a Victorian Society Autumn Symposium.* Philadelphia, Pennsylvania: The Victorian Society in America, 1982.

Russell, Frank, ed. *A Century of Chair Design.* New York: Rizzoli, 1980.

Saunders, J. B. "Camp Furniture of the Victorian Officer," *Army Museum '81*, 50–56.

———. "The Ubiquitous 'X' Chair," *National Army Museum Year Book 1*, Jan. 4, 1988–Mar. 31, 1989, 38.

Sheraton, Thomas. *The Cabinet Dictionary*, 2 vols. (London, 1803).

Shinn, Deborah Sampson, J. G. Links, Paul Fussell, and Ralph Caplan. *Bon Voyage: Designs for Travel.* New York: Cooper-Hewitt Museum, The Smithsonian Institution's National Museum of Design, 1986.

Starke, Mariana. *Information and Directions for Travellers on the Continent.* Fifth ed. London: John Murray, 1824.

Steel, Flora Annie Webster. *The Complete Indian Housekeeper and Cook.* London: William Heinemann, 1909.

Sutherland, Douglas. *Debrett's The English Gentleman.* London: Debrett's Peerage, 1978.

Symonds, R. W. "Pre-Chippendale Furniture at Nostell Priory," *Country Life* (April 25, 1952), 1248–1249.

The Report of the Kabul Committee on Equipment. Calcutta, 1882.

Thornton, James. *Your Most Obedient Servant: James Thornton, Cook to the Duke of Wellington.* Exeter: Webb & Bower, 1985.

Twigger, Robert. "Inflation: The Value of the Pound 1750–1998," House of Commons Research Paper 99/20, February 23, 1999.

Ward, J. D. U. "Furniture for Reclining," *The Magazine Antiques* (February 1953), 128–29.

Young, G. M. *Early Victorian England 1830–1865*, vol. 2, London; New York: Oxford University Press, Humphrey Milford, 1934.

Index

Note: Page numbers in *italics* refer to illustrations

A

Ackermann, Rudolph, *Repository of Arts*, 28, 34, 114
Adam, Robert, 51
advertisements, 157–58
    Allen, *65*, 98, *161*, 162
    Brown Brothers, 168, *168*
    Butler, 34, 76, 88, 98, *100*, *101*, 170–71
    Day, 98, *99*, 159
    Hill & Millard, 159, *184*
    Jarvis, 39, *39*
    Morgan & Sanders, *35*, 76, 98
    Pocock, *28*, 103
    Thompson, 75
    Ward, 212
    see also trade cards
Advice to the Officers of the British Army (Grose), 57, 130, 131
"Aesthetics of Dress. Military Costume" (1846), 57
Alderman, John, 159–60, 213
    brass plaques, *159*, *160*
    Chapman and Alderman, 105, 160
    traveling or invalid's chair, 77, 105, *105*, 212
    washstand, *159*
Alderman, Johnson & Co. Limited, 160, 213
Aldershot camp outfits, 64, 162
Aldershot drawers, *94*, 95
Alexander I, Czar, 154
Allders, 190
Allen, John, 160–62
    barrack room furniture, 160–61
    trade label, *161*
Allen, John, William, and Thomas, 160
    portable chair, *161*
Allen, J. W., 161–62
    advertisements, *65*, 98, *162*

Aldershot camp outfit, 64
    barrack room furniture, *2–3*, *4*, 62, 64, 161–62
    Douro chair, *61*, 64
Allen's, advertisement, *161*
American War for Independence (1775–1783), 109
apothecary's traveling compendium, Victorian mahogany, *130*
Archer, Fulbert, 191
Argles, Edward, 162, 170, 192–93
    brass plaque, *162*
    Regency mahogany caned chair-bed, 162, *163*
"Armchair 905" (Magistretti), 73
Army & Navy Co-operative Society, 69, 163, 181
    Bellamy West African Carrier, 91–92, *92*, 93
    candlesticks, *134*, *135*
    carrying chair, 172
    chests, 61, *63*, 108
    daybeds, 198
    Douro chairs, 61
    lamps, *134*, *135*
    military chest of drawers, *94*, 95
    parlor suites, 41
Army and Navy Stores Limited, 163
Army & Navy Warehouse, 211
Army General Orders, 61
Army List, The, 64
Artist's Ascent of Ram Ghat, Belgaum, The (Bellasis), 92, *93*
Artist's Cabin on the Malabar (Bellasis), *85*
assembly, ease of, 76–87
    disassembly and, 76, 77, *78*, *83*, *87*, *121*
    of Roorkhee chair, 73
    for shipboard furniture, 77, 79, 84–85
    trigger mechanism for, 76, *77*
Atkinson, Capt. George F., "Scenes in Camp," 49–50, *49*
Auckland, Lord George, 43
Austen, Jane, 36
Austin, George, 164
    maker's paper label, *164*
    Victorian brass-bound mahogany spirits case, *164*

B

backgammon, chess, and draught board, *185*
Barker, Albert, Ltd., 165
    late Victorian brass-bound mahogany campaign table, *165*
    late Victorian oak campaign writing desk, *165*
barrack room furniture, 2–3, 4, 62, 64, 73, 99, 120, 146–52, 160–62, 184
Barrackpore, Government House, 55
"Basculant" chair (Le Corbusier), 71, 73
bassinette or cradle, *172*
Bauhaus School, 73
Bayley, William & Co., 166
Bayley & Blew, 166
Bayley & Co., 166
Bayley & Lowe, 166
beds:
    bureau-bedstead, 111, *113*, *114*
    camp, 31, 64, 101, *102*
    chair, 79, *82*, *126*, 162, *163*
    child's, George III brass-bound mahogany and caned, *153*
    convertible daybed or settle bed, *155*
    cushioned, 51
    elegant hangings for, 35, 98, 99, *100*, 120
    field, 32, *33*, 76
    four-poster, 64, 76, *76*, 102, *103*
    George III brass-mounted mahogany four-poster, 102, *103*
    George III mahogany and beechwood patented, *170*
    insects repelled from, 8–9, 101, 114
    invalid, 28, 103, 104, *105*
    light military traveling, *75*
    metallic, 29, 76, 101, 103, 114
    "pack saddle" boxes and bedstead, *48*
    portable camp bedstead, *167*
    Regency gilt-brass, 76, *76*, 101
    traveling throne and, 39
    Victorian caned mahogany adjustable daybed, *198*, *199*
    Wellington and, 103, *104*
    see also sofa-beds
Bellamy West African Carrier, 91–92, *92*, *93*
Bellasis, John Brownrigg, 50, 84
    Artist's Ascent of Ram Ghat, The, 92, *93*
    Artist's Cabin on the Malabar, *85*
    Hunting Party Breakfast, 57, *58*
    Midday Halt: Marching, 8–9
Bengal Club, The, 51
Bengal Lancers, 108
Bengough, George, Robert, and John, 166
    portmanteau, *166*
Beresford, Capt. John P., 77, 79
bidets, early Victorian mahogany, 27
Blades & Palmer, 167
Blair, John, 167
BO (British Board of Ordnance), 59
Boer War (1899–1902), 67, 69, 71, 73
Boethema, or rising mattress, 103, 104
Bofinger, Wilhelm, "Farmer Chair," 73

Bolton, Frances Mary (Simner), 43
Bombay Yacht Club, The, 51
bookcases:
    with chests, 61, 64
    George IV mahogany, *78*
    portable, 74, 76–77, *78*
    Regency brass-mounted mahogany, 21, *127*
    Victorian mahogany open, 74
Boscawen, Adm. Edward, 36, 86
Bosworth, 191
Bowring, Arundel & Co., 167
    "pack saddle" boxes and bedstead, 48, *48*
boxes:
    dressing-table, *142*, *176*
    iron-clamped, 62
    markings on, 61
    "pack saddle," 48, *48*
Boyd, Hugh, 50
Bradshaw, William, 167
    bedstead, *167*
Bramah-type locks, 94
brass beds, Regency, 76, *76*, 101
brass handles, 77, 79, 124
Breuer, Marcel, "Wassily" chair, 71, 72–73, *73*
"Brighton Buns" candlesticks, *134*, *135*
British Board of Ordnance (BO), 59
Broad Arrow stamp, 59
broadsheets, *see* advertisements
Brown, Hamilton, 103
Brown, Joseph, 168
Brown Brothers, 167–68
    advertisement, 168, *168*
Brummell, George "Beau," 57
Burdet, 169
    bedstead, *169*
bureau, mahogany two-part, 79, *80*
bureau-bedstead, 111, *113*, *114*
Butler, Thomas, 169–71, 192–93, 195, 196, 198, 205
    advertising, 34, 76, 88, 98, *100*, 101, 170–71
    bedsteads, 76, 101, 102, 103, *170*
    brass plaques, *170*, *171*
    dining table, *171*
butler's tray, 111, *112*
Byron, Lord (George Gordon), 101, 103

C

Cabinet Dictionary (Sheraton), 29, 31, 32, 36, 77, 206
Cabinet-Maker and Upholsterer's Guide, The (Hepplewhite), 32, 136, 183, 206
Cabinet Makers' and Upholsterers' Drawing Book (Sheraton), 206
Cabinet Maker's London Book of Prices, The (Hepplewhite), 136, 206
Caesar, Julius, 89
Calcutta, Government House, 51, 54, *54*, 56
Caldwell, William, 172
Cambrian, 77, 79

campaign furniture, use of term, *157*
Campaigning in Style (Philp), 98
Campaign in India, The (Atkinson), 49–50
camp equipage:
    austerity of, 73
    balanced load on horse's back, *182*
    domestic demand for, 111, 116
    invoice for, 44, *45*
    mobility of, 69, 88–93, *121*
    prestige of, 44, *45*, 46–48, 59, 62, 64
camp stools, *178*, *179*
candlesticks, *134*, *135*
caning, 97–98
    early Victorian mahogany armchair, *96*, 97
    George III brass-bound mahogany child's bed, *153*
    George III mahogany folding chair, *85*, *86*
    Regency mahogany chair-bed, *162*, *163*
    Regency mahogany sofa-bed, *25*
    Victorian mahogany adjustable daybed, *198*, *199*
Canning, Lady Charlotte, 55, 101
Capper, John & Son, 172
    bassinette or cradle, *172*
Capper, Son & Co., 172
Cardwell, Edward, 64
Carman, John, 172
Carters, J. & A., 172–73
Cavalry and Guards Club, London, 68
chair-beds, 79, 82, 126, *162*, *163*
chair couch, 154
chairs:
    adjusting arm for, 98
    "Armchair 905" (Magistretti), 73
    "Basculant" (Le Corbusier), 71, 73
    camp stools, *178*, *179*
    carrying, 172
    dining, Victorian mahogany (set of four), *152*
    dining, Victorian oak (set of six), *203*
    dining, William IV mahogany, *24*
    Douro, *2–3*, *4*, *6–7*, 61, *61*, 64
    early Victorian caned mahogany, *96*, 97
    elongated portable, *161*
    "Farmer" (Bofinger), 73
    folding rocking, *210*
    George III caned mahogany folding, *85*, *86*
    Georgian officer's mahogany armchair, *125*
    invalid's, 77, 105, *105*, 172, 212–13, *212*
    Irish Victorian mahogany, *200*
    mid-eighteenth-century mahogany, *154*
    for officers, 59
    packing box for, 62
    padded arms for, 97, 98, *98*
    patents for, 116
    reclining, *199*
    recumbent and easy, *191*
    Regency brass-inlaid mahogany, *122*
    Roorkhee, *66*, 70, 71–73, *71*, *72*, 92, *92*

    "Safari" (Klint), 71, 73
    self-propelling, 105
    side, Victorian mahogany, *201*
    upholstered, 51
    Victorian caned mahogany armchair, *151*
    "Wassily" (Breuer), 71, 72–73, *73*
Chapman, T., 105
Chapman, Thomas, 159, 160
Chapman and Alderman, 105, 160
chests:
    in balanced mule load, 61, *182*
    brass-bound military, *18*, 59, *60*, 61, *63*
    bureau-bedstead, 111, *113*, 114
    combinations, *18*, 61, *63*, 64
    dressing case, escritoire, drawers combined, *186*
    English iron-bound leather trunk, *156*
    late George III brass-mounted mahogany two-part *secrétaire*-
        military, *18*
    mahogany two-part traveling bureau, 79, *80*
    maximum size of, 61
    mirrors in, 61, *63*, 79
    Regency teak two-part military, *124*
    sea, 79, *85*
    with *secrétaires*, *18*, 61, 79, *80*, *81*, *124*, *147*
    secret compartments in, 106, *106*, *107*, 108
    stored under bed, 85
    Victorian brass-mounted mahogany, of Aldershot or hut
        drawers, *94*, *95*
    Victorian brass-mounted mahogany two-part with *secrétaire*, *81*
    Victorian brass-mounted mahogany with *secrétaire* drawer, *147*
    Victorian mahogany two-part, *148*
    Victorian military, *204*
chiffonier, Victorian walnut, *40*, 41
Chippendale, Thomas, 29, 117, 173
    chair couch, *154*
    field beds, *32*
    Gentleman and Cabinet-Maker's Director, *32*, 173, 185
Clifton, James, 173
Clive of India, Lord Robert, 38–39, 54–55, 117
clothing, 48–49, 50, 51, 56–59, 68
Cole, J. J., 103, 104
comfort and durability, 94–105
Complete Indian Housekeeper and Cook, The, 94
copying machines, *106*, *107*, 177, 180
Corbett, Lt.-Col. Jim, 72, *72*
Corbusier, Le, "Basculant" chair, 71, 73
Corfield, Edward, 173
cork, furniture in, 61
Cottrell, Alfred, 173
couch, chair, 154
cradle or bassinette, *172*
Crew, Samuel, 174
Crocodile, 84
Crystal Palace, Great Exhibition (1851), 61
Curzon, Lord George Nathaniel, 56, 69, 90, 117
Curzon, Lady Mary Victoria Leiter, 89, 90, *90*

INDEX / 223

D

Day, W. & Son, 174
    advertisements, 98, *99*, *159*
    Douro chairs, *61*
Day, William, 103, 174
daybeds:
    convertible settle bed or, *155*
    Victorian caned mahogany adjustable, *198*, *199*
Dear, Arthur William, 174
    Edwardian mahogany table, *175*
Debonnaire, Ann, 50, *51*
desks:
    carved elm or mahogany, *51*, *69*
    chests with *secrétaires*, *18*, 61, 79, 80, *81*, *124*, *147*
    copying machines and, *106*, 107, 177, 180
    dispatch boxes as, 108
    dressing case, escritoire, drawers combined, *186*
    George III mahogany slant-front, *80*
    George IV brass-mounted mahogany, *209*
    late George III mahogany writing, *20*
    late Victorian brass-bound coromandel, *133*
    late Victorian oak, *165*
    Victorian brass-bound mahogany, *132*
    Victorian oak pedestal, *37*, *38*
    washbasin and, *26*, *27*
Devis, Arthur William, *Hon. and Mrs. William Monson*, 50, *51*
dining chairs, *see* chairs
dining tables, 29
    "Colonial," *39*
    George IV brass-mounted mahogany concertina-action, *30*
    Regency brass-mounted mahogany collapsible draw-leaf, *85*, *87*
    Regency mahogany extending, *171*
    Regency mahogany "Imperial," *193*
    washbasin and, *26*, *27*
    see also tables
dinner wagon or sideboard, *190*
directory, 157–214
dispatch boxes, *106*, *107*, 108
"Double-Purpose Furniture" (Nutting), 114, 154
Douro chairs, *2–3*, *4*, *6–7*, 61, *61*, 64
D'Oyly, Charles, *Summer Room in the Artist's House*, 51, *52–53*
Dragoon Guards, 48, 64, 135
dressing case, escritoire, drawers combined, *186*
dressing-table boxes:
    brass-mounted mahogany, *142*
    Regency brass-bound mahogany, *176*
durability and comfort, 94–105
Durham, John, 174, 193

E

East India Company, 168, 194–95
East Is East And West Is West (Mills), *91*
Eckhardt, Anthony, 175
    George III mahogany table, *175*
Eden, Hon. Emily, 43, 89

Edgington, Benjamin, Limited, 208
Edwardian furniture:
    mahogany and brass-mounted coaching table, *150*
    mahogany campaign table, *175*
Edwards, Clive, 116
Edwards, David, 176
    Regency brass-bound mahogany dressing-table box, *176*
Edwards, Ralph, 136, 185
Edwards, Thomas, 177
Encyclopedia of Cottage, Farm, and Villa Architecture and Furniture (Loudon), 83, 112, 114
enlisted men's furnishings, *see* barrack room furniture; camp equipage
escritoires:
    dressing case and drawers combined, *186*
    hidden drawers in, 108
Euphrates, 84
Express Camel, 10
Eyles, Thomas, 177

F

"Farmer Chair" (Bofinger), 73
Farwell, Byron, 56
Fastenedge, Ralph, 114
Faudel, Phillips & Son, 207
Field, Marshall, 90
field officer's quarters, 43–44, 48
Finden, James, 177
Finsbury Cabinet works, 208
Fitzclarence, Lord Frederick, 34, 36
Flanders Campaign (1793–1795), 44, 46, 211
Fletcher, George & Co., 177
Foot Guards, 64
fork and knife, Victorian, *145*
Foster, William, 194–95
Fowler, W., *Portrait of Lieutenant General Robert Ballard Long*, *45*
Franco-Prussian War (1870–1871), 64
French and Indian War (1756–1763), 109
Fry, C. I., *His Excellency the Viceroy's Bodyguard*, *110*
Fryer, John, 177
Fussell, Paul, 106, 110

G

Gaimes, William, 177
Galton, Francis, 89
games board, *185*
games tables, *22*, *23*, *138*, *139*
Gentleman and Cabinet-Maker's Director, The (Chippendale), 32, 173, 185
George II metamorphic mahogany sofa-bed, 154, *155*
George III furniture:
    brass-bound mahogany and caned child's bed, *153*
    brass-mounted mahogany four-poster bedstead, *102*, 103
    brass-mounted mahogany two-part military chest-*secrétaire*, *18*

caned mahogany folding chair, 85, *86*
mahogany and beechwood patented bedstead, *170*
mahogany occasional table, *129*
mahogany portable table, *175*
mahogany slant-front desk, *80*
mahogany traveling rent table, *115*
mahogany writing desk, *20*
George IV furniture:
    brass-mounted mahogany concertina-action table, *30*
    brass-mounted mahogany traveling desk, *209*
    games table, *139*
    mahogany campaign bookcase, *78*
Georgian furniture, *120*, *121*
    officer's mahogany armchair, *125*
Gillow, 117, 178
Gillow, Robert, 178
Gillow Estimate Sketch Book, 111, *113*
Gillow of Lancaster, games table, *22*
Gillow of Lancaster and London, 178
Goldsmith, Oliver, 114
Government House:
    Barrackpore, 55
    Calcutta, 51, 54, *54*, 56
Grant, Capt. Hope, 90
Great Exhibition, Crystal Palace (1851), 61
Green, Charles, 178
    camp stool design, *178*
    Victorian mahogany folding camp stool, *179*
Grenfell, Capt. Julian Henry Francis, 48
Gresham & Craven, 179
Gronow, Capt. Rees Howell, *Reminiscences*, 58–59
Grose, Francis, 57, 130, 131
guests, extra, 153–56

H

Habitat/Mothercare, 182
Hakewill, James, 179
Hampton & Sons, 179–80
Hancock, Thomas, sofa-beds, 154, *155*
Handford, Thomas, 180
    trade card, *180*
Handford, Thomas, Jr., 180
Handford & Co., 180
Handford & Son, 180
Harcourt, A., *Interior of a Double-Pole Tent*, 6–7
hardware, 77
    Bramah-type locks, *94*
    brass handles, 77, 79, *124*
    iron carrying handles, *124*
    see also specific furniture
Harrod, Charles Henry, 180
Harrods, 180–81
    candlesticks, *135*
    Supplementary Export Price List, 88, *180*
Hawkins, Charles, 181

head-pieces, for West African carrier, 92
Heal, Sir Ambrose, 182
Heal, Fanny, 181
Heal, John Harris, 181, 182
Heal & Son, 181–82
    balanced load on horse's back, *182*
    officer's tent furniture, *181*
Heath, Edward, 104
Heath, William, 103
Hepplewhite, A. & Co.:
    Cabinet-Maker and Upholsterer's Guide, 32, 136, 183, 206
    Cabinet Maker's London Book of Prices, 136, 206
    field bed, *33*, 76
    Roorkhee chairs, 73
    wine table, *136*, *137*
Hepplewhite, George, 29, 183
Hewlin, Peter, 183
Hibbert, Christopher, 64
Hill, John, 183, 191
Hill & Millard, 108, 159, 183–84, 191, 199
    advertisement, 159, *184*
    barrack furniture, 2–3, 4, *184*
Hill & Perkins, 184–85
    Regency mahogany breakfast table, *184*
His Excellency the Viceroy's Bodyguard (Fry), *110*
Holkham Hall, Norfolk, England, staff in, 64
Holmes, Beatrice and John, 88, *88*
Holmes, Mrs., 92
Hornet, captain's cabin in, 36
horse's back, balanced load on, *182*
Household Cavalry, 48
Howe, Adm. Earl, 80
Hunting Party Breakfast (Bellasis), 57, *58*
Hussars:
    "Prince of Wales's Own," 57
    Princess of Wales's Own, 133

I

Ince, William, 29, 185
    Universal System, 32, 185
Ince & Mayhew, 117, 185
incomes, in Victorian England, 64
India:
    camp furniture for, 6–7, 59, 88
    dressing for dinner in, 68
    encampment in, 49–51, 89–90
    Government House, Barrackpore, 55
    Government House, Calcutta, 51, 54, *54*, 56
    hunting party breakfast in, 57, *58*
    insects in, 101, 114
    rule by prestige in, 69
    stream crossing in, *90*
    tent interior in, 2–3, 64
    viceroys of, 56
    wealth in, 54

women living in, 91
India House, 168
Indian Observer, The, 50
Information and Directions for Travellers on the Continent (Starke), 106
insects, 101, 114
Interior of a Double-Pole Tent (Harcourt), 6–7
Interior of My Tent, High Ground, Bangladore (Malet), 2–3, 64
invalids' furniture:
    beds, 28, 103, 104, 105
    Boethema, or rising mattress, 103, 104
    chairs, 77, 105, 105, 172, 212–13, 212
Invoice of Camp Equipage (Trotter), 44, 45
Irish Victorian mahogany chair, 200
Isaac & Campbell, 185

J

Jacques, John, 185
    backgammon, chess and draught board, 185
Jaffer, Amin, 34
James, Charles, *Regimental Companion*, 59
James, John, 186
    traveler's boudoir or dressing case, escritoire, drawers combined, 186
Jarvis, John, William & Matthew, 186
Jarvis, J. W. & M., advertisement, 39, 39
Jefferson, Thomas, 107
Johnson, Edward, 28, 29, 169, 186–87, 191
Johnson, Peter, 91
Johnstone, Captain, 36
Johnstone, Norman & Co., 187
Johnstone & Jeanes, 187
    armchair, 96
Johnstone Jupe & Co., 96, 187
Johnstone Wetherell and Norman, 187
Joy, Edward T., 41, 101, 103, 111, 116

K

Kane, Gregory, 188
    ship tables, 27
Kedleston Hall, Derbyshire, England, 51, 56
Key, Mitchell & Grieg, 188
Kington, Philip Oliphant, 191
Kington, Thomas, 191
Klint, Kaare, "Safari" chair, 71, 73
knife and fork, Victorian, 145

L

Lambe, John, 213
lamps, 134, 135
Lancers, 64, 89–90
Lane & Billing, 188
Lawrence, Sir Henry, 94

Lawrence, Honoria, 94, 97
Layard, Lt. F. P., *Officer's Baggage*, 12
LeCorbeiller, Clare, 47
Le Corbusier, "Basculant" chair, 71, 73
Leicester, Earl of, 64
Leiter, Levi Z., 90
Lennox, Lord William, 59
letter copying machines, 177
Leveson, Edward John, 188
Leveson, E. J. & Co., 188
Leveson, Lewis & Co., 188
Leveson & Sons, 188–89, 198, 213
Levy, Abraham, 189
Levy, Samuel, 189
Life Guards, 48, 64, 68
life under canvas, 19, 122
Loader, Richard, 189
Long, Lt. Gen. Robert Ballard, 44, 45, 46, 48, 211
looking-glasses, *see* mirrors
Loudon, J. C., *Encyclopaedia of Cottage, Farm, and Villa Architecture and Furniture*, 83, 112, 114
Lowndes, J & W, 189
    trade card, 189
Lowndes, James & William, 189
Lucan, Earl of, 64

M

Macaulay, Thomas Babington, 54–55, 194
McGuffie, T. H., 46
Mackenzie, John, 198
McQuoid, Percy, 136
Magistretti, Vico, "Armchair 905," 73
Maiden, Sydney J., 43
Malabar, 85, 85
Malet, H. E., *Interior of My Tent*, 2–3, 64
Manning, Henry, 190
Maple, John & Co., 190
Maple and Co., 190
Maples, 190
Martin, Thomas, *New Circle of the Mechanical Arts*, 97, 111
Mason, George, 154
Mason, Lt.-Col. Kenneth, 69
Mayhew, John, 29, 185
    Universal System, 32, 185
Mead, John, 190
    dinner wagon or sideboard, 190
Meadmore, Clement, 71–72
Mercer, Gen. Cavalié, 98, 101
Merlin, John Joseph, 105
Merriman, G., 190
Merriman, G. F., 190–91
Merriman & Sons, 190–91
Midday Halt: Marching (Bellasis), 8–9
Miles, Edward Peach William, 191
Miles, Henry Cruger William, 191

Miles, Philip William Skynner, 191
Miles & Kington, 191
Miles Kington & Co., dining chairs, *152*
Mileses, Brothers & Co., 191
Millard, Richard, 183, 191
 recumbent and easy chair, *191*
Millard, William, 192
 trade card, *192*
Mills, Thomas, 192
Mills, Wallis, *East Is East And West Is West*, *91*
mirrors:
 in chests, 61, *63*, 79
 late Victorian teak pivot-folding, *145*
 Victorian mahogany, *202*
Monson, Hon. and Mrs. William, 50, *51*
Morant & Co., 187
Morgan, Thomas, 169, 195
Morgan & Co., 174, 193
Morgan & Sanders, 79, 169–70, 174, 192–94, 195, 196, 205
 advertisements, *34*, *35*, 76, 98
 bedsteads, 76, 101, 103
 brass plaque, *194*
 chair-beds, *82*, *126*
 chairs, *122*
 dining table, *193*
 trade card, *34*, *35*, 98
Moroccan leather arm pad, *97*
Morris, James, 67
mule load, balanced, 61
Murphy, James Ross, 199, 201
Murphy, Patrick, 199
Murphy, Veronica, 39
Myerly, Scott Hughes, 56, 57

N

Napoleonic Wars (1793–1815), 103, 110
native head load, 91–92, *92*
Navy "At Home," The, 36–37
Nelson, Adm. Lord Horatio, 79
New Circle of the Mechanical Arts, The (Martin), *97*, 111
Northcote-Bade, Stanley, 34
Nutting, Wallace, 114, 154

O

Officer's Baggage (Layard), *12*
officers' commissions, purchases of, 64
officers' furnishings, *see* camp equipage; tents; *specific items*
Officer's Quarters At Newry, Northern Ireland, *146*
Overley, William, 194–95
Oxenham, Hugh & Henry, 196
Oxenham, Samuel & Co., 196
 trade card, *195*
Oxenham, Thomas, 169–70, 192–93, 195–96

P

packing cases:
 for chairs, *62*
 as chest of drawers, *94*, *95*
 markings on, 61
pack loads, balanced, 61, *182*
"pack saddle" boxes and bedstead, 48, *48*
parlor suites, 41, *42*, *43*
patents, numbers of, 111, 116
Paulet, Admiral, 86
Peale, Charles Wilson, 107
Peninsular War, Spain, 46–47, 61, 103, 109
Penzer, N. M., 136
personal kits, 141–45, *186*
Persuasion (Austen), 36
Phillips, Lawrance, 196
Phillips, Lawrance & Son, 196
Philp, Peter, 29, 98
"Pig War," 55
Pioneers of the King's Own (Royal Lancaster) Regiment, 59, *60*
pistols, 106
Plassey, Battle of (1757), 38–39, 54
plate, Wellington, *47*
Pocock, William, 28–29, 196
 advertisements, *28*, 103
 invalid bed, *28*, 103, *104*
 sofa-beds, 79, *84*
 trade card, *28*
Pocock & Co., 196
Pocock & Son, 196
Pole-Carew, Maj. Gen. R., *66*, 71
port, passing clockwise, 136
portmanteaus, *162*, *166*
Portrait of Lieutenant General Robert Ballard Long (Fowler), *45*
pot cupboard, Victorian mahogany, *202*
Powell, Mrs. Elizabeth, 196, 197
Powell, John, 196, 197
Powerful, 37, *38*
Pratt, Edward, 197
Pratt, Henry, 197–98
Pratt, Henry, Jr., 198
Pratt, Samuel, 103, 197–98
 receipt, *197*
"Prince of Wales's Own" Hussars, 57
Princess of Wales's Own Hussars, 133
Pryer, George, 198
Pryer, Steains & Mackenzie, 169, 198
Pryer & Mackenzie, 198
Punch, *91*, 91

Q

Queen Charlotte, 80

R

razor case, Victorian brass-bound oak, *144*
Regency furniture:
    brass-bound mahogany dressing-table box, *176*
    brass-inlaid mahogany chairs, *122*
    brass-mounted mahogany bookcases, *21*, *127*
    brass-mounted mahogany collapsible draw-leaf dining table, *85*, *87*
    caned mahogany chair-bed, *162*, *163*
    caned mahogany sofa-bed, *25*
    gilt-brass officer's field bed, *76*, *76*, *101*
    inlaid mahogany traveling rostrum, *131*
    mahogany breakfast table, *184*
    mahogany center table, *123*
    mahogany extending dining table, *171*
    mahogany folding billiards table, *140*
    mahogany games table, *22*, *23*
    mahogany "Imperial" dining table, *193*
    mahogany metamorphic chair-bed, *82*
    mahogany occasional table, *128*
    mahogany sofa-bed, *83*
    mahogany wine table, *136*, *137*
    oak chair-bed, *126*
    portable bagatelle table, *140*
    teak two-part military chest with *secrétaire* drawer, *124*
Regimental Companion, The (James), 59
Regiment of Native Infantry, 50
Regiments of the Line, 64
Reminiscences (Gronow), 58–59
Report of the Kabul Committee on Equipment, 59
Repository of Arts (Ackermann), 28, 34, 114
Richmond, Duke of, 59
Robinson, Charles, 198
Robinson & Sons, 198
    Victorian caned mahogany adjustable daybed, *198*, *199*
rocking chairs, folding, *210*
Roorkhee chairs, *66*, *70*, 71–73, *71*, *72*, 92, *92*
Rosoman, Treve, 36, 80, 84, 86
Ross, E., of Dublin, 69, 199
    brass-bound military chest, 59, *60*, 61
    brass plaque, *201*
    camp furniture for officers, 59
    parlor suite, *42*, 43
    reclining chair design, *199*
    Victorian mahogany side chair, *201*
Ross & Co., 199–204
    chiffonier, *40*, 41
    Irish Victorian mahogany chair, *200*
    ivory plaque, *203*
    parlor suite, *42*, 43
    Victorian mahogany pot cupboard, *202*
    Victorian mahogany traveling mirror, *202*
    Victorian military chest of drawers, *204*
    Victorian oak dining chairs (set of six), *203*
rostrum, Regency inlaid mahogany, *131*

Rouch, William White, 204
Royal Artillery, 98
Royal Dragoon Guards, 48, 64, 135
Royal Horse Guards, 48–49
Royal Lancaster "the King's Own" Regiment, 59, *60*
Rudall, Rose, Carte, 204

S

Saadat Ali, Nawab of Oudh, 38
"Safari" chair (Klint), 71, 73
Sanders, Joseph, 169, 192, 193, 195
San Juan Island, 55
Savory & Moore, 205
"Scenes in Camp" (Atkinson), 49–50, *49*
Schnell, William, 205
Schoolbred & Co., 206
sea chests, 79, *85*
secrétaires, chests with, *18*, 61, 79, 80, *81*, *124*, *147*
secret compartments, 106–8
Seddon, 117, 205
Seddon, Charles & Co., 205
Seddon, George I, 205
Seddon, George II, 205
Seddon, George III, 205
Seddon, Sons & Shackleton, 205
Seddon, T & G, 205
Seddon, Thomas I, 205
Seddon, Thomas II, 205
Seddon & Co., 205
Sedley, Angelo, 205
Shackleton, Thomas, 205
shaving kit, *143*
Shearer, Thomas, 29, 206
Shepherd, John, 206
Sheraton, Thomas, 206
    Cabinet Dictionary, 29, 31, 32, 36, 77, 206
    Cabinet Makers' and Upholsterers' Drawing Book, 206
    camp bed, *31*
    field officer's quarters, 43–44, 48
    on shipboard furnishings, 77, 79
    sofa-bed, *32*, *33*
    tent and marquee, 43–44, *44*
    on trestle tables, 36
Sheraton Furniture (Fastenedge), 114
shipboard furniture, 36, 37, *38*, 77, 79, 84–85, *85*
Shoolbred, Cook & Co., 206–7
Shoolbred, James, 206–7
shower, Victorian, *141*
sideboard or dinner wagon, *190*
Sikh wars, 103
Silber & Fleming, 207
Silver, Stephen Winckworth & Co., 207
Silver, S. W., 207–8
    parlor suites, 41
Silver, S. W. & Co., 207–8

Simner, Capt. Benjamin, 40, 41, 43
Siraj-ud-daula, Nawab of Bengal, 38–39
Smee, William & Sons, 208
Smee, William A. & Sylvanus, 208
Smith, Thomas, 101, 103
Smith & Cobay, 208
Smythe, George Augustus, Viscount Strangford, 142
sofa-beds, 32, *33*, 84, 88
    expanding, *169*
    George II metamorphic mahogany, *154*, *155*
    Regency caned mahogany, *25*
    Regency mahogany, *83*
Southgate, John & Co., 208
Southgate, John & Sons, 208
Southgate and Alcock, 208
Spain:
    Douro River in, 61
    Peninsular War, 46–47, 61, 103, 109
spirits case, Victorian brass-bound mahogany, *164*
Starke, Mariana, 106
Steains, James, 169, 198
Steel, Flora Annie, 90–91
Stewart, Charles, 29, 208–9
    brass plaques, *209*
    dining table, *30*
Storehouse PLC, 182
Summer Room in the Artist's House, The (D'Oyly), 51, *52–53*
Sutherland, Douglas, 58
swords, 48
sword-sticks, 106
Symonds, R. W., 154
Symons, Charles, 209

T

tables:
    bagatelle, Regency portable, *140*
    billiards, Regency mahogany folding, *140*
    breakfast, Regency mahogany, *184*
    coaching, Edwardian mahogany and brass-mounted, *150*
    dining, *see* dining tables
    folding, *112*
    games, George IV, *139*
    games, Regency mahogany, *22*, *23*
    games, Victorian mahogany, *138*
    gentleman's social, *136*
    George III mahogany, *175*
    George III mahogany rent, *115*
    George IV brass-mounted mahogany concertina-action, *30*
    late Victorian brass-bound mahogany, *165*
    occasional, late George III mahogany, *129*
    occasional, late Regency mahogany, *128*
    for officers, 59
    packing and carrying, 36
    Regency mahogany center, *123*
    ship, *27*
    trestle, 36, 59
    wine, late Regency mahogany, 136, *137*
    writing, Victorian mahogany, *149*
Tait, Margaret, 209
    George IV brass-mounted mahogany traveling desk, *209*
    maker's paper label, *209*
Taylor, Benjamin & Sons, 210
    furniture in cork, 61
teak, 97
tents, 43–44, *44*, 46, 49
    furnishings for, *2–3*, *6–7*, 64, 88, *120*, *181*, *182*
    heat inside, 50
Thompson, Henry Edward, 210, 211
    folding rocking chair, *210*
Thompson, John Thomas, 210–11
    advertisement, *75*
    metal tubes for beds, 103
Thornton, James, 34, 36
throne and bed, traveling, 39
Tipu, Sultan of Mysore, 39
Tomkinson, Lt.-Col. William, 46–47, 48
trade cards:
    Butler, *100*, *101*, *170–71*
    Handford, *180*
    Lowndes, *189*
    Millard, *192*
    Morgan & Sanders, 34, *35*, *98*
    Oxenham, *195*
    Pocock, *28*
Trafalgar, Battle of, 79
transport, ease of, 73, 88–93
Trappes family of Nidd, 107
Trevenen, Lt. James, 84
trigger mechanisms, for folding furniture, 76, 77
Trotter, John & Co., 211
    camp equipage invoice, 44, *45*
Trotter, John & Coutts/Army and Navy Warehouse, 211
trunks:
    English iron-bound leather, *156*
    portmanteaus, *162*, *166*

U

Universal System of Household Furniture (Ince and Mayhew), 32, 185
Uxbridge, Lord, 103–4

V

Valentia, Lord, 38, 54
Vaughan, William Henry, 211
Verrinder, John, 211
Vickery, John Collard, 211
Victoria, queen of England, 67
Victorian England, incomes in, 64

Victorian furniture:
    brass-bound coromandel traveling desk, *133*
    brass-bound mahogany spirits case, *164*
    brass-bound mahogany table, *165*
    brass-bound mahogany traveling desk, *132*
    brass-bound oak razor case, *144*
    brass-mounted mahogany chest of Aldershot or hut drawers, *94*, *95*
    brass-mounted mahogany chest with *secrétaire* drawer, *147*
    brass-mounted mahogany two-part chest with *secrétaire*, *81*
    brass-mounted washstand, *159*
    brass traveling candle holder, *135*
    butler's tray, *111*, *112*
    caned mahogany adjustable daybed, *198*, *199*
    caned mahogany armchair, *96*, *97*
    early, *120*, *121*
    Irish mahogany chair, *200*
    knife and fork, *145*
    mahogany apothecary's traveling compendium, *130*
    mahogany armchair, *151*
    mahogany bidet, *27*
    mahogany dining chairs (set of four), *152*
    mahogany folding camp stool, *179*
    mahogany open bookcase, *74*
    mahogany portable games table, *138*
    mahogany pot cupboard, *202*
    mahogany side chair, *201*
    mahogany traveling mirror, *202*
    mahogany two-part traveling chest, *148*
    mahogany washbasin, *26*, *27*
    mahogany writing table, *149*
    military chest of drawers, *204*
    oak dining chairs (set of six), *203*
    oak pedestal desk, *37*, *38*
    oak writing desk, *165*
    shaving kit, *143*
    shower, *141*
    teak pivot-folding camp mirror, *145*
    walnut chiffonier, *40*, 41
Victory, 79, 84, 86

W

Ward, John, 212–13
    advertisement, *212*
    invalid chair, *212*
    self-propelling chairs, *105*
Ward, John, Ltd., 160, 188–89, 212–13
War Department (WD), 59
Warren, Kenneth, 68
washbasin, Victorian officer's mahogany, *26*, *27*
washstand, Victorian brass-mounted, *159*
"Wassily" chair (Breuer), 71, 72–73, *73*
Waterloo, Battle of, 30, 58–59, 98, 103–4, *110*
Watney, Norman, 68
WD (War Department), 59

Wellington, Duke of (Arthur Wellesley):
    and Battle of Waterloo, 58–59, 103–4, 110
    campaign bed of, 103, *104*
    campaign plate of, *47*
    dressing-table box of, *142*
    and Government House, 51
    Halifax Regiment of, 43
Wells, J., 213
Wells, J. & Co., 213
Wells, John & Co., 205
Wells & Lambe, 213
Whiteaway and Laidlaw, 68
Wilhelm I, Kaiser, 55
William IV mahogany dining chair, *24*
Williams, George Langford, 213
Wilmot, Thomas, 213
Wilmott, Thomas, 213
Wilson, William, 213
Winfield, Robert W., 214
Winfield, R. W. & Co., 214
Winfield, R W & Son, 214
Winfield & Simms, 214
Wolfsky & Co., Ltd., 208
woods, 97
World War I, 67–68
Wren, John, 214
Wren Brothers, 214
Wyatt, Capt. Charles, 54

Y

Young, G. M., 64
Younghusband, Gen. George, 56

Photograph Credits

Patrick Adam, Galerie Le Scalaphré, Paris: 81; Bonham's, London: 102; Boulton & Cooper (Fine Arts), Malton, England: 141; By Permission of the British Library, Oriental and India Office Collections: 2, 3, 6, 7, 54, 72, 90; © Copyright The British Museum: 35, 100, 180, 189, 192, 195, 196; Peter Bronson: 37, 65, 99, 132, 133, 135 (bottom), 143, 144, 145, 161 (bottom right), 164, 168, 179, 184 (left); The Anne S. K. Brown Military Collection, Brown University, Rhode Island: 10, 12, 89, 110; © Christie's Images New York, 2001: 30, 176; Christopher Clarke (Antiques) Ltd., Stow-on-the-Wold, Glos., England: 86, 151; Philip Colleck, Ltd., New York, NY: 153; Courtesy Martyn Gregory Gallery, London: 8, 9, 58, 85, 93; Ross Hamilton Antiques, London: 165 (top); W. R. Harvey & Co. (Antiques) Ltd., Witney, Oxfordshire, England: 63, 80, 87, 120, 121, 130, 147; Christopher Howe, London: 61, 62, 126; Los Angeles County Museum of Art, William Randolph Hearst Collection: 51; Mallett, London: 115; David McAlpine: 45 (right); Courtesy of the Director, National Army Museum, London: 38, 45 (left), 60 (top), 66; Art & Architecture Collection, Miriam and Ira D. Wallach Division of Art, Prints and Photographs, The New York Public Library, Astor, Lenox and Tilden Foundations: 33 (top); Phillips Fine Art Auctioneers, London: 42, 131, 140; Phillips of Hitchin (Antiques) Ltd., Hertfordshire, England: 18, 20, 21, 22, 23, 24, 25, 27, 40, 60 (bottom), 74, 78, 82, 83, 94, 95, 105, 112, 114, 122, 123, 124, 127, 128, 129, 138, 146, 148, 149, 152, 154, 159 (right), 160, 162, 163, 171, 194, 202, 203, 204, 205; Private Collection: 26, 70, 71, 77, 79, 88, 91, 92, 96, 97, 106, 107, 134, 135 (top), 137, 139, 150, 156, 161 (top right), 165 (bottom), 175 (left), 198, 199 (left), 200, 201; Courtesy of Public Record Office, Kew, Surrey, England: 28, 48, 98, 161 (top left), 166, 167, 169, 172, 178, 185, 186, 190, 191, 199 (right), 210; Michael Sim Fine English Furniture, Chislehurst, Kent, BR7 5PG, England: 193; Sotheby's: 170; Victoria & Albert Museum; V&A Picture Library: 31, 32, 33 (bottom), 39, 44, 47, 49, 73, 104, 136, 142, 175 (right), 181, 182, 212; Westminster City Archives, London: 113; Neil Wibroe: 184 (right); Professor and Mrs. John Ralph Willis: 76, 125, 155, 159 (left); Yale Center for British Art, Paul Mellon Collection: 52, 53.

"The British Army is a social institution prepared for every emergency except that of war."

—H. O. Arnold-Forster,
Secretary of State for War, 1903